Sport Aviation Se

COMPOSITE CONSTRUCTION

FOR HOMEBUILT AIRCRAFT

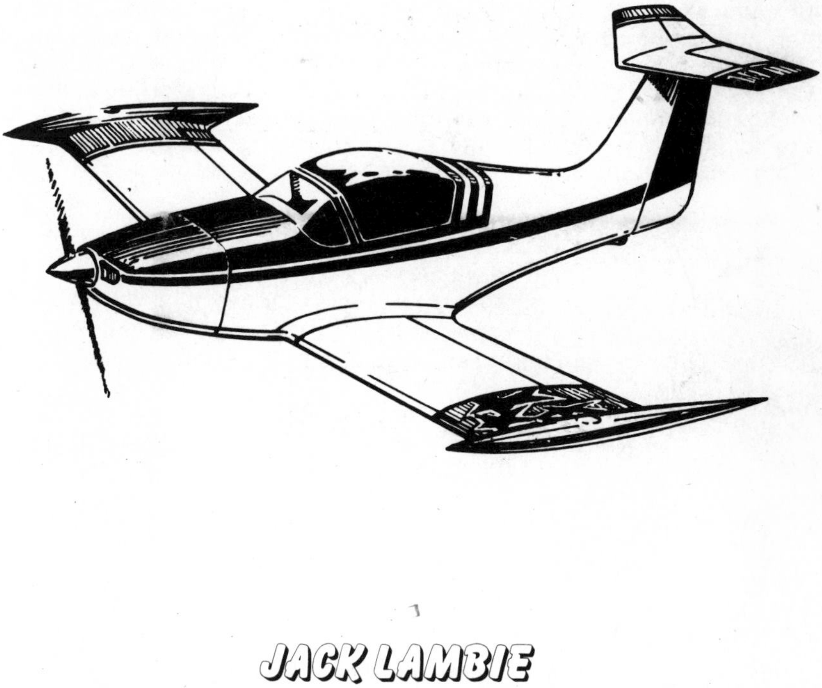

JACK LAMBIE

AViation Publishers

One Aviation Way
Lock Box 234
Hummelstown, PA 17036 USA

COMPOSITE CONSTRUCTION
For Homebuilt Aircraft
Jack Lambie

Copyright © 1984 by Michael A. Markowski

FIRST EDITION
First Printing — May 1984
Second Printing — September 1985

Published by:

Aviation Publishers

Ultralight Publications, Inc.
One Aviation Way
Lock Box 234
Hummelstown, PA 17036 USA

Books by the Author
BUILDING AND FLYING SAILPLANES AND GLIDERS
ULTRALIGHT AIRMANSHIP
COMPOSITE CONSTRUCTION FOR HOMEBUILT AIRCRAFT

Library of Congress Cataloging in Publication Data

Lambie, Jack H., 1935 —
Composite Construction For Homebuilt Aircraft
(Sport Aviation Series/Book No. 6)

1. Airplanes, Home-built. 2. Composite construction. I. Title.
TL671.2.L27 1984   629.133'340422   83-51736
ISBN 0-938716-14-X (Paperback)

On The Cover

The *Polliwagen* is a two-place, side-by-side, composite structured light sporting aircraft, designed for amateur construction. It can be powered by the 75 hp Revmaster Turbo VW, the 100 hp Continental 0-200, or the 150-160 hp Lycoming 0-320. Plans and a kit of extensive pre-molded parts are available from: Polliwagen, Inc., 40940 Eleandra Way, Murrieta, CA 92362. (714) 677-7877.

About the Author

Jack Lambie is on the frontier of so many diverse activities the usual question is, "What are you doing next?" A lifelong love of the air and things that fly and move through it has been the focus and concentrated energy of Jack Lambie's life.

In 1978 he received the Soaring Society of America's Exceptional Achievement Award as a member of the design team of the Gossamer Condor, which performed the first successful sustained, maneuverable, man-powered flight. He has worked with Dr. Paul MacCready and Dr. Peter Lissaman previously as chief consultant, designer and vehicle tester on a National Science Foundation project to develop devices that reduce air drag on large trucks.

A student of bird flight, Jack raised many soaring birds. He has built models and full size sailplanes and gliders, as well as replicas of the 1901 and 1903 Wright Gliders and Flyers. With over 6,000 hours in 67 kinds of aircraft, holder of commercial and instructor ratings, he has also gained international soarings of highest badge—the Diamond C (USA #20). A winner in many soaring contests, he was also the co-pilot on the flight that holds the current U.S. two-place goal record for gliders.

One of the founders of hang gliding, his "Hang Loose" design was built by the hundreds in 1970-71. As pilot, technical advisor, plane designer and builder, he has worked on many films and ads such as the PBS special "Orville and Wilbur," and the NBC "Winds of Kitty Hawk."

Jack and his wife Karen are the first couple to have ridden around the world on a tandem bicycle. Their 515-day journey covered 30 countries. He built one of the earliest streamlined bikes and co-organized the first of what are now annual human-powered speed contests. Almost 60 mph has been reached with the streamlined, advanced bicycle-like machines.

Aided by the National Geographic Society, he completed an 8,000 mile flight during 1980, in a motorglider to Paraguay, South America, exploring the Andes and searching for the great Condors.

Jack has degrees from the University of Illinois, USC, and UCLA and has been an educator for 15 years in primary, elementary, high school, adult and university graduate science programs. He was the first Director of Education for the California Museum of Science and Industry at Los Angeles, where he developed many innovative programs.

He has had 130 articles published in various magazines, a book on gliding and one on ultralight flying. Jack prowls the skies in his Fournier motorglider. He lives in Orange, California, where he divides his time between lecturing, writing books and working on fascinating projects.

Acknowledgement

Special thanks go out to the following individuals and companies for their cooperation and permission to use certain information: Aeroviornment, Inc., Aero Gare, Inc., *Aeromodeller* Magazine, Aircraft Spruce and Specialty Company, Inc., Jack Ashcraft, Dupont, Goldwing, Inc., Pat Lloyd, Michael A. Markowski, Polliwagen, Inc., Quickie Aircraft Corp., Rand/Robinson Engineering, Inc., Rutan Aircraft Factory, Inc., Stoddard-Hamilton Aircraft, Inc., Molt Taylor, Viking Aircraft, Inc., War Aircraft Replicas, Inc.

WARNING — A WORD OF CAUTION

Flight, in and of itself, is not necessarily dangerous, however it is most unforgiving of errors, sloppiness and misjudgement on the parts of the designer, builder, and pilot. Whenever a man builds and/or flys an aircraft, he accepts the risk that he may be injured or even killed. It is each individual's decision to either accept or reject this risk in light of its potential hazards, challenges, and rewards. Flying can be, and is done safely every day of the year by paying strict attention to the details.

This book is a source of information to be used as a reference guide. If there is anything you don't understand, don't hesitate to ask an expert. It is further recommended that you join your local EAA chapter. With over 600 chapters worldwide, there's no reason you can't get involved and be guided by those in the know.

PUBLISHER'S COMMENT

The opinions expressed in this book by the author are not necessarily shared by the publisher. Authors, of course, see things through their own eyes and base what they say on their personal experiences. You may either accept or reject the author's opinions, but they will hopefully lead you toward a greater understanding of the subject.

Contents

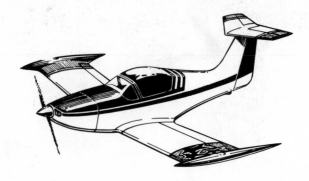

Introduction

Plastic composite construction is a wonderful advance in homebuilt airplanes because form and function are the same, something that has been dreamed of for years.

The fast, smooth and unique new personal planes are within reach of anyone with average skill, persistence, spare time and a moderate amount of money. In this book you will see how to work with composite materials. You'll learn the basic ideas behind layups, sandwich designs, carbon fiber, Kevlar, and paper. Several different materials and techniques for mold and non-mold forming are discussed.

Airplanes are a kind of sculpture — shaped to slip easily through the air. Our artistic sense often has good judgement. A beautifully sleek airplane is usually aerodynamically sound.

Nature has been using composite construction for millions of years. Look at a section of bamboo, a feather, palm fronds or an insect. You will see how the outer structure is hard, with a lighter bulky inside for compression resistance.

In the past, combining structures with streamlined shapes was always a problem. Fuselages were made of wood, braced with piano wire. Ribs were fitted around the wing spars to make the wing's airfoil. Light bulkheads and stringers were added to the body to smooth it aerodynamically. All was then covered with cloth and painted for the final finish.

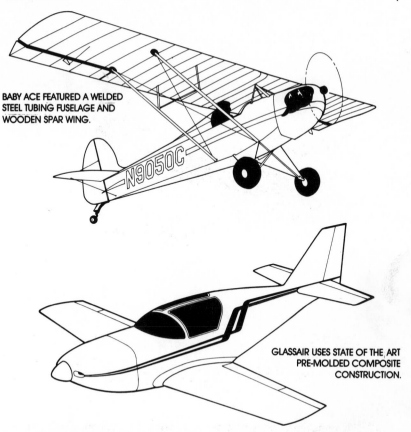

BABY ACE FEATURED A WELDED
STEEL TUBING FUSELAGE AND
WOODEN SPAR WING.

GLASSAIR USES STATE OF THE ART
PRE-MOLDED COMPOSITE
CONSTRUCTION.

Fig. I-1. Composite construction has allowed homebuilt aircraft design to develop from the strut
braced, open cockpit Baby Ace of the mid-Fifties, to the cantilevered, totally enclosed Glassair.

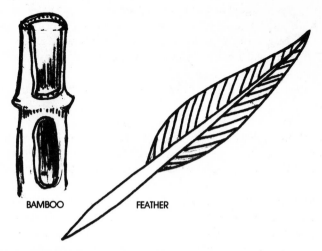

BAMBOO   FEATHER

Fig. I-2. Nature has been using composite construction for eons.

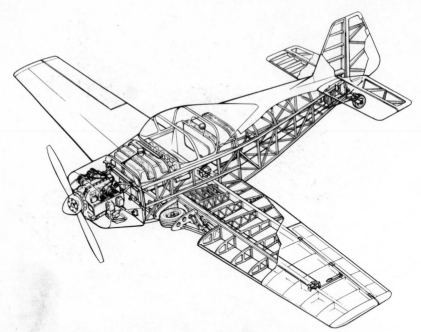

Fig. I-3. CA-65 SkyFly is a good example of an all wood homebuilt airplane.

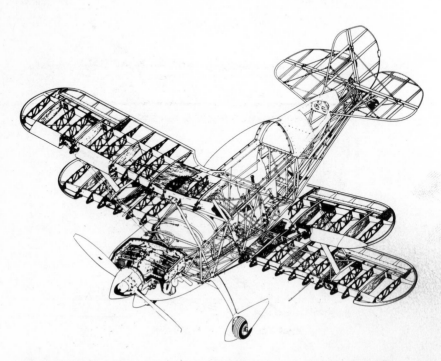

Fig. I-4. Christen Eagle features a welded steel tubing fuselage, and wooden spars and ribs.

Fig. I-5. Pazmany PL-2 is perhaps the epitome of the all metal homebuilt aircraft.

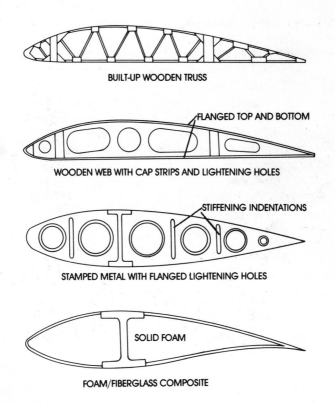

BUILT-UP WOODEN TRUSS

FLANGED TOP AND BOTTOM

WOODEN WEB WITH CAP STRIPS AND LIGHTENING HOLES

STIFFENING INDENTATIONS

STAMPED METAL WITH FLANGED LIGHTENING HOLES

SOLID FOAM

FOAM/FIBERGLASS COMPOSITE

Fig. I-6. The various types of homebuilt aircraft wing rib construction.

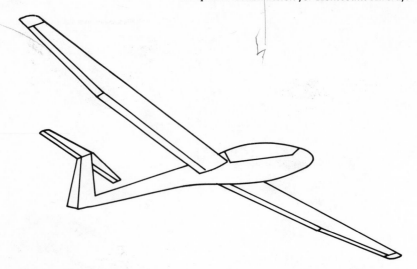

Fig. I-7. The West Germans pioneered composite construction with high performance sailplanes. They proved to be light, strong and appropriately flexible.

As progress was made, the wooden frameworks gave way to welded steel tubing. Even so, the steel frames had to have wooden formers and stringers to fair the final shape, the same as the older airplanes.

Riveting sheets of aluminum together into a shell was a great advance. There was no need for covering or paint because the aluminum itself was both. This is known as "monocoque" construction. It was marvelous for mass production because the aluminum could be formed perfectly with large presses. Parts could then be fastened in special jigs for line-up and a fairly easy assembly. All production aircraft are still made this way.

For the homebuilder, the "one-off" metal airplane is very difficult. Most of us don't have presses, shears, and other metal working machinery. With careful design, some very nice all metal homebuilt planes have been built —made mostly with flat sheets or simple one-way curves. Most of these aircraft tend to be angular looking, unless they are made from a kit with specially formed parts available.

The perfect airplane should have every component devoted to smooth aerodynamics and structural strength. The ideal way to make the complex curvaceous shapes of airplanes has finally come about by using plastic resins combined with very strong fibers. Both the shape and the structure are the same piece.

The West Germans pioneered plastic construction when they made the Phoenix sailplane almost entirely fiberglass. Now, most of the top sailplanes are German and made of composite plastic.

In the United States, fiberglass was first used in less stressed parts, such as wing tips and fairings. But now, composites are major structures. Sometimes a plastic foam or balsa wood core is covered with fiberglass on each side, making a much stiffer part. Steel or aluminum fittings can be fastened into

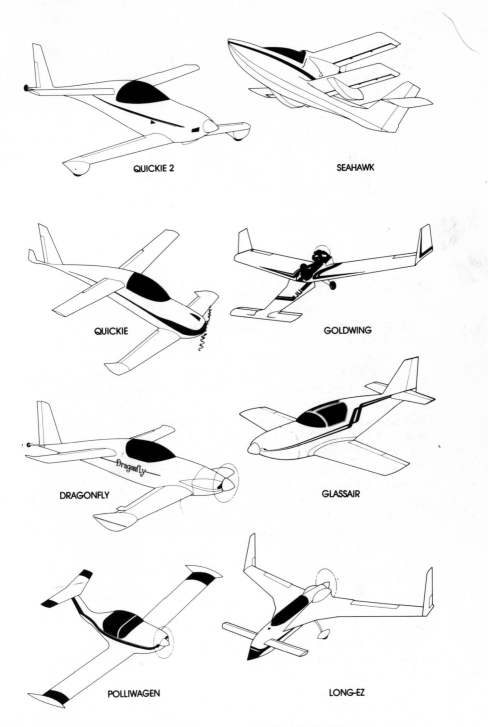

Fig. I-8. Some of today's most popular Composite construction homebuilt airplanes.

Material	Ultimate Tensile (PSI)	Maximum Compressive (PSI)	Modulus of Elasticity (10^6 PSI)	Weight cu. ft.
Expanded Polystyrene	22	15	.0008	1
Balsa	100	1,700	0.55	9
Pine	470	3,510	1.12	32
Spruce	345	5,000	1.3	28
Fir	375	7,000	1.7	34
Aluminum	30,000	10,000	8.0	165
Magnesium	40,000	26,000	6.5	114
7075 T6	55,000	13,000	10.0	175
4130 Steel	95,000	28,000	30.0	489
Carbon Fiber	130,000	126,000	24.0	100
E-Glass	500,000	62,000	10.5	162
S-Glass	650,000	65,700	12.6	156
Kevlar	525,000	40,000	19.0	86.4
Graphite	360,000	over 40,000	30.0	106

Fig. I-9. Relative physical properties of various materials.

the composite as "hard points" to transfer loads. Super strength carbon fibers and Kevlar cloths and filaments are available to make airplanes that reach undreamed of perfection both structurally and aerodynamically.

This book will give you a practical knowledge of the new materials and techniques of working with plastic composites. You will be able to design and make many non-critical parts. For an entire airplane however, the subtle complexities of structural analysis are such that you should seek advice from an expert.

A chapter on basic design and the importance of aerodynamics, stability and control in relation to the new methods of structure is presented. While not intended to be a design manual, it will help you understand the advantages of plastic materials. You will certainly be better able to judge the kind of flying machine you wish to build.

The similarities and differences between such popular plastic homebuilt airplane kits as the *Quickie, LongEze, Dragonfly, Pollwagen, Glassair* and *Micro Imp* are explained. You'll be able to decide which would suit your ideal of aesthetics, performance, and building methods.

Discussions of comparative costs of the pre-pregs, carbon fiber, Kevlar, and S-Glass will help in that important phase of deciding what's best for your particular project. Also, since many of us are sensitive to the various glues and resins, health and safety in handling them is emphasized.

Whether you are considering building one of the new kits, thinking of an original design, interested in making fairings to improve your present airplane or just want to learn more about the *new wave* in airplane construction, this book is the place to start.

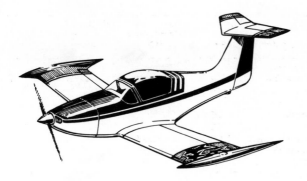

1

Why Airplanes Are Shaped The Way They Are

Before we look at plastic airplanes and the methods of making them, let's see how some of the basics of design can effect the structure.

Wings

Most important are the wings. Why are there so many different shapes? (Long and skinny, short and wide, swept back, tip plates, various kinds of twist, tapered and curved.) Controls of various sorts such as flaps, ailerons, spoilers and rudders are attached or built in. Let's discuss all these and their significance to composite construction.

Lift

Wings sustain an airplane by accelerating air downward. This causes a reaction upward as Isaac Newton explained many years ago, with his third law of motion. There is an equal and opposite reaction to every action.

Some students of flight have been ingrained with the theory of flight as described by using the Daniel Bernoulli ideas of the eighteenth century. He

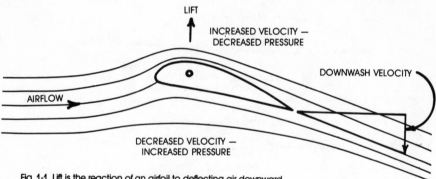

Fig. 1-1. Lift is the reaction of an airfoil to deflecting air downward.

correctly noted that when air speeded up the pressure dropped, and when retarded the pressure increased. You can demonstrate this yourself by blowing across the top of a straw immersed in a glass of water and watching the water move up the straw. The air pressure in the faster air over the straw is less, causing the atmospheric pressure to raise the water level in the straw. That's how most paint sprayers work. Bernoulli lived from 1700 to 1782 when there were no airplanes or wings to which his theory could be applied. In 1738 he certainly never thought of the airplane in relation to his discovery.

In later years, Bernoulli's theory was used to describe how an airplane wing lifts, causing confusion for many. Most texts, including FAA manuals, use a description of lift which says: "A wing airfoil is shaped so the air must go farther over the top than the bottom. Since the air molecules must meet at the back of the wing the air goes faster over the longer curve of the top of the airfoil Most of the lift of a wing comes from this air speeding up over the curved top of the wing, creating low pressure, which sucks the wing up."

Unfortunately, Bernoulli's Theory only describes the secondary effect of how the forces are transferred to the wing. It does NOT describe the basic

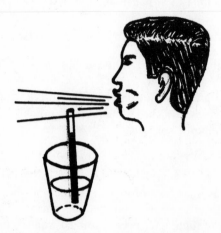

Fig. 1-2. Low pressure is created by blowing air past a soda straw, causing the liquid to rise.

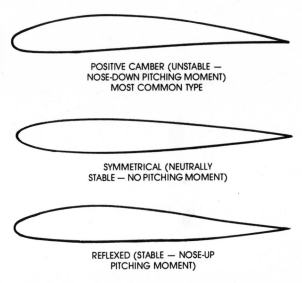

POSITIVE CAMBER (UNSTABLE —
NOSE-DOWN PITCHING MOMENT)
MOST COMMON TYPE

SYMMETRICAL (NEUTRALLY
STABLE — NO PITCHING MOMENT)

REFLEXED (STABLE — NOSE-UP
PITCHING MOMENT)

Fig. 1-3. Airfoils develop lift regardless if the bottom is flat or curved. All that's necessary, is for the air flowing past it to be deflected downward.

phenomena. By using it as a primary description, many pilots can't understand how an airplane flys upside down, or why an undercambered airfoil produces more lift than one with a flat bottom. In a convoluted way, Bernoulli can be used to understand those effects. But, it has been such a poor choice of lift descriptions that has set back the simple understanding of basic aerodynamics for over a generation.

There are, of course, other theories as well. The Prandtl-Lanchester Lifting Line explanation and the Kutta-Joukowski Circulation Principle. Their descriptions for some reason have not been used as much as the Bernoulli Theory in attempting to explain how an airplane flies. They picture air moving around a wing airfoil something like that of a moving, spinning cylinder. The result is an acceleration of the air above and a retarding effect below thus creating an upward force. Robert Jones of NASA also developed a description of lift by accounting for the flow changes ahead of a wing. All these later aerodynamicists make very clear that it is the downward momentum imparted to the air by the wing that creates lift. And they are well aware their theories describe the secondary effect of transferring the forces to the wings in order to make mathematical predictions of the lift...depending on speed, wing area and lift coefficient.

Some pilots become almost violent defending their particular understanding of lift, but really they are all quite accurate descriptions of the same thing.

"Come on now, they can't all be true," you might think. Yes. But note, I said all are accurate, but all are not "true". So what is the "true" theory of lift?

In science what is considered "true" is the simplest explanation that covers the most phenomena. Newton's "Action-Reaction" lift explanation wins

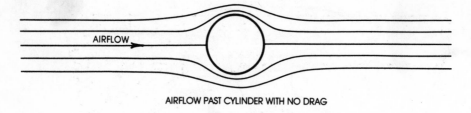

AIRFLOW PAST CYLINDER WITH NO DRAG

AIR CIRCULATION AROUND ROTATING CYLINDER

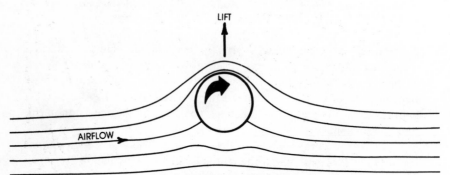

AIRFLOW COMBINED WITH ROTATION

Fig. 1-4. A rotating cylinder generates downwash and therefore, lift.

easily. It covers every motion from running, (pushing back on the ground drives you forward) to swimming and propellers, (accelerating water or air in one direction drives you in the other), and rockets (which blast out a great mass of fuel down to react them upward).

Another test of a "true" theory's simplicity is considering how close it is to human experience. Describing lift by pressures and suctions is often confusing because we can't physically sense the air pressure, unless it's when our ears pop on a fast elevator — but hardly around a wing. The action-reaction, or acceleration, explanation is better because we can (with our hands) feel the equal and opposite reaction of trying to shove something and having it push back.

Yes, the narrowness of the Bernoulli theory has resulted in confusion to many pilots, and writers, who must use different and often complicated

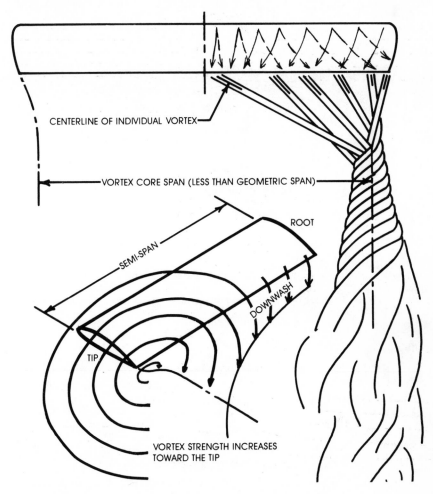

CENTERLINE OF INDIVIDUAL VORTEX

VORTEX CORE SPAN (LESS THAN GEOMETRIC SPAN)

ROOT

SEMI-SPAN

DOWNWASH

TIP

VORTEX STRENGTH INCREASES
TOWARD THE TIP

Fig. 1-5. A lifting wing experiences spanwise flows and develops tip vortices.

explanations of how propellers, rockets, controls and high lift devices
work...or even how an airplane flies upside down. (Note that on airliners,
such as a DC-10, the inboard wing sections, out to the jet engines, are curved
more on the bottom than the top, in defiance of a (Bernoulli-type
explanation).

So, to understand aerodynamics, and lift in particular, the basic and far
more meaningful idea is Action (air being accelerated down) and Reaction
(lift). A wing is like a vane that turns air. It grabs air from above and pushes it
down. You don't need an airfoil curved more on the top than the bottom. A
square edged plank will lift if it deflects air down (but its poor shape will
make for high drag). A properly curved airfoil is simply the best way to create
lift with the least drag for a given amount of lifting force.

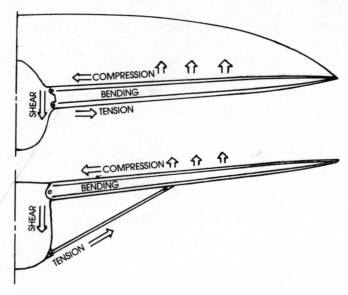

Fig. 1-6. Lift load distribution over a wing, and the major forces generated in cantilevered and strut braced wings.

Induced Drag

The energy lost to gain lift is called induced drag. It is the word needed to "induce" the air to accelerate down and thus create the reaction of lift. It is sometimes called vortex drag. It must be overcome by thrust in an airplane, or gravity in a glider.

For maximum efficiency, Nature likes to have things done gently. A long wing will push a mass of air equal to the weight of the plane down more softly than a short wing. The air that flies out around the ends making big swirls, called tip vortices, absorb energy but don't do anything to hold the airplane up. A long, slender wing can capture more air to thrust down, at the same speed and angle of attack as a short wing. Because a long wing obviously encounters more air as it moves along it doesn't have to bend it down so sharply and the reduced downwash angle makes for less tip vortices.

To gain the same amount of lift with a short wing, of the same area as a longer wing, it must be moved through the air faster or angled up more, making larger tip vortices. A longer wing with the same wing loading can move slowly and at a lower angle for equal lift, so induced drag is decreased because tip swirls are less.

Aspect Ratio

If two airplanes have the same wing area but one has its area spread over a longer span it is said to have a higher Aspect Ratio. The aspect ratio is the span divided by the average width (chord), of the wing. For example, a forty foot span, four feet wide wing would have an aspect ratio of 10. An AR of 10 is considered rather high for an airplane but gliders go as high as 30.

Another way to describe this important performance factor is the span loading—the weight each foot of span must carry. With equal power the airplane with the lowest span loading will climb faster.

But look at fighter planes and aerobatic competition machines. If a high aspect ratio is good for efficiency, why do most airplanes seem to have short wings? The reasons are size, cost, weight and because power is relatively cheaper than aircraft structure.

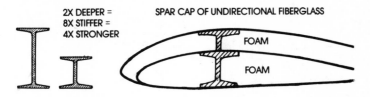

Fig. 1-7. Spar stiffness increases as the cube of its depth. Strength increases as the square of its depth.

Wing Size and Weight

A long wing weighs more than a short one. Why? For the same thickness, a long ruler is easier to break than a short one. To be of equal strength, a long wing must be much heavier. The center of the wing lift is out farther, giving it more bending leverage. If the wingspan is doubled while its thickness is not increased, the same strength requires eight times the weight! The extra weight is tough on the landing gear which in turn, must be made stronger. The engine has more weight to accelerate on takeoff. Weight compounds itself.

It is an interesting situation, especially with respect to the new composites. Wings can be made *long* and *light* with the new, thicker laminar flow airfoils. They can also be made accurate more easily with plastics. Later we'll discuss the possible compromises and solutions to the wing weight problem.

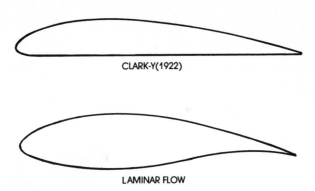

CLARK-Y(1922)

LAMINAR FLOW

Fig. 1-8. New laminar flow airfoils offer higher lift, greater thickness and greater strength potential than old Clark-Y section.

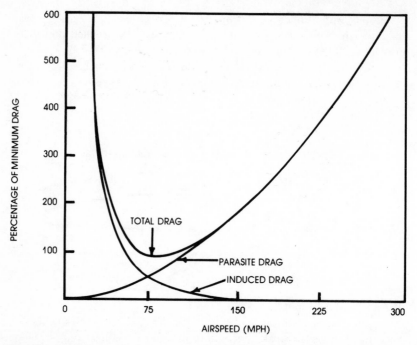

Fig. 1-9. How parasite, induced and total drag vary with airspeed. (Curves not for any particular homebuilt aircraft.)

Power and Span

To see the relationship between power and span, lets look at lift and drag versus airspeed. A basic fact of air forces is their increase as the square of speed. This basically means that when the speed is doubled the lift as well as the drag is quadrupled. The air molecules are being hit twice as hard at double the speed — two times two is four. A wing that creates 800 lbs of lift at 50 mph, generates 3200 lbs at 100 mph...assuming the angle of attack is the same. An airplane weighing 800 lbs would require a lesser angle of attack at the higher speeds.

A fast airplane with short wings needs relatively more power however, because its drag increases as the square of the speed. If you want an airplane with short, light wings you will fly fast. But, when you go fast, you don't need as much angle of attack. There is a squared increase in parasite drag from the airplane pushing through the air. However, the drag due to lift, called induced drag decreases. This can be shown graphically to picture how it happens. The least drag and therefore, least power required, occurs when the parasite drag is one-third the induced.

Parasite Drag

Drag not involved in lifting an airplane is called parasite drag. It is the result of air flowing past the struts, wires, wheels, door handles etc. It can be reduced by shaping the parts (streamlining) so the air will go back into

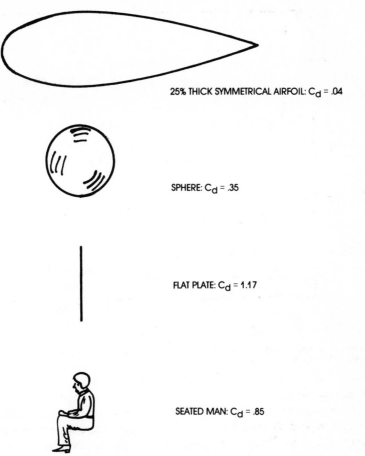

25% THICK SYMMETRICAL AIRFOIL: C_d = .04

SPHERE: C_d = .35

FLAT PLATE: C_d = 1.17

SEATED MAN: C_d = .85

Fig. 1-10. The coefficient of drag for various basic shapes.

position after the airplane passes. The shape of the object is important. For the aerodynamic comparison of shapes, a number called the Drag Coefficient (C_d) is used. (It's called "C_x" in automotive literature.) In all other applications it is quite properly called "C_d". During the 1920's and 30's it was sometimes called the "K" factor.

Studying these examples lets you understand how streamlining reduces drag. The more evenly the air can be made to move aside as the object passes through it, and the more carefully it is returned to its still position after the object passes, the less energy is used. In the turbulence behind any shape is left the residue of the energy: Making the wake less turbulent by having smooth slow changes in contours, and therefore pressures, is the way to move through the air with minimum drag.

Power is one answer to short wings. An aircraft can takeoff and climb quickly if it has lots of thrust. Once it is level it can go fast and the relatively light structure will help it climb well.

Conversely, with low power the wings must be longer for good performance. Low power means slower flying parasite drag is less.

Increasing the span while keeping the weight, thrust and wing area the same, will increase the rate of climb. A homebuilder making an airplane of an estimated gross of 1300 lbs., can get identical climb performance with a 100HP engine and 30 foot span. Only a 24 foot span is needed if the power is increased to 125HP. The extra 25 HP often doesn't cost as much or weigh more than the weight due to the increase in spar strength, plus man-hour and materials cost to make the extra six feet of wing.

During the 1930s "Golden Age of Flying," many light-planes used only 50 HP engines with close to 40 feet. Since they were also very slow flying, the long wings could be made lightly and still be safe. Now, with engines of 100HP and more we can obtain good performance with almost half the span.

Efficiency

There are still some important flight conditions that still favor the high aspect ratio (AR) wing. When the engine stops, the glide angle of the low aspect ratio ship is very steep because of the higher induced drag. If you are near an airport, fine. But, if there are a few miles to go, the "brick-like" gliding qualities of the low AR wing could be scary. Higher aspect ratios are also favorable for high altitude and long range cruise at slower, economy speeds. The high aspect ratio wing gives the aircraft a better lift divided by drag ratio (L/D) compared to the low aspect ratio wing.

Airliners, which must make money, use a high aspect ratio wing. Powerful, factory made light aircraft have increased spans for more efficient flying and long range, particularly turbo-supercharged models such as the Beech V36TC, and Rockwell 112 turbo. Some airplane types have increased spans from one model year to the next. The Cessna Citation business jet series grew ever longer wings as pilots found how higher aspects ratios at higher altitudes contributed to improved climb and efficiency. When flying the Citation 500, which has the shortest wings, I find the speed must be kept up for the wing to be at the best lifting angle of attack. When loaded and flying over 25,000 feet the plane hardly climbs. The Citation One has a few feet longer wing which greatly improves its climb because it can be flown more slowly at its best climb angle. More of the power is used to climb instead of pushing it through the air.

High speed turns favor the long, slim winged machine. The turning aircraft creates centrifugal force which increases the load on the wings. For example, a thousand pound airplane may weigh over 1500 pounds in a turn. The wing with the smallest induced drag can make a sharper turn without losing altitude, given the same power. Shorter wings have a quicker roll to start into the turn but must make a wider circle unless a lot more power is used.

Powerful fighter planes have no problem turning tight, but light planes and homebuilts do. With comparatively less thrust, they lose altitude making tight turns when they reach full power. Short wings may make it seem to have

Fig. 1-11. Paper busting is easier with a long-winged, low powered airplane because, it turns quicker than short-winged, high powered airplanes.

good manueverability because a little aileron movement rolls the plane quickly, but it may not go around the circle as well.

From personal experience, I can say how much fun it is to have high performance manueverability with low power. I have owned a Fournier RF-4D motorglider for many years. It has only about 32 HP but a 38 foot wing. It loops from its normal cruise speed of 105 MPH and also does a complete circle in under 10 seconds, including the roll in and out. To equal that performance with a short winged aircraft, like a bi-plane, takes about three times the horsepower. Coming back from airshows with my friends, they in their 100 HP little bi-planes, I get a kick out of doing a quick loop and continuing right where I left off. When they try it, their bi-planes always seem to end up a hundred feet below — their short, little wings have such high induced drag pulling them down. I can easily turn inside them in our mock dogfights even though they have a much quicker roll to start the turn.

My Fournier has won every paper cutting contest I have ever entered by using its superb circling performance. The contests usually work like this. The flyers circle, at perhaps 3000 feet above the ground, until their turn. Each pilot then goes to the place designated by the judges, and throws out a roll of toilet paper. As the roll drops, streaking out its paper, the flyer tries to cut it as many times as possible in 90 seconds. A good pilot can do four. An outstanding performance would be six to eight. The Fournier will cut it into eleven to thirteen neat little three foot sections.

So why not make a very tiny airplane with a little high aspect ratio wing? Because at lightweight landing and takeoff speeds the air flowing over small wings behaves differently. Lift is less and drag higher because of the relative stickiness of the air. An understanding of Reynolds number effects explains this most important part of airplane design.

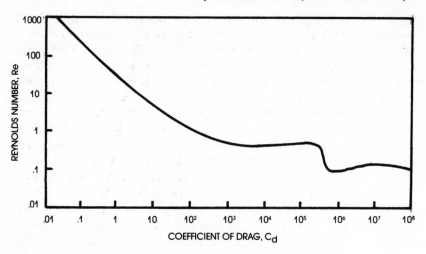

Fig. 1-12. How the coefficient of drag of a sphere varies with Reynolds number.

The Reynolds Number

One of the fascinating parts of aerodynamics and airplanes is the subtle turns and twists of what at first glance seems straightforward. Why do flys and bumblebees have hair on their wings and bodies? Why do they tend to be round instead of streamlined? How come a Frisbee has ridges running around the edge and why are golf balls made with dimples? Does airflow and drag per unit area change with the shape of an object, as well as with size and speed? What has all this got to do with homebuilt airplane design anyway?

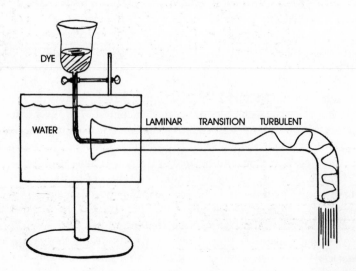

Fig. 1-13. Osborne Reynolds' experiment showing how laminar flow transitions to turbulent flow with increasing length and fluid flow speed.

In 1883 Osborne Reynolds did some experiments with water flowing through a glass pipe. He added a fine stream of dye to picture the flow. A straight dye line showed smooth movement. He slowly increased the speed of water until some critical point, which he found depended on the size of the pipe, its roughness and the speed of the fluid, the line of dye suddenly became turbulent. He demonstrated two kinds of fluid flow: laminar (streamlined) and turbulent (irregular). He made rules describing this phenomena as the ratio of viscous (stickiness) to inertial (flow energy) forces. It turned out to be a most important and far reaching observation of nature that has been used to describe and predict all kinds of what had been aerodynamic mysteries.

He discovered that fluids, which air is, change their flow characteristics depending on the speed and the size of an object in the fluid flow. At very low speeds, air is likely to cling so well it will not separate into turbulence, even if the object is not streamlined. Hey, that sounds great, you might think. Even a round ball should have no drag with the air going all around it. Not so, however, because the air rubbing along the sides is almost glued to the object.

The result is that at low speeds and small sizes, i.e., at "low" Reynolds numbers, the drag per unit area is extremely high. As the speed is increased, the air's relative "stickiness" decreases, but the drag due to the air breaking away into turbulence increases. At a certain speed known as "critical"

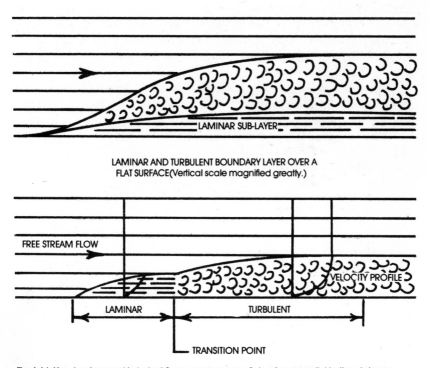

LAMINAR AND TURBULENT BOUNDARY LAYER OVER A
FLAT SURFACE(Vertical scale magnified greatly.)

Fig. 1-14. How laminar and turbulent flows appear over a flat surface parallel to the airstream.

Reynolds number, the air doesn't know exactly what to do. This is the so-called transition zone, where the flow goes from laminar to turbulent. A number of things can cause transition to occur.

The Reynolds number (Re) is found by multiplying the length of an object in feet by its speed in MPH by 9360. I always use 10,000 to do it in my head. With a ball, for example, the drag per unit of frontal area becomes lower as the Rn is increased.

One way to make the total drag less at slower speeds (lower Rn's) is by roughening its surface. This seems to go against what you would think intuitively, but remember how sticky air is at low speeds? The way to decrease this "clinging" is by having a bumpy surface to chop up the air. The turbulence thus generated,energizes the thin layers of air close to the surface, enabling the air to flow around the ball more completely. At the particular speeds and size of a golf ball the bumps make it go farther by helping the air get around the ball, decreasing the drag of its wake. The skin friction drag is increased,while wake turbulence is decreased enough to lower the overall drag, allowing the ball to travel further.

Lift is increased and overall drag decreased on Frisbees, models and bumblebees by making the air turbulent before it moves past the surface. That is why flying insects don't have well streamlined bodies and wings. Insects fly very slowly. They are also very small. For them, viscous drag is greater than inertial drag. This means the air doesn't whirl off into turbulence as it would behind a large, fast-moving object. Instead, it sticks to the surface and slides closely around. This "stickiness," or viscous drag, depends more on area than shape. A round object has the smallest surface area for its volume. Therefore the lowest drag shape in tiny insects will be for the round instead of streamlined body.

The highly tapered homebuilt airplane wing runs into the problems of low Reynolds numbers. A tip with an average width of a foot at 40 MPH would have a Re of 1 x 40 x 10,000 = 400,000, which is very low. The lift is much less per unit area with small chord wingtips so, when the airplane approaches a stall one tip or the other drops. The plane rolls suddenly and the pilot may have to take more time and altitude to recover than if the wing root stalled first and the airplane began dropping straight ahead.

The Spitfire pursuit of England's World War Two Battle of Britain fame, used an elliptical wing. The idea behind such a shape is that the tips don't have to lift as much as the center for best efficiency (the lift distribution is optional), and better roll performance. The American Thunderbolt fighter, considered one of the best all-around planes of that war, also used an elliptical wing. If it's so good then, why don't all airplanes use it. If nothing else, it surely is aesthetically pleasing.

Here's one of the reasons most airplane haven't used elliptical wings. Efficient lift distribution can be obtained by altering the angle of attack of the tip, that is twisting it down (called washout) slightly so it will stall later than the center section. Another way is to locate a stall strip near the inboard section of the wing so the root stalls while the tips remain flying.

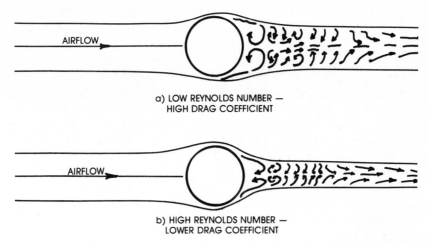

a) LOW REYNOLDS NUMBER —
HIGH DRAG COEFFICIENT

b) HIGH REYNOLDS NUMBER —
LOWER DRAG COEFFICIENT

Fig. 1-15. Airflow behind a sphere shows decreasing turbulence, and therefore lowered drag, with increasing Reynolds number.

Another reason elliptical wings are not made is that, despite their aerodynamic efficiency, they don't perform much better than moderately tapered planforms. The extra manufacturing costs can not justify it. The P51 fighter was a good example of a superior airplane without elliptical wings. This is because the fuselage intersection, aileron cutouts, flap leakage and other such discrepancies did not give a smooth lift distribution. No sense making an elliptical wing when the lift wasn't spread that way. A wing designed to match its lift distribution seems a better way to go, and its planform may or may not be an ellipse.

Wing Sweep

For stability in airplanes without a tail, the wings are swept back like an arrow with the tips washed out. The idea is to get a surface that will change its center of lift to keep the aircraft flying at its trimmed speed. In some airplanes with a stabilizer, a swept wing is used to increase stability even more. In airplanes that approach the speed of sound, sweep allows it to do so with less drag. This, of course, does not concern homebuilt lightplanes. Let's look at how the flying wing uses sweep.

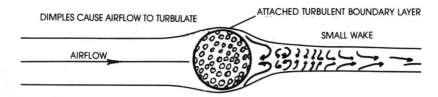

DIMPLES CAUSE AIRFLOW TO TURBULATE   ATTACHED TURBULENT BOUNDARY LAYER

SMALL WAKE

AIRFLOW

Fig. 1-16. The airflow behind a golf ball at low Reynolds numbers is like higher Reynolds number flow around a sphere. Dimples cause the flow to go turbulent making for a smaller wake, decreasing drag, and allowing the ball to travel further.

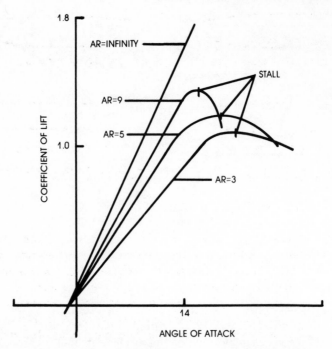

Fig. 1-17. The tip of a highly tapered wing operates at a lower Reynolds number than the root, giving it inferior lifting qualities.

Flying Wings

Stability is gained primarily by locating the center of gravity, i.e., balance point, ahead of the center of lift. This would tend to make the plane dive except the ends of the wing push the nose up because the air doesn't lift them as much as the central parrt of the wing. The pilot can control these tips with elevons (combined elevator and aileron) on their trailing edges to nose up or down. Most airplanes must have some stability so human beings can control them. Birds and bats however, are not automatically stable. They do very well by using instinctive reflexes. Although we can hop along on one foot, this would be an unstable way to move around. Humans don't have the reflexes to fly completely unstable airplanes. Unless there is a very quick acting autopilot, the airplane must be stable to be pleasant to fly. Remember, the air forces change as the square of the speed? This, in combination with the weight ahead of the center of lift is basic to stability.

Now, with the advent of plastics and foams, you can make just about any wing shape you want. So, lets discuss the aerodynamic efficiency and structural possibilities of various planforms.

Rectangular Wings

The rectangular wing is one of the most common planforms on airplanes today. It's easy to manufacture because most parts are parallel or at right angles and all the ribs are the same size. It is deficient aerodynamically and

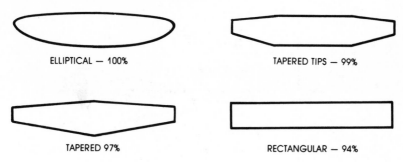

Fig. 1-18. Basic wing planforms and their relative efficiencies as lifting surfaces, at an aspect ratio of 7. Elliptical is assumed to be 100% efficient for purposes of comparison.

structurally however, because not every part carries its share of the aircraft's weight. For example, a 120 square foot wing on a thousand pound airplane would have an 8.33 pounds per square foot wing loading. But, it is only an assumption that each square foot of wing lifts the same amount.

The lift distribution is an ellipse, even though the wing is rectangular. The tips aren't lifting according to their area, yet the drag is still equal across the entire span. This is inefficient because the wing is bigger and heavier than need be for the lift generated.

When some areas of the wing are not working as hard as others, induced drag increases. Furthermore, the part of the wing not doing its share of lifting, is still dragging through the air, adding its skin friction and profile drags. More so with the rectangular than a tapered wing, the tip vortex makes the angle of attack at the tip less than inboard. The whirl of the vortex results in the tip being in a slight downcurrent.

Another disadvantage of the rectangular wing is greater roll damping than the tapered or elliptical planform. This results in more sluggish response to aileron forces and less maneuverability. The extra weight on the tips and the mass of air that must be moved when the wing rolls is the cause. A wing, in other words, is not just a wing — it includes the air around it. For example, moving a canoe paddle that weighs two pounds is very easy through the air, but trying to move it in water takes a lot more force. You are not just moving the paddle but a mass of water as well. This is the so-called "apparent mass" and is a factor in airplanes, too.

This is not to say airplanes with rectangular wings are unacceptably slow in roll. Many are fine because they use very short wings and large ailerons. But they would be even better with a tapered wing.

An important advantage of rectangular planforms is the ease with which the center section can be made to stall first. The large tips work at relatively less angle of attack than the center of the wing. They have a reserve of lift when the center is already above its stalling angle. Thus, it has a built in safety feature. At the stall, the airplane will tend to sink straight down instead of rolling over to one side or the other.

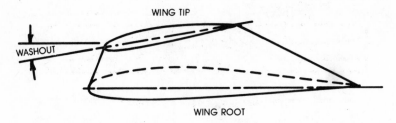

Fig. 1-19. Twisting the wingtip to a negative angle of incidence, compared to the root, can provide a better lift distribution. Its primary purpose in homebuilt aircraft is to prevent tip stall. This technique is known as washout.

Tapered Wings

If you take the area at the tips and add it to the center, is it possible to have the entire wing lift the same? This is structurally good because it can be made lighter but not very aerodynamically efficient. Why? The highly tapered planform is unstable because the tips are loaded more than the center. And, the tips small Reynolds number, due to its narrow chord, results in less lift and a quicker loss of lift as the speed drops and the tips stall before the root.

There are many fixes used to make sure the center section quits flying first. Stall strips, triangular pieces about a foot long by half an inch wide fastened along the leading edge, are one. As the airplane noses up and flies more slowly, the air becomes turbulent as it goes around the sharp corners of these strips. At a moderate angle of attack the section behind them loses lift before any other part of the wing, insuring a root stall first.

The opposite approach to stall strips inboard is "lift" strips outboard. The VariEze and Beech 36TC, force the tip to lift more near the stall by putting a device on the end of the leading edge to create vortices which energize the stalled boundary layer.

The strips cause drag, so one way to eliminate them and still have the center stall first is by constructing a twist into the wing. The tips are built to fly at a lesser angle. Since they are always operating at a lower lift compared to the center section they will be far from their stall angle when the root stalls. When the rest of the wing has stalled the tips will still be lifting, keeping the plane from rolling over. Twist is called "washout" and can reduce the overall wing drag due to lift, because it will spread the lift more elliptically. The disadvantage is that the improved lift distribution works at only one speed. Here's a personal experience with washout to explain.

The BG-12A sailplane I flew for many years had such a wing twist. It worked fine until I flew over 70 MPH. Then the tips started to bend down. By 80 to 100 MPH I could look out along the wings and see them bent like an arch! The extra download of the tips had to be carried by the center section, creating a lot of induced drag. As you can imagine, I was careful not to fly over 70 MPH. In competition, it was a great problem especially on strong lift days. Everyone was going fast between thermals and I had to plug along slowly to keep a good L/D ratio.

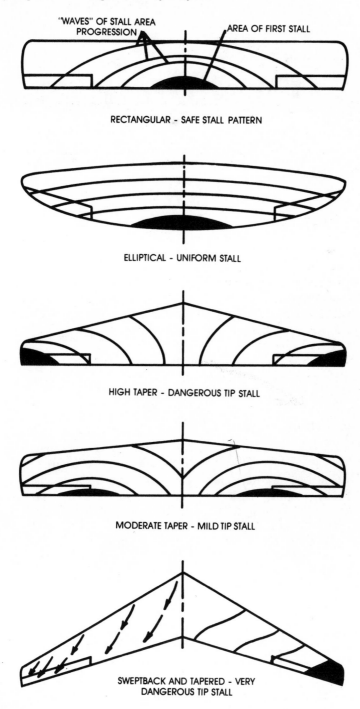

Fig. 1-20. Initial stall patterns for various wing planforms with no twist. Adding twist (washout) will drive the stall inboard.

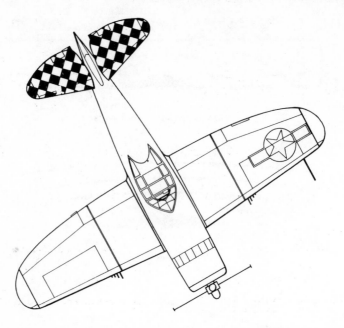

Fig. 1-21. Top view of W.A.R. P-47 shows clipped ellipse wing, with advantages as discussed in text.

The elusive perfect lift distribution was thought to be attainable with the classic elliptical planform. When ribs were hard to build and wings had to be simple, only those most interested in super performance made elliptical wings, like the pre WWII race planes. However, with modern understanding, it is not quite the wonderful planform as supposed because the tips are small, resulting in Reynolds numbers that are too low. The lift of a normal airfoil is greatly reduced at low Re. Thus, like the sharply tapered wing, the tips lose lift radically as the plane slows and it is likely to roll over as the lift on the tips drops off. The small tip problem can be reduced simply by cutting off the tip of the ellipse, as in the P-47.

Lift distribution is also complicated by the fuselage cutting across the center of the wing. A wing-on-top airplane keeps a smoother lift distribution than the low wing. A low winged plane uses a wider chord in the center section to increase the lift lost by fuselage interference. This not only evens out the lift distribution but it also allows a thicker spar with the same percentage airfoil.

The best wing then is an ellipse modified by being wider at both the center and the tips. Furthermore, it can be made with straight lines with only a slight loss in efficiency. The Cessna 150 series is typical of the tapered wing machine with a slight tip washout for extra stall safety. Late model Piper Aircraft use a tapered wing as well, to gain snappier aileron control and more efficiency.

Sweeping the wing forward in conventional tailed airplanes, is done to keep the rear, or instructor, pilot ahead of the wing with tandem two seaters.

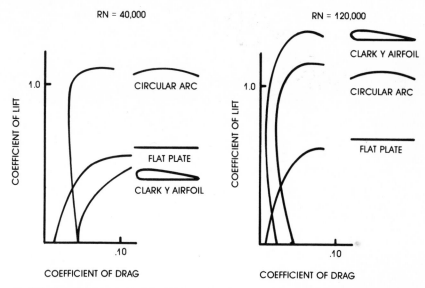

Fig. 1-22. Lift and drag characteristics of thin sections at very low Reynolds numbers. Flat plates and circular arcs are superior to airfoils in the realm of insects.

Forward sweep is sometimes used in very light planes. The pilot's weight is a great percentage of the total and the aviator doesn't want to sit in the middle of the wing with a poor view.

Airplanes designed for aerobatics, such as the Great Lakes Bi-plane and the Polish ZLIN often use a swept back planform. It can make an airplane more laterally stable without using dihedral (wide "V" as seen from in front). The airplane can be flown up-side-down or right-side-up without so much tendency to roll and slip sideways. For most aircraft it is easier to use a little dihedral instead of sweepback to keep the plane steady. High speed jet aircraft use the sweep to advance their critical mach number. Sweepback on lightplanes is limited by the problem of crossflow near the tips which thickens the boundary layer toward the ends of the wings. This results in tip stalling, causing dangerous slow speed wallowing, as each tip stalls and rolls the wing back and forth. Sweep is used in tailless airplanes which I'll discuss later in the section on stability and control.

Conventional Airfoils

Modern plastic composite construction methods have made a great impact on the homebuilder's choice of airfoils. To see how this has helped, let's take a look at the changes in airfoils since the beginnings of flight.

The Wright brothers thought a thin undercambered airfoil was best. This was a mistake although they decided this on the basis of extensive wind tunnel tests. Their problem was using a wind tunnel too small and too slow to get realistic results for their full sized airplanes. It's the old Reynolds number problem of air acting very differently at slow speeds. Only at very slow speeds

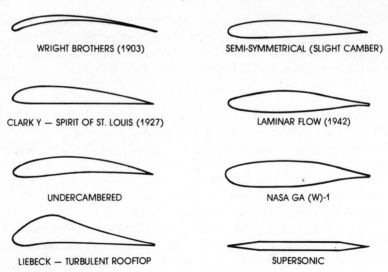

WRIGHT BROTHERS (1903)   SEMI-SYMMETRICAL (SLIGHT CAMBER)

CLARK Y — SPIRIT OF ST. LOUIS (1927)   LAMINAR FLOW (1942)

UNDERCAMBERED   NASA GA (W)-1

LIEBECK — TURBULENT ROOFTOP   SUPERSONIC

Fig. 1-23. Airfoils come in a variety of shapes, depending on the designer's goals.

and small sizes is a curved plate more efficient than a thicker rounded airfoil.

An advance occurred during WWI when the Dutch manufacturer of many German planes, Tony Fokker, made a thick sectioned wing. It has far less drag than the thin ones everyone was using because he could make a deep spar strong enough to eliminate the many wires and braces all the other planes needed. It is interesting to note in passing that an unbraced wing was so radical the powers in charge made Fokker put a strut between the wings on one of his biplane models, to make it look stronger. Fokker's wings were strong enough in bending without the phony struts. In actuality however, the officially required bracing probably saved many a pilot's life because the Fokker wing was not strong enough in torsion. The struts kept the wings stiff. Later, it was also found the wings needed cross ply veneer covering to be safe.

By the time of the 1920's and 1930's, the Clark Y was the most popular airfoil. Nicely rounded at the front it had a flat bottom making it easy to manufacture, while its performance was very good. The old Piper Cub used this section and it is still found on many homebuilt airplanes today.

In general, you can increase the lift coefficient of a standard airfoil, by curving it more or by making it thicker. Of course the profile drag increases too. That's why a designer tries to find the thinnest most streamlined shape

Fig. 1-24. A laminar flow airfoil cannot tolerate waviness. This reduces lift and increases drag. Canard configuration designers must be particularly aware of this critical requirement. See text for details.

that will lift the plane at cruising speed. The plane must take off and land slowly for safety and use short runways. The shape giving the most lift coefficient at high angles of attack usually has high drag at cruising speed. An airfoil that can be altered in flight is needed.

Flaps

Flaps at the trailing edge of the wing are the most popular fix. By being able to change camber (the curve of the airfoil) in flight from a high to a low lift position, there is a good widening of the aircraft's performance. All flaps increase the lift coefficient of the wing. Some can even be used to decrease the lift by putting them up, in a negative "cruise" position. The idea behind a negative flap setting is to reduce the lift coefficient of the wing airfoil at high speed so the profile drag, due to the camber, is less.

Flaps come in three basic styles, SPLIT, PLAIN and FOWLER. The SPLIT flap has only the bottom of the aft part of the wing going down. A PLAIN flap has the entire edge going down. The FOWLER flap actually slides out behind the wing adding area as well as increasing camber.

A gradual stall is developed by a fat, gently curved leading edge because near the stall angle, air can flow around it better than a sharp edge. The idea is to get the back edge of the wing to stall first and the nose last. A sharp edged airfoil may have lower drag but the stall may start at the leading edge. That makes for a very sudden stall as the air breaks away from the wingfront at the wing.

The standard Clark Y type airfoil with flaps was considered about the best that could be done until just before WII when a new, almost radically different airfoil was developed.

Laminar Flow Airfoils

These airfoils are easily recognizable from others because the thickest part is farther back from the leading edge. For them to work properly, the contours must be within a few thousandths of an inch accurate.They offer a tremendous advance in aerodynamics for homebuilders since the new composite building techniques can approach the smooth surface contours necessary to get the full benefit of the laminar shape.

Why are these airfoils better? Laminar flow over a greater percentage of the wing compared to standard airfoils is the secret. This means the air slides smoothly past the wing in unmixed layers, creating less turbulence. The shape causes the air to accelerate over a greater percentage of the airfoil. To visualize how this works, throw a deck of cards along the rug and see how they spread out. Note the cards easily slide over each other in "layers". Similarly, air made to accelerate over most laminar flow wing surfaces tends to keep sliding smoothly in layers just like the cards.

Experimenting with a funnel can demonstrate the effect of acceleration in making smooth flow. Hold it under the spigot in the sink so you can see the water running out of a funnel. No matter how turbulent it is when it splashes in, it will smooth out into a laminar stream by speeding up as the funnel narrows. Conversely, a fluid being made to slow down will roll up into turbulence. Put a hose into a swimming pool and you can see the vortices as the fast moving water decelerates in the still water.

Freeway driving conditions are an interesting example of how laminar flow can be visualized. During normal traffic, cars will stay in their particular lanes, with only minor shifting around. This would correspond to laminar air flow. If there is a disturbance to the flow of traffic, say someone brakes suddenly, or a car stalls, you will see vehicles changing lanes every-which-way as the traffic slows. The high speed lanes mix with the slower outside lanes, and vice versa. This corresponds to turbulent airflow. Once past the incident, the motorists accelerate and, the freeway clears quickly. Cars now stay in their lanes according to speed. This is like laminar flow. Air moving over the wing can be pictured similarly. The idea is to keep the velocity gradient (speeds of the various layers of air moving past) smoothly increasing as far back as possible, while not separating too much at the rear of the wing.

Today, this all important velocity gradient is designed by computers to keep the flow moving so each layer of air slides smoothly over the other. Using computers and potential flow theory, specific shapes can be designed to fit exact airplane design requirements. The designer gives the computer a particular airfoil and the machine works out the pressure distribution based on the acceleration or deceleration of the airflow. It then draws a picture the aerodymnamicist can use to predict how smoothly the air will flow over the wing.

Once the air is accelerated back past the 50 percent point of the chord, there is nothing much that can be done because it must now slow down as it approaches the rear of the wing. The boundary layer thickens and the air readily becomes turbulent. But, in the new airfoils this happens much farther back so there is less drag overall.

An important feature of the laminar flow airfoil is its thickness, which can be more than conventional types, while still keeping a very low drag. This, of course, allows a deeper spar. Remember, doubling the spar depth, leaving all other dimensions the same, makes the wing eight times stiffer! Thus, a laminar flow airfoiled wing can be made either lighter or longer with the same weight for greatly increased efficiency.

It must be said in favor of the older airfoils that, the minimum drag of a thin airfoil is slightly less than for a laminar section with the same camber (a line drawn halfway between the upper and lower curves). But, the thick wing has a wider speed range. Plus, the strength advantages will make the longer, or lighter, wing outperform the thinner, conventionally airfoiled wing.

If these new airfoils are so good, why haven't they been used for homebuilts? A poorly made laminar flow airfoil may be arguably worse than a conservative design is the common reason given. Buy why?

Laminar flow airfoils must be made accurately to achieve optimum performance. This does not mean super polished. A surface equal to smoothly doped cloth is all that is necessary for lightplane speeds. What is vital is that it be geometrically smooth. There can be no bumps or hollows.

The air will speed up slightly over a ridge as small as 4 thousandths of an inch. It will slow down going into an equally tiny hollow. This constant speeding up and slowing down drains energy from the boundary layer, just as going through a town full of stop signs uses more fuel than driving steadily along the open road. This slowed and speeded up layer becomes thicker and starts mixing with the higher speed flow. The air moving relative to the wing is no longer laminar, but draggy and turbulent.

Using the conventional spar and rib methods of wing making, causes a small wavy bump at the spar. The ribs, spar and leading edges must be superbly fitted or the air becomes turbulent at the spar position and laminar flow is lost far ahead of where the airfoil design specifies. The foam covered with fiberglass and unidirectional filament spar, results in a wing more all-of-one-piece. There is less opportunity for lumps between the sections. Thus, the new composite wings are far more able to produce the performance improvements of modern airfoils.

Stability

Natural fliers such as birds, bats and insects don't have built-in aerodynamic stability. They use automatic nervous reflexes to make subtle shifts of their wings and bodies to control themselves. Think of how we humans can hop along on one foot naturally, using our sense of balance and the feedback from our eyes and muscles. Flys have a false wing or "haltere" that buzzes up and down making a vibrating reciprocating "gyroscope" to send feedback sensations to their change in position. Flys can beat their wings to manuever the way they wish. This is similar to the new fighter planes that are aerodynamically unstable but very easily flyable by human pilots, because they have a quick acting auto-pilot. Aerodynamic stability is important in homebuilts because they don't have expensive servos, gyros and sensors to augment stability.

Longitudinal stability is the tendency for an airplane to return to the trim angle of attack after a disturbance. The airplane should continue to point the way the pilot aimed it without sliding all over the sky and speeding up or slowing down unless the pilot moves the controls. Since we humans haven't evolved to fly naturally, we need an airplane that "wants" to be steady.

Free flight model airplanes are a good example of self-stable flyers. Those of us who have flown models a lot understand automatic stability because, until the adding of radio control, model airplanes must have been able to complete the entire flight uncontrolled.

The flight path of a normal wing airfoil tends to follow its average chord line and dive if there is nothing to keep it level. This can be stopped by putting another wing, a tail, behind it at a lesser angle of attack. By putting the balance point ahead of the center of lift of the wing a most interesting automatic stability results.

If, for example, a model glider is dropped into the air at a low flying speed, the weight being forward tries to pull the wing into a dive. When it dives it speeds up. The tail begins pushing down since it is set at a negative angle. The

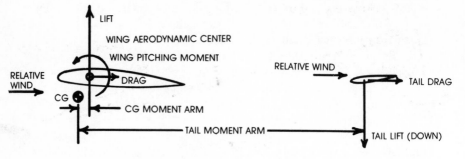

Fig. 1-25. The basic criteria for longitudinal stability in a conventionally tailed aircraft.

airplane rotates nose up. The wing has a higher angle of attack so the plane pulls out of the dive and climbs. Why doesn't it keep right on going up? Gravity pulls back and slows it down.

Remember, aerodynamic forces change as the square of the speed, so very little slowing will greatly reduce the down push on the tail. The forward weight does not change with airspeed. This weight is always the same no matter what the speed. (Unless it approaches the speed of light and the Einstein increased mass effect takes place, which hardly is a factor here).

This balancing act is a clever and wonderfully automatic method of keeping pitch at a set angle. If the airplane slows or speeds up, the tail force is increased or decreased as the square of the difference in speed. That means that very slight changes in airspeed make far greater modifications in the downforce on the tail.

The weight ahead of the aerodynamic center of the wing does not change no matter what the speed. Thus if the plane slows, the downforce on the tail quickly decreases. As it slows the weight pulls the nose down which results in a slight dive. As it speeds up the tail force quickly pulls down more than the weight. Then the nose goes up. The plane climbs slightly and slows. After a few oscillations it steadies down to smooth flight until upset again. Its like a self correcting teeter-totter because the slightest changes in speed makes the correct change in forces on the tail.

The heavier the weight in the nose the more the tail is set at a negative angle versus the wing, the greater the pitch stability. When the airplane stalls, the smaller angle of attack of the tailplane means there is little danger that it will stall before the wing. Since the wing will always drop before the tail the plane will pitch down for an automatic recovery.

Did you ever notice the extreme angle the tail slot is cut on those packaged balsa wood throw gliders? That is so anyone can get stable recovery no matter how awkwardly the glider is thrown.

The farther forward the plane is balanced and greater negative angle between wing and tail the more stable an airplane will be in pitch but at a cost. The harder the tailplane must react with the air the more drag it creates.

To help reduce this trim drag, airplanes use a fairly long fuselage and a small tailplane. With the center of gravity very carefully set back as far as

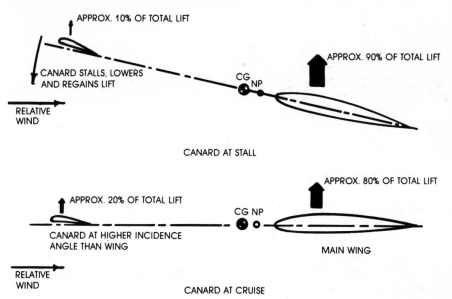

Fig. 1-26. The basics of conard longitudinal stability.

possible, there is only a slight download necessary to balance the airplane. The ultimate of such design is found in sailplanes, because efficiency is so important to motorless flight. They have a small tailplane set at the end of a long slim fuselage. If the tail can be set in the downwash of the wing it will have a greater restoring force in slow flight where it is most necessary to keep the wing from pitching down, while in normal cruise, or high speed, flight it will have no loads on it. The downwash angle varies enough with the airspeed to cause this.

An airplane can be made stable with a lifting tail, but this is dangerous. The tailplane may stall before the wing, causing the airplane to fall backwards uncontrollably. There is nothing to be gained by having the tailplane lifting anyway because the efficiency of a wing is determined by its aspect ratio not its wing loading. The slight extra weight the wing must carry due to the downforce on the tailplane is not nearly as costly in drag as trying to create lift with a small low Reynolds number wing such as a tailplane. This lesson has been forgotten by canard enthusiasts.

Tail In Front

Some designers put the tailplane ahead of the wing as the Wright brothers did in their 1903 KITTY HAWK FLYER. This is called a CANARD after the French work for duck. With its long neck stretched out, this water bird looks as if it is flying backwards. The term has also come to mean any backward statement or reversed idea as in the sentence, "Nixon offered his usual canards in defending his Vietnam policies."

Canard stability is achieved by balancing the plane so the canard carries relatively more per unit area than the wing. The forward surface, being more highly loaded, is designed to begin losing lift before the wing. Thus, when the canard hits an upward gust or is flying too slowly, the nose drops. The plane picks up speed and returns to its trimmed angle of attack. As in the tailplane-in-back airplane, the more the canard is loaded and angled up compared to the wing, up to a point, the more stable it will be.

The reasons canard enthusiasts say airplanes are made with the stabilizing plane in front are varied. Some believe that having the stabilizing surface lift the airplane is more efficient. "Instead of making parasite drag, as does a rear tailplane, a canard lifts so it carries its share." They say, "The downforce on the tail is just so much extra weight the wing must carry. The conventional type airplane wing flies at a slightly greater angle to carry that weight so the induced drag must be higher." They also may say, "The canard cannot be stalled and is a safer design because of this feature." To the amateur flyer the logic of a lifting canard seems very appealing.

Quite the opposite is true however. All things being equal a tailplane in back design is safer and more efficient. Why? There are many reasons.

Two lifting surfaces have four tip vortices so there is more induced drag.

The canard's rear wing must be *limited* to a lift coefficient less than the foreplane because if the wing stalled first the plane would fall backwards. Thus more wing must be dragged through the air to have the same landing and takeoff speed as a conventional. The tail-in-back airplane can have a much higher lift coefficient and thus get the same performance with a smaller wing.

A wing operating at high Reynolds number and aspect ratio is far more efficient than trying to get lift from anything smaller, such as a stabilizer.

The old fallacy of creating lift from various non-wing parts of the plane so the wing doesn't have to carry so much has tricked designers into making less efficient airplanes in the past. In WWI days, some planes even had airfoils between the wheels to make extra lift. In the twenties and thirties some fuselages were "airfoil" shaped to get lift. Even door handles were shaped like little airfoils.

The idea doesn't work. The lift so generated is at the cost of very high drag due to the air whirling into vortices from the low aspect ratio of a non-wing shape. A good wing is such a superior way to create lift that modern designers take special care that no part of the plane, other than the wing, lifts. That is why the wing is set at a slight angle of attack compared to the fuselage. The air will part to flow equally over all sides of the body during cruise flight and insure there is no lift from the fuselage. All other parts are shaped symetrically to the expected on-coming air.

Some proponents of canards understand their basic inefficiency, but say prevention of spins by the inability of the main wing to stall is the greatest advantage of the design. This may be so, but a tailplaned airplane can be rigged so there is not enough elevator movement to pull the wing into stall. Several airplanes have been made with this feature, such as the Ercoupe, but they have no significantly better safety record than stallable aircraft. Why? Isn't the dreaded spin the cause of most fatal crashes?

When a non-spinnable airplane is flown slowly enough it sinks very fast. If it smacks the ground, the results are about the same as if it had spun. If all airplanes were non-spinnable, the statistics might not change but the cause from the spins would be simply changed to "impact from high sink descent."

All things being equal (span, wing loading, etc.), the non-spinnable airplane, whether canard or conventional, will begin a high rate sinking at a higher speed than a plane that can be stalled or spun. A good pilot can therefore get more performance from a plane that can be stalled in the form of slower landing, better climb angle and tighter turns, by flying nearer the stall which simply can't be done with airplanes of limited wing lift coefficient. At high speeds, the difference between the two types isn't as significant because they are both operating at low lift coefficients.

Flying Wings

Some of the composite planes, such as the Mini-Bat, are flying wings. With the smoothness of plastic and ease of making any shape, the simplicity of a flying wing is appealing. No tail to make and a compact airplane for easier storage. How are they stable and what compromises must be made with this design compared to others?

The flying wing can be swept forward or back and even a simple straight wing can also be made stable. A special airfoil with the trailing edge turned up, called a "reflex airfoil", is used in a tailless airplane. A cambered airfoil tends to pitch down, so it needs a stabilizer to hold it at the proper angle of attack. A reflexed airfoil will tend to keep a set angle of attack all by itself. A straight winged tailless airplane will fly stably on the reflex airfoil alone. However, the greater the reflex for stability, the less the wing will lift. There is, quite obviously, less downwash generated with the trailing edge of the airfoil bent up.

Some tailless planes use an airfoil that can lift more because it is less reflexed and less stable. To keep the teeter-totter stability of changing forces with speed they use a negative angle of attack, or "washed out" wing tips with a swept back wing. The tips are behind the center of gravity. If the plane speeds up the wind hits the tips pushing them down so the nose goes up and the plane slows as it tries to climb. The weight ahead of the aerodynamic center then becomes the greater force and brings the nose back down to its pre-set trimmed position.

The flying wing stability principle is identical to the conventional plane but, depending on the sweep angle, the distance between the center of gravity and the downforce on the tips is much less than for a plane with a long tail. This means more washout must be used, with its attendant increase in drag, just as a plane with a very short tail must use greater negative angle for stability. This, combined with the stable airfoil, limits the lift. The airplane must be made with extra wing area for performance equal to a tailed airplane. The swept and twisted wing is more complicated to make with all the angles and once again, the twisted wing is at lowest drag at only one speed. At very slow speeds the controls on the tips or trailing edge of the wing are deflected up considerably, reducing the lift and increasing the drag. When the tailless plane is going fast, the tip controls are flexed down to counteract the effect of the washout in the wings, again increasing drag, so there is only a narrow speed range for good efficiency.

Directional Stability

A large fin in back is necessary in all aircraft to have a good flying feel and directional steadiness with less yaw when using the ailerons. The rudder area can be small if the fin is long and large enough because, deflecting the rudder changes the lift over the entire vertical tail.

In the old days, most airplanes had a very tiny fin and large rudder which made them more difficult to fly because a lot of rudder had to be used, coordinated with aileron movement, to keep from yawing and skidding. I believe this was because most of the early plane designers were model airplane builders. A model needs far less fin and uses more dihedral, (bent up wings), than full sized planes. Most striking about the more modern airplane designs, compared to those of the 1930 s, is the larger fin area and much less dihedral.

Many planes use a swept back tail for jet-like styling. The tail sweep has no effect aerodynamically except slightly more drag than a straight tail. The swept structure is harder to build with difficult angles and twisting moments to plan for, but its the style.

Since flying wings and canards are shorter than conventional aircraft, directional stability requires more vertical tail area. They offer less leverage in the distance between the center of gravity and tail. The situation calls for very large fins on the end of swept back wings, to get the tails back further, and special drag flaps on the tips for turning by dragging a wing back to counteract the adverse yaw of ailerons.

Biplanes

A biplane is a delightfully historic looking airplane that was predominant in the earlier days of flying. Airplanes with two wings continue to be popular among homebuilders. Besides the looks, advantages are less weight and span for the same wing loading as a single winger. Surprisingly enough, a biplane can also have greater aerodynamic efficiency IF compared with an airplane of equal span, despite the four tip vortices and interference between the wings. If equal wing areas are considered the monoplane is easily better, of course. Biplanes are lighter because the wings can have external bracing to make a trussed structure. It's as if the spar is as deep as the space between the wings. With the light, strong, short wings, biplanes may have a very peppy takeoff and rapid aileron response.

One disadvantage is that the extra set of wings takes more manhours to produce. Also, monoplanes of only five percent greater span, say a half foot longer on each tip, (a 21 foot monoplane compared to a 20 foot biplane), is more efficient. The five percent longer span monoplane is far easier to make than the extra set of wings for a biplane of similar performance.

One popular composite airplane is a so-called tandem winged biplane which uses the front wing for control. The fin and rudder are set on the back of a reasonably long fuselage so it has good directional characteristics. It gets its pitch stability by having the front wing at a higher angle of attack and loaded more than the back wing. Thus at slow speed, or high angles of attack, the plane will nose down automatically as it approaches the stall, the same as with the canard.

The tandem wing bi-plane, like the canard and flying wing, suffers from a low maximum lift coefficient. Longer takeoffs and faster landings, combined with wider turning, are the tradeoffs for the elimination of a tailplane.

All things being equal, neither the canard, tailless, tandem wingers, or biplanes, have advantages over the conventional designs. They are of worse performance in every case because of high trim drag. The canard surface must lift with a less efficient wing of low Re (Reynolds Number) and high induced drag, while the wing is limited in lift coefficient to less than the canard. The flying wing also cannot create as much lift for its size because part of the wing must be used to insure stability.

But what about all the records held by some of the canards and the success of tailless airplanes, particularly in hang gliding and ultralights? Haven't biplanes won many speed races and aerobatic contests over the years? Yes, of course, but not because they have aerodynamic efficiency over the conventional monoplane. It's simply because the proponents of these designs took the time and care to set the aircraft up for the particular achievement, while the competition did not.

Remember, I said, ALL THINGS BEING EQUAL, which is seldom found between airplanes. A very streamlined unconventional design that sacrifices short field landing and takeoff to all-out cruise performance may seem to be outstandingly efficient when compared to a very draggy conventional plane or even a clean one with slower landing and takeoff speeds.

A tail-in-back airplane designed for efficient cruise will easily best a canard or tailless designed to the same performance band. As an example, consider an international soaring champion, A.J. Smith, who knows his aerodynamics. He created a conventional tandem (seats one behind the other) specifically for the Oshkosh 500 speed and economy race. Smith's well streamlined and detailed tail-in-the-back, motor-in-front taildragger, swept the race in both economy and speed by a very big margin over many of the equally streamlined but less aerodynamically efficient canards.

However, it is also true that unusual airplanes are fun. I owned a Fauvel flying wing sailplane for many years, won contests and trophies, got one of my Soaring Diamond Badge achievement awards with it and had a great time flying the unique-looking wing. There is no question unconventional designs can be made to work very well but crediting their achievements to unusual design is a fallacy.

Engine Position

To put the engine in the front or rear has been a question ever since airplanes were invented. It has been pretty well settled for the great majority of airplanes by having it in front. It is such a nice weight with which to balance the rest of the airplane. The pilot and cargo or passengers can then be distributed around the center of gravity with less effect on balance, no matter how light or heavy. A front propeller pulls in clean undisturbed air for high efficiency and thrust. Another feature I like is being able to see what is happening to the prop or exhaust pipes so I can manage the mixture or pitch controls or watch for oil leaks etc. — an observation seldom possible with the engine behind. In an accident, the engine and its mount absorb some of the crash energy, protecting the pilot.

A disadvantage is that the wind from the prop blows turbulent air along the fuselage creating more drag. This is especially true while flying slowly, when the difference between the airplane's airspeed and the wind behind the prop is greatest. The forward prop is broken more easily in a noseover and in some cases it is more danger to ground people while it is turning.

The pusher has slightly more efficiency than a tractor. It doesn't blow turbulent air back over the fuselage and it can make up the losses of accelerating turbulent air at the back of the fuselage by lowering the drag of a short or blunt body. It pulls the air together which would ordinarily be starting to separate.

In an open cockpit plane, or an ultralight, a pusher makes for more comfortable piloting because the wind-in-the-face is less. Put your hand in front and then behind a fan and you will see what the difference is. Now picture yourself sitting behind a propeller.

The balance problem has been minimized in one airplane by having the engine at the CG and the prop at the end of a long shaft from the tail. One canard has the pilot put the nose down on the ground by retracting the front wheel. If the pilot simply forgot to drop the nose the engine, which is mounted in the tail, would pull the plane over backwards. More than one canard flyer has suffered this embarrassment. A nut or bolt, piece of the exhaust system or a stone kicked up by the wheels may take out a pusher prop far more often than a puller.

Wing Position

The high wing is more aerodynamically efficient than a wing put on the bottom of the fuselage — there is less disturbance of the flow over the top. The pilot is usually placed at the CG about a third of the way back from the leading edge. This creates the problem of being able to see out in a turn. Exactly where the pilot needs to look first before banking. With the wing on the bottom seeing into a turn is much better. Most people like to look down while riding in an airplane so the high winger is preferred if the windows are low enough.

The wing is a very strong part of the airplane so a low mount position allows the pilot and passengers to sit on it, making for a good crash absorbing structure. Mounting the wheels to the low wing is efficient too. The high winger must make extra strength parts in the fuselage to attach the wheels as well as carry the loads to and from the wings.

The features of high versus low wings are so balanced it is almost even, depending on how you value certain features. This is obvious by going to the local airport and seeing how evenly divided are the types. By putting a window in the cabin roof, and having the pilot's seat slightly forward with the engine close to the CG, a highwing pilot can have very satisfactory viewing. The Cessna Cardinal was a good example of this. A low winger with fairings in the roots can eliminate most of the problems of airflow disturbance at the fuselage joint. If the windows are carried well above and below the pilot a low wing can have better downward viewing than some poor highwingers.

Ultimate Airplanes

The great joy of composite airplanes is the freedom they give to designers and builders. Never has a method of making airplanes so suited to toolless amateur construction been possible. Interesting canards, tandem winged bi-planes, pushers and flying wings are being built by many fliers who would have never considered these types with conventional materials.

I think the ultimate design might combine fast cruising with slow landing and takeoff. This can only be done with extendable wings. Flaps are fine for landing but they create so much drag, takeoffs are better with flaps up. To make slow takeoffs, one must have more wing area operating at a lower drag coefficient. This is not possible with flapped airplanes.

Nature is difficult. A big wing makes for great weight if there is to be enough strength for high speed gust loads. The answer would be a telescoping wing. It is moved out for takeoff and climb giving more wing area and low induced drag. When the pilot wants to go fast, the wing tip is pulled in. The short wing is much stronger for high speed bumps. Great weight can be saved by having the wing-out position limited to slow takeoff and climb speeds so the plane need be strong only in the short wing position. Flapped planes have speed limits on the flaps down speed as would a telescoping wing machine. Will something like this be made?

That's the fun of this modern age of composite construction. The freedom to try so many ideas in aerodynamics and styling. Now let's look into the materials themselves and how they are worked.

Summary
- An elliptical lift distribution is ideal. The wing planform to achieve this varies.
- A high aspect ratio has lowest induced drag.
- Composite wings with laminar flow airfoils can be longer and lighter.
- A wing is the best device for gaining efficient lift.
- Tailplane-in-back has most potential performance.
- A telescoping wing might be the ultimate in a wide speed range on limited power.

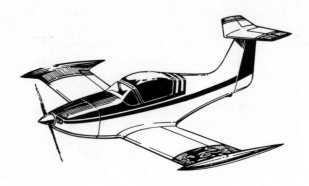

2
Foam/Fiberglass Technique

There are many ways to do the same thing, each with its enthusiasts. It is impossible to know which is "right". Much of it depends on the kind of item being made, tools, type of equipment you have, and the experience of the worker. What may be a superb method in a shop with experienced people may be not possible for the average person in a home workshop. The need for low weight and reliable strength is not important in auto body finishing, for example, so different materials and methods than these used for aircraft, may be fine. The Long-EZ manual, Dragonfly instructions, Spruce and Specialty supply company catalog, *Sport Aviation* articles, talks with homebuilders working on their plastic airplanes and personal experiences, have all been combined to describe the way experts work with aircraft.

Here's a step-by-step, basic description of making airplane parts of foam covered with fiberglass. This, and the following re-cap and emphasis chapter on finishing, should be read carefully before making test pieces or actual parts. The first thing we'll do is shape the foam, keeping in mind that foams are different and not shaped the same way.

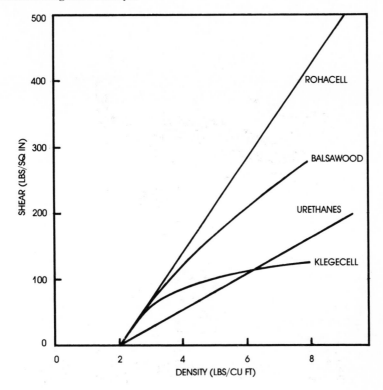

Fig. 2-1. The shear strength of various foam cores.

Urethane Foam

This rather costly, $1.12 per cubic foot, foam is easy to work and fun to use. It is impervious to most solvents and thus, can be used with easier safer, less expensive polyester resins. The green color changes to brown with exposure to air and sun. It is cut with a big knife to rough shape, then sanded with other bits of urethane foam to the final design. I find it useful for making wing tips or wheel fairings, and small streamlined parts with lots of curves. Inside curves can be made with a wire brush, then final finished with curved scrap blocks.

Urethane foam is dangerous to your lungs, especially when sanding large parts, because so much dust is created. Use a vacuum to draw the dust away. Wear a mask to keep from breathing the stuff. The sharp little particles are furious on the lungs. It is simple to work outside on a windy day when the dust will blow away. It is silly to use urethane foam on large parts with gentle curves, such as tail and wing sections, because a quicker and easier way to make parts is by hot wire cutting. Urethane is used for fuel tanks because it is not dissolved by gasoline.

Warning

Urethane gives off a poison gas when it melts, and it should not be cut using the hot wire method. Don't try to burn scraps either.

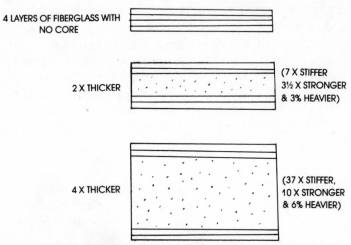

4 LAYERS OF FIBERGLASS WITH
NO CORE

2 X THICKER   (7 X STIFFER
                               3½ X STRONGER
                               & 3% HEAVIER)

4 X THICKER   (37 X STIFFER,
                               10 X STRONGER
                               & 6% HEAVIER)

Fig. 2-2. How foam/fiberglass sandwich strength varies with core thickness.

Clarkfoam

This is a denser and more expensive, $1.20 sq. ft., 4 pound per cubic foot, white, sheet urethane that comes in 1/8th to 4 inch thicknesses. A wonderfully versatile material used as the center for sandwich sections, it can be purchased with fine lines scored in one or both sides to easily form compound curves. The original Viking Dragonfly tandem winged bi-plane used it for the fuselage, which could be made without a full mold. The Clarkfoam can be bent into a simple set of formers to hold the curves in position while the fiberglass is applied over it to fix its shape. It is frequently used in regular molds after the gel coat and first two glass layers are put in. Then the Clark urethane is put in and another layer of glass added for a strong, light sandwich. The Glassair and Q-2 have their fuselages made this way.

Styrofoam

Blue or orange styrofoam is the principal core material for wings, canards, and control surfaces. It weighs 2 pounds per cubic foot and is often strong enough in compression to be used for parts with no internal structure. Cost is only fifty cents per cubic foot. It is an insulation material in the real world, so it is often easy to get from insulation companies. However, just about anything except water and epoxy will dissolve it. It cuts easily with a hot wire.

Polystyrene

Orange polystyrene can be seen as floatation foam around the boating industry. The boating type is not affected by sunshine which makes it fine for airplanes. The lightweight Goldwing uses Polystyrene foam for its flying surfaces. Cost is only fifty cents and weight 2 lb per cubic foot.

Expanded polystyrene looks like a lot of little balls pressed together. It is also 2 lbs per cubic foot, soft, weak and easily eaten away by solvents. My friend Bill Watson uses it to make radio control model airplane wings by hot wire cutting the airfoil, insetting strips of spruce on the top and bottom for strength then gluing on that shiny paper for the surface finish. I like polystyrene for making model airplane fuselages. It carves with a sharp knife or hot wire. Of course, Polyester resin will eat up the foam. But, you can use the cheaper and less irritating polyester resin without melting the foam by sealing it first. Cover it with silkspan model tissue and white glue mixed with a little water for thinning. If epoxy resin is used you can go right over the foam.

After the fiberglass cures, pour any solvent on to the foam inside to make it disappear. You then have a very light fuselage, suitable for flying models. Ducting for cooling air, and weird internal shapes such as wheel wells, can be made rather quickly. Carve your shape, epoxy the fiberglass over it, and eat away the core plug, this saves applying mold release, and prying the part off after the cure.

Wheel fairings or fancy wing tips for full sized airplanes can be made by this method, since it must be hollow inside for the wheel.Great bending loads are not applied to a streamlined wheel cover or tips, so it works out fine.

Klegecell

This is standard "aircraft quality" foam that meets all the Federal Air Regulations for fire proof, as well as the aviation industry's engineering needs. It is little effected by the sunshine and, polyester resins won't melt it. Cost is over $1.80 a cubic foot for the 2 lb/cu ft density, with higher prices for the denser foam which goes up to 15 lbs/cu ft. It is cut with a fine saw and shaped in one-direction, and bends with a heat gun.

At 200°F, the material can be vacuum formed in a mold to compound shapes. One problem with this material is the variation in pronunciation, some say the word with a hard "G" and some with the soft. Klegecell as in "keg" or "leg" is common as well, Klegecell as the G said with a sound like "ledge."

Balsa wood is one of the strongest and least expensive sandwich centers. Its main problem however, is the great variation in strength. As you may know from building models, it can be heavy and hard or light and soft. Unless a very skilled balsa selection is made, its outstanding strength to weight ratio cannot be counted on reliably, so it is simpler to use the foams.

Rohacell is a German foam much used in sailplanes. Resistant to most chemicals, strong and expensive, it is a fine material but not necessary for most applications in USA kits and plans.

The Work Table

Presuming you are going to build one of the aircraft mentioned in this book, or design your own, an important part of the tooling is a work table. It is truly surprising how important a large stiff table is for making anything, certainly as accuracy critical as an airplane. The table should be as long as you can comfortably fit into the workplace with a minimum of 18 feet up to

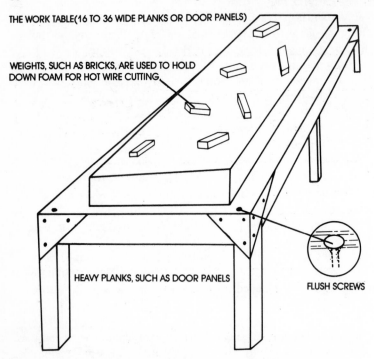

THE WORK TABLE(16 TO 36 WIDE PLANKS OR DOOR PANELS)

WEIGHTS, SUCH AS BRICKS, ARE USED TO HOLD DOWN FOAM FOR HOT WIRE CUTTING.

HEAVY PLANKS, SUCH AS DOOR PANELS

FLUSH SCREWS

Fig. 2-3. A large, sturdy worktable is essential for working with composite structures.

25 feet long, by 16 inches wide. The 16 inches is narrow, so get some of those ten dollar, hollow doors at the building supply store to use for laying on the big table for extra work space as needed. When you don't need the door tables, put them up against the wall to conserve space. By making the table top a box of 4 to 10 inches depth, stiffness will be adequate. Glue the parts with countersunk screws to hold them together. This is to make a smoother, non-catching surface for cutting glass cloth. If you prefer, it is perfectly logical to make a three foot wide table if you have the room and want lots of space. But, the need is for only the size of the foam blanks used.

MAKING AIRFOIL FOAM CORES

Templates

To create wing sections, a pattern of the airfoil is made of some material over which the hot wire cutter can slide easily, such as thin plywood, masonite, or aluminum. Whatever you use, the edges should be smoothed and accurate to be sure the wire doesn't hang up and mar the cut. The kits being marketed today, have full sized airfoils either as templates already, or able to be cut out and traced on the template material. The template of the root and tip airfoils are cut according to the design of the wing.

White Wallite tempered masonite is my favorite material. It is available at the building supply house. Its slick surface should be sanded a little so the

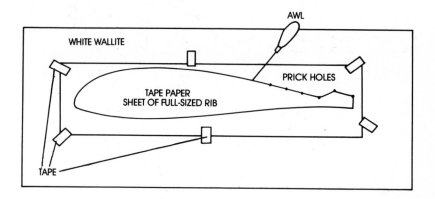

WHITE WALLITE

AWL

PRICK HOLES

TAPE PAPER
SHEET OF FULL-SIZED RIB

TAPE

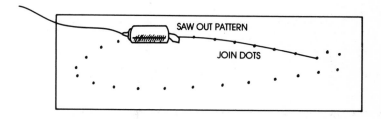

SAW OUT PATTERN

JOIN DOTS

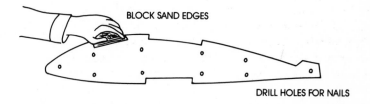

BLOCK SAND EDGES

DRILL HOLES FOR NAILS

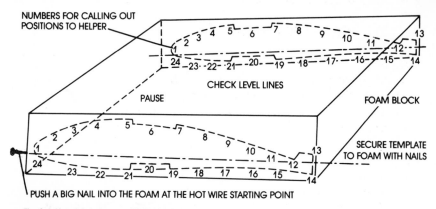

NUMBERS FOR CALLING OUT
POSITIONS TO HELPER

CHECK LEVEL LINES

PAUSE

FOAM BLOCK

SECURE TEMPLATE
TO FOAM WITH NAILS

PUSH A BIG NAIL INTO THE FOAM AT THE HOT WIRE STARTING POINT

Fig. 2-4. How to make an airfoil template.

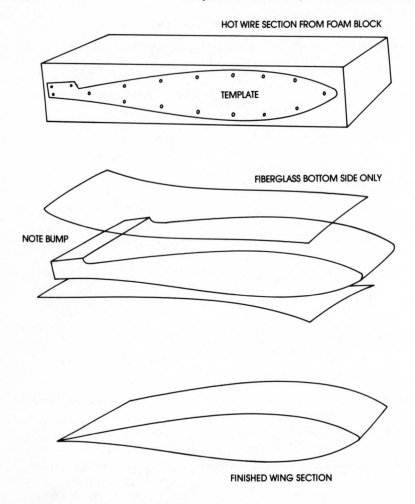

HOT WIRE SECTION FROM FOAM BLOCK

TEMPLATE

FIBERGLASS BOTTOM SIDE ONLY

NOTE BUMP

FINISHED WING SECTION

Fig. 2-5. How to make a thin trailing edge.

marking pen or pencil will show up well. Put the airfoil pattern over the Wallite fastened with double sided cellophane tape.

Use a very sharp awl or pick to mark through the pattern and into the Wallite every quarter inch. Be sure the tape is holding so the pattern doesn't move. Over the curves of the leading edge, the marks are made closer together, about ⅛ in. Remove the paper airfoil pattern and connect the prick marks with a pencil line. Now cut the template from the Wallite. Notice, that to make a proper thin trailing edge, a funny bump is put on the foam blank now which is cut off after one side is glassed. Hand sand the template to its final shape with blocks. Put the template over the pattern to insure everything was lined up when it was made. Now you have a smoothly edged and accurate template.

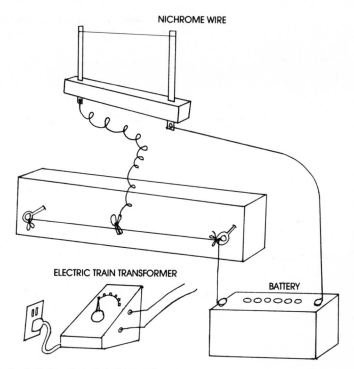

NICHROME WIRE

ELECTRIC TRAIN TRANSFORMER

BATTERY

Fig. 2-6. The basic design of a hot wire foam cutter.

Drill 6 to 12 nail holes in the template, and using lathing nails, fix it to the end of the foam block. Draw a level line on the template with a carpenter's level, when the template is fastened to the foam with the nails. The tip template is also adjusted with the carpenters level so the relation of the root to the tip is proper. For example, washout twist in the tip. If none is called for however, make sure there really is no change in the angle of attack.

The block is now on the table, the templates fastened and leveled, and 80 to 100 lbs. of weights are set on the block to hold the foam steady. A couple of sheets of half inch foam, plywood or wood shelving can be laid full length under the blocks to give working room between the edge of the foam and the table. If more than one block is needed, tape or center glue the blocks into one. The tool used to shape the block is a hot wire.

Foam Wire Cutters

A foam cutter is simply a wire strung tightly between two posts connected to a source of electric current. The friction of the electrons moving through the wire makes it hot. By moving it through a foam block it will melt a smooth line cut. It can be freehanded for rough cuts but generally a pattern is fixed to each side of the block and the wire carefully run around it to make an accurate shape.

A foam cutter 65 inches long will be fine to make wing sections, while 45 inches is fine for rudder and elevator pieces. By using two twelve volt

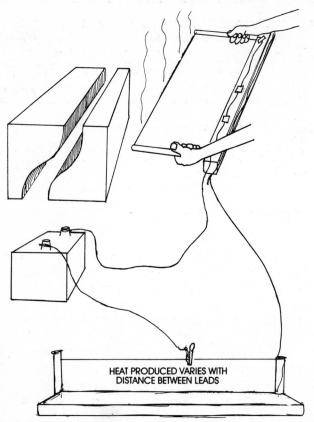

HEAT PRODUCED VARIES WITH
DISTANCE BETWEEN LEADS

Fig. 2-7. Make practice cuts on scrap foam, until you get a feel for the proper heat and speed.

batteries or a twelve volt battery charger, a cheap power supply can be made for heating the wire.

The transformer from a model train set that converts 110 volt 60 cycle standard house current to a direct current of variable voltage works beautifully. Two ordinary twelve volt chargers with a homemade regulator will suffice to do most of the cutting. Current required is 4 amps. A variable transformer for foam cutting operations is available for $47.50 (see suppliers in the Appendix).

Nichrome wire can be used for the foam cutter. It will get just as hot as stainless wire on only 2 amps, but I use stainless steel(.032 inch) wire because it can be pulled tighter. This is important because you don't want the wire to stretch and sag while pulling it through a foam block. The flex may make a badly shaped part, especially in a sharply curved section.

The waste of two amps using stainless instead of nichrome is inconsequential. Despite the cries for conservation it seems the less electricity we use the more the utilities raise rates to cover their claimed fixed cost, so who cares.

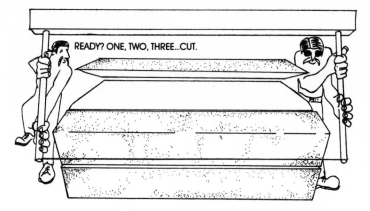

READY? ONE, TWO, THREE...CUT.

Fig. 2-8. Two people are needed to cut a wing core.

Twang the wire and listen to the sound as you heat it and tighten (increase the tension). The tone will become higher pitched until just before it starts to stretch and fail. When you find the pitch staying the same stop tightening or it will break.

After practicing with scraps you can set the current properly. A wire too hot, will melt out a wider slot than the wire diameter. It may also make little pits or craters in the foam. When you stop briefly a rut will appear in the cut because of the excess heat.

If the wire is not hot enough, it takes too long to cut and when pushed hard the wire stretches and bellies, making an inaccurate sagging cut in a curve. However, this is not as serious when on a straight section.

Turn up the current until the wire is glowing, then back off until it is dark. Check the temperature by sliding a three inch foam cube into the wire. Do several cuts, slowly increasing the voltage, until the wire makes a long hair of melted foam as it exits the cut. If it is too hot, you will hear a loud hissing sound and the foam may even stick back together behind the wire. There should be a small but noticeable drag on the wire during a cut and little increase in foam melt if you stop for a moment. A steady hiss and sizzle as the wire cuts and the long fine plastic hairs streaming from the wire at the end of a cut, shows it is the best temperature. The faint hiss of the foam melting is a good sign of the correct wire temperature. As I said, secure it with heavy weights, like bags of lead shot, steel gears and such. This keeps the block from twisting, flexing or moving around during the cut.

The reason your table should be sized to fit is so you and your helper can walk around it to move the wire smoothly. Reaching far out over a too large table is conducive to tiring arms and perhaps poor cutting.

If the section desired is too large to be made with one block, which is usually the case, put several chunks together. They may be temporarily glued with fast setting epoxy at the centers. But, it is important that there is no chance the hot wire will hit the glue and interrupt it during the cut. Nails struck in at an angle are not as good because the hot wire cutter may bump into them resulting in problems starting up again and making ridges in the foam shape. A trouble free way to fasten blocks is with wide masking tape.

The templates are held to the block on each end by pushing nails through the holes into the foam. If there is a twist in the wing it must be done during the cut. The Long-Ez, for example, has the tips at less angle of attack than the center section. To do any twist properly a baseline is marked on the foam so the pattern can be placed according to a centerline on the airfoil template.

A mark is made every inch around the circumference of the template so the helper can stay with you by calling out the numbers as the wire is moved. The hot wire should be moved through the foam an inch for every slow count of five.

Turn on the current and call out "Position." That means you both hold the cutter almost touching the foam. Then say, "Ready——CUT!" Together, with your helper, start the wire into the foam slowly. Call the number position of the wire on the template every five seconds. Use light pressure.

A sharp curve takes special technique. For example, the leading edge of an airfoil requires care to keep the wire straight. Go very slowly as you cut around the curve to be sure the sag, or delay in the middle of the wire, doesn't make a bow in the leading edge of the foam airfoil.

To make unbowed sharp curves, push wire rods into the foam at the apex of the curve and cut to that point. Then, start on the other side of the block and cut to the same place. Take a doubly slow cutting pace as the point of the curve is approached and pause at the rod marker. A thin line, the thickness of your marker rod,will be left at the completion of the cut but that is easily sanded or sliced off with a big knife.

Mistakes

If you or your helper accidently lifted the wire from the template don't panic, stop, or start over. Move the wire back to the template and keep going. Simply sand off the resultant ridge later.

Rarely, but possible, the wire may snap while cutting, in which case you must stop. Re-attach a new wire and start again by going into the foam at the break. Sand and fill that place later.

If the wire snags on a nail, bit of epoxy, or anything impossible to cut through, stop the heat and remove the object. If you can't get the obstruction out, start over going the other way and cut to the other side of the blockage. Now the foam blocks are ready to be joined for good. They were glued by globs of five minute epoxy or tape, remember. So after gently pulling them apart, check the fit again and prepare for a micro slurry sealing.

Mixing Epoxy

There are many kinds of epoxy. Thick, thin, slow or quick setting, and brittle or flexible. In this section, you will be using the standard type used in homebuilt aircraft, as sold by the suppliers. The chapter on materials discusses epoxies and other resins, costs and sources.

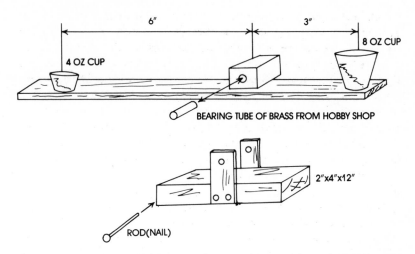

Fig. 2-9. A simply-made proportional balance is all you need to properly mix epoxy. Cups shown for two-to-one mix.

Simplest is the quick, 5 min cure, epoxy that needs estimated equal globs of resin and catalyst mixed to cure and harden successfully. On all other epoxies, use a scale to set the proper ratio of catalyst to resin. Always mix ratios accurately according to the designers directions. For example, the Long-Ez and Quickie use fast and slow setting resins. Both epoxy types use the same weight ratio of 22 parts of catalyst to harden 100 parts of resin. The hardeners are different to vary the rate of curing.

The idea is to use a slow curing epoxy where the heat generated by the catalyst action might build up. Heat will ruin the foam or joint. Too fast a cure may result in heat building up in thick blocks or layups. In thinner areas, the heat can escape easily so, a faster curing hardener can be used.

To insure exact ratios for mixing epoxy, I like to use a proportional pump. This device pushes out the right ratio of resin to catalyst with one stroke of the handle. It is simpler and more error free than the weighing method. Some are fancy affairs with variable ratios, while others have a simple pump-lid that fits into the place of the cap on your can. Compared to the cost of the complete airplane, it seems penny wise and pound foolish not to buy one. Get them at the aircraft resin suppliers. Still, a home-made scale is fairly easy to make, is free, and can be made to work well.

Slurrying The Foam

Before the foam is glassed, it must be covered by a coat of epoxy-microballoon slurry. This is to fill the tiny voids so the resin doesn't soak in too much and make the part too heavy. It is also to insure the glassing adheres to the shape. First check for twist and any ridges that may have been made by uneven hot wire movement during the cut. Use a sanding block a foot or two long with medium or rough sandpaper to keep the sanding even. High performance laminar flow airfoils require an accurate shape. Air does

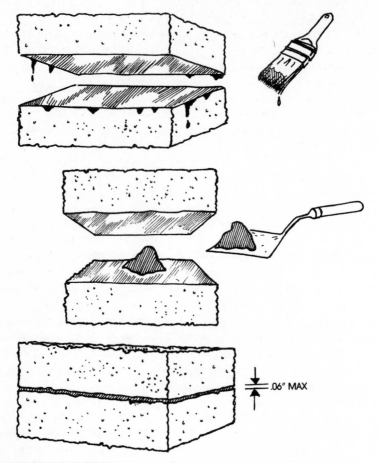

Fig. 2-10. How to slurry the foam.

not like to go up and down hills and valleys, even as small as a few thousandths of an inch. But more about this in finishing.

Now, back to our wing section. We have a block of foam that has been hot wire cut into an aerodynamic shape for a wing panel or control section. It has been lightly sanded to accuracy. The blocks that have been temporarily glued with five-minute epoxy or tape are now permanently bonded. Make a six ounce batch of resin. That's the same as half a can of beer. By cutting your cans two thirds from the top and cleaning and drying the inside you can have an endless supply of mixing cups. The usual alternative is waxless paper cups. That they be plain paper is important, because any wax coating will contaminate the resin and degrade the mix to the point where it may not harden.

Caution: Before even touching epoxy resin and hardener always put on your safety goggles and rubber gloves or skin barrier cream as emphasized in the safety section.

Limiting batch mixes to 6 ounces keeps it from getting too hot during curing, and is about all you can work with before it begins to gel.

Try to make exact mix ratios and stir with a tongue depressor. Scrape the sides and bottom of your cup, using two to three minutes by the clock. That's a long time and your hand may get tired, but it is very important for a proper epoxy batch.

Next, the microballoons are put in, and mixed 50% with the resin to make a thin slurry. These microscopic glass balls lower the density of the resin and if enough are put in, can make it putty-like for filling foam dents and holes. The surface is done with thin micro to keep it from soaking up so much resin when the glass is laid over. It is also used to fill holes and notches as well as glue blocks to one another.

The micro-slurry should be about like molasses. After spreading it on, let it sit for 4 minutes while it flows in the foam crevices. You can hear it clicking and crackling as it fills. Then work the mirco back and forth with a 5" squeegee before wiping most of it off and putting it in the small container to discard. This will save much weight. There should still be the pattern of the styrofoam when you finish slurrying. Urethane does not have the large cells of styrene foam so this step isn't necessary. Instead, use the resin only on the foam to aid wetting the first layer.

On a fancy curved part that is hard to drape with fiberglass, it is possible, but more difficult, to resin on top of the already positioned cloth. Gently stipple and spread the resin lightly.

Glassing

The fiberglass is put on the foam in layers depending on how strong the part needs to be in each area. Since bending forces on wings are greatest near the center, more layers of glass are used inboard with less toward the tips.

Unidirectional fiberglass is a special weave with the thicker bundles of glass filaments going one way. It is used where strength in tension, in one direction, is needed.

For parts stressed in many ways, another weave called bi-directional, has equal filaments both ways. It is best for compound curves as it can be smoothed over the foam in any direction.

Temperature should be 70° to 80° F for glassing. You should have helpers and enough resin and hardener. The fiberglass or Carbon Fiber cloth should be kept clean. Any dirt, oil or solvents on it may make the resin bond poorly. A clean, smooth table for cutting is necessary. Using the floor is ok if it is clean. Measure and mark the pieces oversize. Cut the cloth with sharp scissors. Sharpen them every series of cuts. A good file or a fine grinding wheel is very useful.

Cut the cloth pieces in the order they will be used, and label them with your felt pen. Using masking tape to label cloth is ok if you put it along the edge where it will not leave residue or distort the fabric when you pull it off. Cover the cloth with a plastic sheet to keep any resin drips off before you are ready

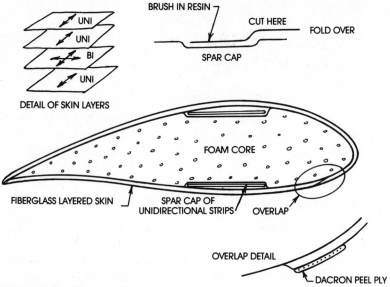

Fig. 2-11. Laying fiberglass over a foam core wing.

to lay it on the foam. A drip of resin would make a little bump on the fabric which will likely be sanded through during finishing, and weaken the shell.

Caution: Always wear your special coveralls and safety goggles. Why safety goggles? To keep from thoughtlessly rubbing your eyes with even a trace of epoxy. **It could blind you!** Don't forget to have your helpers wear protection, as well.

The main tool in glassing is the squeegee, made of beer carton cardboard. The venerable brush is seldom used except for edges, and little parts that need several layers piled up, such as reinforcements around fittings. The brush is used in a poking stroke, called stippling, to wet the little pieces.

Lay the cloth according to the fiber direction called for and pour on the epoxy. Using fast, light sweeps spread it with the squeegee. Too much resin may allow the cloth to move around when you lift away from the foam.

It's a good idea to have some small parts and sections ready, aside from the major glassing operation. Making the preparations to epoxy, such as having clothes on, hand protection, eye protection, gloves, proper temperature and so forth, is too much to do for little parts alone. Have them ready in case you have some still cool epoxy left over which you can use for these little items.

Peel Ply

Lay strips of Dacron cloth along places that are designed to have another layer of glass. This is usually called out in the plans, but may take some thinking ahead. Use the excess resin you squeegeed off to put on the Dacron.

When ready for the next layer, peel off the dacron ply. The roughened surface will glue well to the new layers. This technique saves a lot of time compared to sanding the edges with 100 grit paper to prepare the bond area.

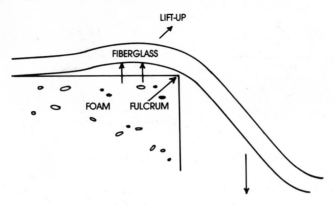

Fig. 2-12. Trim the cloth to within a half inch of the part's edge, to prevent it lifting-up.

Trim

When the glass is hard enough not to flex too much, yet soft enough to cut easily (say after four or five hours cure), trim off all the extra glass.

The part can be now turned over and the process repeated on the other side.

Summary

- Make a stiff smooth work table.
- Make accurate templates.
- Align and attach templates to ends of foam blocks.
- Move slowly around sharper corners in wire cutting.
- Measure hardener precisely and stir epoxy 3 minutes.
- Glue blocks in centers.
- Micro Slurry, wait 4 minutes, squeegee excess.
- Cut cloth oversize at a clean place.
- Pour on epoxy, spread, squeegee excess.
- Aim for even translucence in layup.
- Eliminate dry (white) glass, excess resin, (shiny) bubbles or separation of layers.
- Clean all epoxy from tools, hands and carefully change clothing.
- Trim edges after 5 hours.
- Pull peel ply ready for next side.

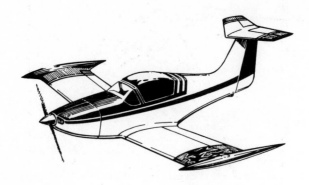

3

Foam/Fiberglass Finishing

Humans are fascinated by making things smooth and contoured. Statues, monuments, jewelry and furniture are finished as part of their appeal, not their utility. We seem to like using our hands for this activity. Backrubs, petting, picking pimples and scabs are in this "natural affinity of humans for" category. Rubbing on your beautiful sky machine should be exciting and satisfying. It only becomes drudgery when the work seems to be getting better only incrementally and out of proportion to the amount of time you are pouring into it. The sanding and finishing "work" is as delightful as any of the construction of an airplane.

A homebuilt airplane is an exciting and emotionally attractive creation. It may be the most satisfying project you will ever carry out and how it looks is very important. Recognize that sanding and finishing is truly great fun, but it must be well planned and properly done to get the most joy from the process.

This chapter on finishing underscores the chapter on how to work with foam and glass and should be studied at the same time. The emphasis is on the total finish, not just the final priming and painting. Details that begin when you start your project will insure a fine aircraft both in looks and aerodynamics.

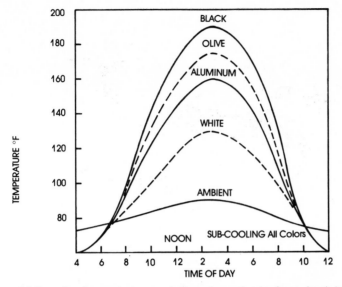

Fig. 3-1. The surface temperatures generated by various colored surfaces when in bright sunlight.

Every step of the construction process leads to a finish which will be only as good as the previous work. If the preliminary stages of foam shaping aren't done properly the only recourse is many hours of filling, sanding and reshaping to cover up the first mistakes. We will review the construction process but with stress on the little tricks and details that add up to a superb finish without such a crushing burden of time.

The paint job on a plastic airplane is the same as a car or metal airplane, with the exception that the color is limited to very light on the top surfaces.

White is preferable on homebuilt composites because the resin is cured at "normal" temperature. Otherwise the sun can heat the material so much on a hot day the plastic will lose strength. The major sailplane manufacturer in Finland, PIK, uses big ovens (autoclaves), to cure the higher temperature resins of their fiberglass airplanes, giving them much greater heat resistance. The gliders they make can be painted or gel-coated with red, yellow or other reasonably light colors besides white. They make their gliders with a good "Finnish", of course.

A good appearance is quicker if the base work is done correctly from the start, but it does require a lot of time. Plan on at least a hundred hours. Pace yourself so you don't get discouraged and stop before you are truly satisfied in your fondest fantasies of how it should look. I sanded and filled and sanded on my Fournier motorglider, with my brothers Mark and Rick, for days. Then late one afternoon, when they weren't around, I got impatient. I was tired and not thinking clearly. I decided to start painting. The paint sprayer nozzle was set wrong and the paint came out looking like a stuccoed wall. Boy, were they mad the next day! After hours of sanding off my premature enamel job, we started again. So take it easy. Relax and pace yourself. Be satisfied with each section. Don't go rushing on unless you are

SPANWISE CURVE FROM WIRE SAG

SANDING BLOCK

Fig. 3-2. If your hot wire is not hot enough, it will sag and cause a depressed contour spanwise. This can be prevented with proper hot wire temperature. A long, stiff sanding block can be used to correct it, provided the airfoil contour is maintained.

really pleased with the results so far. Wait until the next work session if you tire. What was acceptable at the end of a long day may look different the next morning.

Cured fiberglass is hard to sand and is part of the structure. Foam is much easier to work. Make up your mind to have perfect cores before you even think of glassing.

A word about finish and the air. 99.9 percent of the air the plane flies through does not touch the surfaces. Those glasslike finishes are for the pilot's emotions, not the air. **The shape** not the finish of the surface **is** important. A few thousandths of an inch in the airfoil curve can make a great difference in the performance. If the wing is uneven, the air closest to the surface must speed up over the hills and slow down in the valleys. This thickens the boundary layer and results in earlier separation than with perfect countours.

In sailplanes, careful tests show a sanded, dull finish along the leading edge is better than a polished one. Sailplane pilots improve wing performance by block sanding their perfect airfoils with fine grit paper, making it dulled and finely scratched. This reduces the overall drag and improves the glide angle.

Ever notice those pictures on the covers of flying magazines where they take the photographs at sundown so every rivet and skin lap on production airplanes stands out? It is a dramatic and interesting way to show the airplane. But, it is very disheartening for the aerodynamic enthusiast. The many lumps, bumps and skin laps in the aluminum structures of most lightplanes detract from the performance, no matter how shiny the paint.

Because the airplane's parts are one piece, composite construction can, if properly contoured, eliminate the discontinuities of aluminum-and-rivets aircraft. The results are better performance using composites instead of aluminum, given the same size and horsepower.

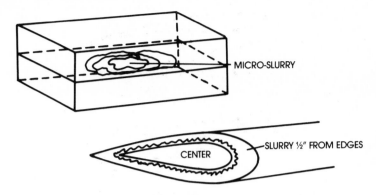

Fig. 3-3. When smearing on the micro-slurry, keep the half inch from the edge bare.

Foam Core Preparation

Aircraft made of foam cores have a different beginning than molded planes like the Polliwagen and Glasair but, the techniques for final filling and painting are the same. Using the moldless construction method of the Quickie etc., it is most important that foam cores be perfectly made. The airplane should be like you want it *before* the fiberglassing. The fiberglass is very thin compared to the foam and, since the strength comes from the glass in tension, each layer is important and *cannot* be sanded through or thinned without reducing strength. **Therefore, create good contours by making perfect cores, not sanding after glassing.**

Important to shaping foam well is having an easily handled hot wire cutter. One trick is to hang it from the ceiling with a spring to take the weight. Another is to make it very light. A fiberglass bow-and-arrow with the wire pulled as tightly as possible without stretching when hot, is easier to use than a heavy oversize-for-the-job cutter.

Start the hot wire cut where the curves are sharpest, at the leading edges of airfoils, for example. Hold the foam rigidly during cutting with lots of weights or clamps so it doesn't move and possibly result in wavy cuts.

It seems obvious, but handle the cut cores as if they were precious sculptures. Gouges and twisting can be prevented by putting your completed cores in a protected spot and insuring they're evenly supported to prevent warping.

Use extra time and care lining up blocks you must slurry-glue together. To insure twist and taper are accurate make lots of sightings and use string-lines to check the lineup of the foam blocks.

Misalignment, bumps or ridges can be more easily corrected by checking the contours with a metal yardstick laid along the surface. Use a light shining toward the ruler so any dips or humps can be seen under the edge.

Most discrepancies happen during hot cutting when the wire is allowed to sag. These result in the center being lower than the ends. They can be smoothed with a long sanding block moved along the span.

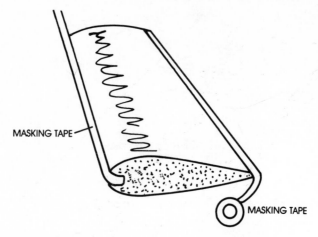

MASKING TAPE

MASKING TAPE

Fig. 3-4. Use masking tape over the edges of the foam, where the glass is to go.

One of the most difficult problems is the joints where the foam blocks are joined by micro-slurry. Cured slurry is much harder than the foam and equal sanding will leave a bump. Bumps are the worst kind of defect in foam. If glassed over, the only way to level it is to sand away some of the fiberglass layers. That is a "No-No" for composite planes since the structure depends on fiberglass strength in tension. The area all around the bump must be filled with micro balloons mixed with resin. This is a heavy and time consuming fix that can be prevented by careful core preparation.

When smearing on the micro-slurry to glue the blocks, keep half an inch from the edges bare. The blocks will be acceptably joined yet the micro-slurry glue doesn't squeeze out so any joggles or misalignments can be sanded smooth without having to cut through the glue. If the slurry is exposed over the foam use a low angle block plane, like the Stanley 60-1/2 P, to shave it away. The foam is much softer, so sanding a micro-slurry joint makes low spots on each side and the glue is left high in the middle. It is, of course, easier to correct exposed micro before it is fully hard. Scrape off any drips of micro before they harden. A drop of the stuff on the foam is removed with difficulty. Usually you end up tearing out a bit of the foam on which it has hardened.

Glassing Edge Treatment

Glassing over the perfectly shaped foam should be approached with care to stop drips on the unglassed foam. The overlapped edges of the glass are most likely to need extra finishing. Repairs and fixes on sharp curves are easier than on long, gently curved places, so the edges of the fiberglass should be at the sharpest curves.

Use lots of masking tape over the edges of the foam where the glass is yet to go. Run a couple strips of three quarter inch tape exactly along the leading edge of the wing or tail surfaces. This serves as a line to start the fiberglass

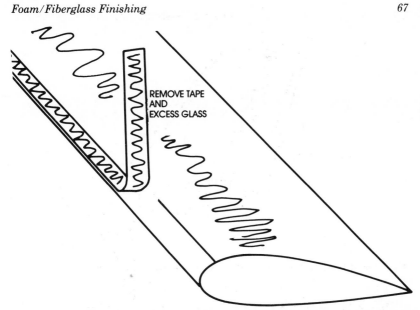

REMOVE TAPE AND EXCESS GLASS

Fig. 3-5. After cutting the edge of the glass when it's in the "rubbery green stage", simply lift-off the excess with the masking tape.

cloth. On a fuselage, run the tape along the corner. If it is round or oval, put the tape along the bottom where imperfections are less noticeable.

After the cloth is applied in the layers specified by the designer, the edge is trimmed before it hardens. This is the rubbery "Green" stage. The tape line is now used to define the place to cut the edge of the rubbery fiberglass. After the cut is made, pull off the tape, carrying the trimmed fiberglass with it.

Now use a Stanley Shurform blade to fair the edge of the fiberglass into the foam. Do this carefully so you don't cut into the foam. Pull toward you at an angle to keep from hooking the edge of the glass and ripping it off the foam.

When the part is turned over, check to be sure it is true. Again, put a couple strips of masking tape along the already glassed section edge giving room for the overlap. Put "peel ply" tapes only where you expect to attach another part because the roughened area is hard to sand smooth. Glass the side with an overlay of one to two inches, depending on what the plans callout. Use the masking tape to guide the trim cut and then pull off the waste portion of glass. With your trusty Shurform blade pulled at an angle away from the fresh edge, smooth the overlap into the older fiberglass. The older glass is harder so there is less danger of damage as the blade slides over it while tapering the new layer.

The pattern of laying several strips of masking tape on the edge of the surface to be fiberglassed, trimming to the tape line and blending the edge, is done throughout the glassing. A couple dozen rolls of masking tape are used on a typical foam-fiberglass aircraft. Since runs or blobs are usually made on the edges of the fiberglass, the tape helps to greatly reduce that problem which is particularly difficult to repair on bare foam without making a hole.

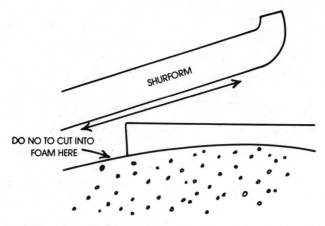

Fig. 3-6. Fair the edge of the glass into the foam with a Stanley Surform blade.

Some highly stressed areas have more than one layer of fiberglass. Use the same technique. Put double lines of tape around the piece being glued. Trim the edges when rubbery and pull off the waste with the masking tape. A nicely defined straight line edge is much easier to taper with a shurform file. Again, this is made less critical because the layer underneath has become much harder than the fiberglass piece on top and is not harmed by the shaving tool. Well tapered overlays can almost eliminate later filling.

Filling

Dry sand the part, say a wing, with forty grit sandpaper to make a good bond surface for the filler. If you use a foot long sanding block you can start to see the low spots. Also bend a metal ruler over the wing chordwise, from front to back, to see the dips. Many people can develop skill in running their hand across the surface to feel waviness. Some people can consistently sense a millionth of an inch and I think we can train ourselves to distinguish between differences in texture and contour. While sanding keep feeling the wing to check and sense its contour.

Sanding a wing blindly will make it smooth, but just as wavy as before. To fix low spots, mix a small batch of resin with the proper amount of catalyst, and smear some in the depression for better bonding. Next make a very dry mix of resin and micro-balloons. Micro is the filler used most for finishing. It should be mixed very dry when used for filler, because it will be easier to sand. Unfortunately, the dryer the micro-fill is applied, the harder it is to apply. It rolls into crumbs and doesn't want to stick very well. When gluing blocks together, you might think that using micro that is much more liquid is the way to make it flow into the depressions. Not so. Dry mixed micro is lighter and far easier to sand than runny micro.

Filling a depression in one try is seldom successful. Plan on filling and sanding three times. Only low spots can be filled and sanded. High spots

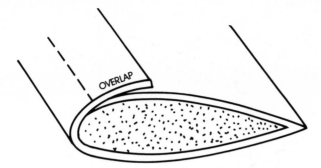

Fig. 3-7. The glass from the upper and lower surfaces of a wing must be overlapped sufficiently to assure a good bond for proper strength.

cannot be sanded down because you'll cut through the fiberglass making a weaker structure. Be careful to sand only the filler.

In some very micro overfilled places, use the Shurform plane to save time cutting down the extra thickness. Wet or dry 320 sandpaper does the fastest job on the filler. A hose gently running water on the part lubricates the sandpaper and the surface so it is easier to move the block. The sandpaper lasts longer as the water washes the dust away thus, keeping it from filling with grit.

You can make a block using a 9 inch by 2-1/4 inch piece of wood, which will then use one-third of a sheet. Also the Standard Brands chain of paint stores sells a hard rubber block with split ends to hold the paper, for $3. It uses a size that allows four strips to be cut from each sheet. Best for filler sanding is aluminum oxide sandpaper. Expensive, high quality sandpaper is

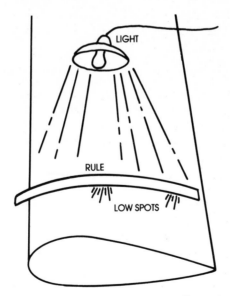

Fig. 3-8. Use a metal rule and a spotlight to check for bumps and low spots.

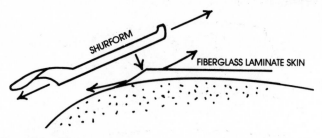

Fig. 3-9. Use a Shurform plane to save time in cutting down micro-slurry overfilled areas.

worth the price, considering the cost of the finished project and the ease of using good working materials.

Sanding is more pleasant if you know what is happening and see progress toward a good contour. With wet sanding the only way to tell is by sliding your hand back and forth to feel for the high spots. The flow of water makes the true surface indistinguishable. To really see it, the part must be dry. Sand at least a minute between dryings or it will seem nothing is being accomplished.

Some finishers dry sand so the results can be examined immediately. Starting with wet sanding and finishing the last bit dry is one way to compromise.

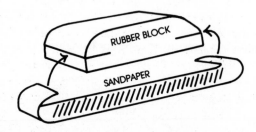

Fig. 3-10. Standard Brands makes a hard rubber block for holding sandpaper.

Tapered fiberglass laps are easy to finish and can often be done in one fill, but spar caps and multiple tapered laps may take several fillings. The front third of the wings and control surfaces are aerodynamically most important, so constant checking with the hand and a ruler is necessary for a good contour.

Pockets may form in the micro due to the dry mix. Since you are doing one section at a time, go back to the last part and fill the holes with the micro being used in the immediate section. The next day go back to sand the filled little craters.

Another method is to use automotive filler, such as Bondo or White Knight. The canned body fillers set quickly so you can finish the holes as you go along. Automobile fillers are too heavy for large amounts of contouring on homebuilt aircraft. Use as little as you can to get a good surface.

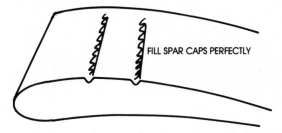

FILL SPAR CAPS PERFECTLY

Fig. 3-11. Be certain to fill the spar cap perfectly to preserve the proper airfoil contour.

Part Fitting

Sections of the airplane are removed for maintenance and transport or, have been made separately and must be attached at least once. The line joining them should be sealed to reduce air leaks into the boundary layer. If not they may result in separation and high drag in critical places, such as the wing-fuselage intersection.

At the contact areas of the parts, such as the canopy edges and the fuselage, cowling and firewall or wing and fuselage, put a layer of duct tape on the moveable part and micro fill the fixed section along the tape. This gives a uniform gap-line. Finish filling the fuselage over the edge of the tape. To have a super fine line, I use plastic sheeting taped over the fixed part of the joint. Butt a layer on the moveable part and join in finished position. After the partial hardening it can be trimmed and sanded to a perfect fit. Removal is easy, with the layer of plastic to keep it from sticking.

In some joints, such as the wing-fuselage joint, a larger gap is desired, because of the shifting required during assembly. Use three layers of duct tape over the wing then tape the plastic sheet over that. Putty in lots of micro-balloons and push the parts together to squeeze the mix out. Scrape off the excess putty and sand the joint. Disassemble and peel off the tape. The result is an even smaller gap that can be taped over with one strip of colored or white plastic tape to stop air leaks when the plane is assembled and readied to take to the air.

The wings and stabilizer are best worked with the part you are sanding. Final assembly is after painting. Trying to sand and paint the bottom of a wing after it is mounted on the fuselage is almost impossible.

Featherfilling

When the shape is proper and evenly contoured, and the pin holes and little craters filled, spray on the featherfill. This material is used in auto painting and gets its name from the ease with which it can be sanded to a feather edge that can't be seen after final painting. It is very heavy and should not be used for contouring. I assume you have a powerful compressor and quality paint gun. If not, hire the job out or rent a compressor and a good gun. Mix the MEK catalyst precisely with the featherfill using an electric drill and paint stirrer.

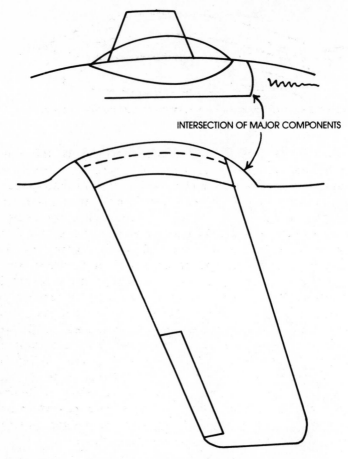

INTERSECTION OF MAJOR COMPONENTS

Fig. 3-12. The intersection of parts must be properly sealed to minimize air leaks.

Use your air gun to blow all the dust from the part. Spray paint it wet for the first few passes, and a bit thinner for the final coat. When the filler cures, use #100 grit paper in the half sheet size on a block for a good sanding. Lots of paper changes are required because this part is done dry. Finish with #150 and even more sheets, as the dry sanding fills the paper quickly. Tiny blemishes and holes can be fixed with lacquer spotting putty from the auto finishing paint store.

Primer

The featherfill should be sanded off down to a faint hint of the fiberglass weave. But isn't that most of it? Right. It will either be on the floor or filtered out by the mask you should be wearing while sanding the stuff. Take time to be satisfied every part of the surface is the way you want because, it is not possible to go over primer with featherfill. The juxtaposition of many colors, fillers, micro balloons and spot putty gives such a mottled surface it is hard to

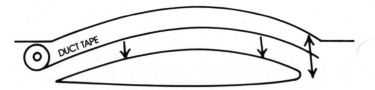

Fig. 3-13. Put a layer of duct tape over the wing section that contacts the fuselage.

see how it is going to look. The moment of truth comes after the first coat of primer, because you at last see the surface as it will appear when painted.

Spray painting is a relatively common skill and it seems always possible to get someone that can do it better than yourself, or at least they say so. If you have no experience get someone to help, read a book on spray painting cars, or go watch at the body shop and ask questions. In its simplest form, it involves getting the material on evenly. Spray by moving the gun back and forth over the part, shutting off just before the end of each stroke then pulling the trigger to start the flow when moving the spray gun at a steady speed for the next stroke. With the gun moving pull the trigger. Move smothly at a steady distance from the surface and shut off just before you stop movement.

Now go back to wet sanding with the primer, using standard #220 wet or dry, a rubber block and a gentle stream of water. Again, sand most of the primer away. Prime again, use #220 wet then #380 for a silky feeling finish. This second primer coat may be all you need. Some places may take more layers to be as nice as you like but the final primer coat should not be sanded off completely. This is the layer that makes the surface opaque to sunshine. At this stage all scratches must be finished out with nothing coarser than #380 because paint will not fill anything of greater depth.

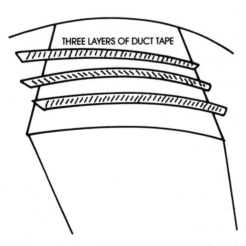

Fig. 3-14. In some joints, a larger gap is required because of the shifting that occurs during assembly. Use three layers of duct tape here.

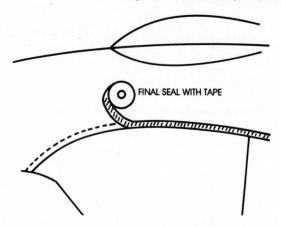

Fig. 3-15. After the parts are mated and structurally fastened together, final seal the intersection with tape.

Painting

If you have the final paint done professionally at this point, I'd say it is worth it. Ask them to put on Polyurethane paint. This paint is so brilliant you can forget about having to rub it out or even wax later. If planning to do the job yourself, use acrylic enamel. It produces a fine shiny finish without having to buff. Use a good grade of auto enamel, Dupont, Ditzler or any standard product. If an experienced person is doing the spraying or helping, you should let that person pick the product he likes to use.

If there is a place where the paint has run, it will usually be in a concave area where the spray becomes concentrated. An experienced spray painter is aware of the tricky places and is governed accordingly. If there is a run, wait a couple weeks, or even a year if it doesn't show too much and, wet sand it with a rubber block and #400 paper. Rubbing compound applied briskly will polish it to match its luster. Smear it on and rub it with a towel or use a buffing pad on an electric drill or one of those special buffers.

Paint striping for decor and style is serious business on these modern composite airplanes. Do not make spanwise trimlines in the front part of the airfoils. Along the fuselage or chordwise is less critical. Here's why. The lip of the paint line, unless sanded judiciously and rubbed out, will trip the boundary layer on the first third of laminar flow airfoils. At high attack angles the drag increases while the lift is reduced.

Remember, the contour is what the air "sees" and the shine is what you and your friends see. Don't waste time on areas of aerodynamically purposeless obscurity. Also, remember good sealing is very important. An airplane in flight accelerates the air near its surfaces as it passes and therefore has low pressure surrounding all but front edges and the bottom of the wings. A flying airplane is "pressurized", so to speak, like a balloon. Air flows out of every crack. The leaking flow may easily push away the boundary layer, especially in critical places, resulting in separation and high drag. A small slot

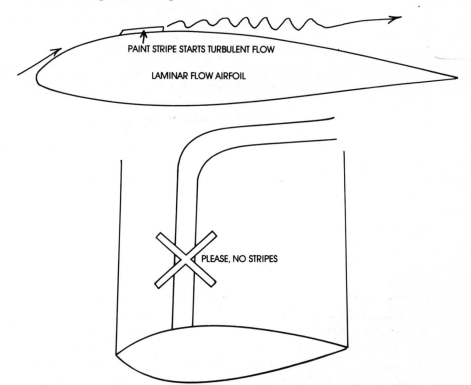

PAINT STRIPE STARTS TURBULENT FLOW

LAMINAR FLOW AIRFOIL

PLEASE, NO STRIPES

Fig. 3-16. Do not apply paint stripes or striping tape to the wing, as they can reduce the lift and increase the drag tremendously.

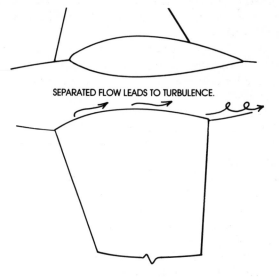

SEPARATED FLOW LEADS TO TURBULENCE.

Fig. 3-17. If part intersections are not sealed, air will leak into the boundary layer flow. This causes separation and turbulence, leading to reduced lift and increased drag.

where the wing joins the fuselage will raise the stall 5 mph and reduce the climb rate 50 to 100 feet per minute, because of the loss of lift and increased drag. Your aircraft should be a paragon of envy if this chapter is followed.

Summary
- Finishing continues throughout the project.
- Slurry joints are harder than foam so sand them separately or keep the joint edges clear of glue.
- Eliminate high spots and smooth all foam block discontinuities before glassing.
- Do glass cloth overlaps on corners and sharply radiused edges, never on flat or gently curved surfaces.
- Use masking tape on the foam at glass edges and overlaps, to stop drips.
- Overlap the glass cloth an inch or two after glassed edges are tapered.
- Pre-taper all lap joints while green.
- Find lows and highs with a ruler; correct with micro-balloon-resin filler mixed and put on very dry.
- Use a small block for hard filler, a large block for very soft.
- Plan three fills and sandings for each section.
- Bondo or lacquer putty fills pits fastest.
- Featherfill spraying is done after the contours are perfect, not as a correction technique.
- Primer and featherfill should be almost completely sanded off with wet 220 and finish sanded with 380.
- Acrylic enamel is easy and satisfactory for painting.
- Don't paint trim lines along the first third of the flying surfaces on laminar flow airfoils.

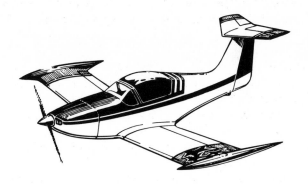

4

Foam/Fiberglass Kit Planes

Four popular canards, the Quickie, Dragonfly, Long-EZ and the ultralight Goldwing use moldless composite construction. Basically, they are made with plastic foam covered with layers of fiberglass.

Will these suit the flying you would like to do and is this construction technique for you? Since the building methods are similar, we can discuss working with them together.

To help explain these "moldless" airplanes, let's discuss the difference between molded and moldless. Does one method have any advantage? Many early all-plastic airplanes were made using molds. This is time consuming because an accurate shape of the part desired must be made and smoothly finished. To review the process briefly. A special mold release wax is applied to the shape, called a "plug", and fiberglass laid over and allowed to cure. The part removed from the plug is made into a "female" mold. (That's because the fiberglass is "laid" inside the mold. Something you put something into is "female", and something that sticks out with the part formed over it is called a "male" mold.)

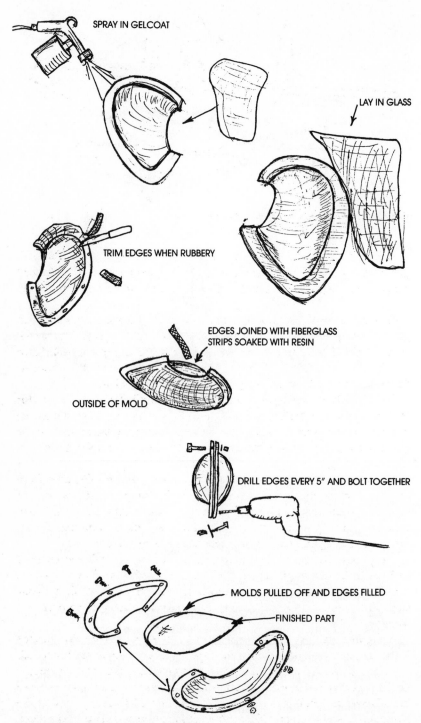

Fig. 4-1. How to make a molded wheel fairing.

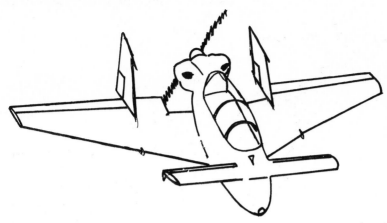

Fig. 4-2. The original Vari-Viggen was built of wood.

The mold is stabilized by a frame, usually of steel tubing. Hours are spent fine finishing the inside of the mold. When it is complete, many indentical parts can be made and the quality is as good as the mold in which they were laid.

To make a part, the mold is waxed and a coat of special resin, called gelcoat, is sprayed in. It is usually white in plastic airplanes to keep them cool while in the sun. Fiberglass fabric is laid in the mold and resin brushed into the fabric. The number of fabric layers and their weave orientation is determined by the strength needed for the part being made.

For example, in a wing panel, unidirectional (parallel) rovings are used for the spar caps. All the fittings for the ailerons and flaps would then be installed. When everything is cured, the wing halves are taken out and the ailerons, etc. sawn out and then joined and finished, resulting in a perfectly contoured wing.

A plug usually takes more time to make than an entire wing does from scratch. Factory made molds cost tens of thousands of dollars but are amortized over many airplanes. For the homebuilder making one airplane, the time to make plugs and molds is a long way beyond fun, although several notable planes by dedicated constructors have been made this way.

The increased popularity of plastic planes came with the development of moldless construction. By using light, easily shaped, plastic foam covered with fiberglass, the part is made without a plug or a mold. It's all done in one step. The plastic plug is itself a part of the structure used for compressive strength.

A big disadvantage is that each airplane must be individually finished —the outside is not shaped by the mold. But, since these are homebuilt airplanes, it doesn't matter. For greater production, the mold procedure would probably be more cost effective as we shall see in later chapters when the Glassair and Polliwagen are considered. Now, let's take a look at the planes made with this moldless method and the time it takes to make them.

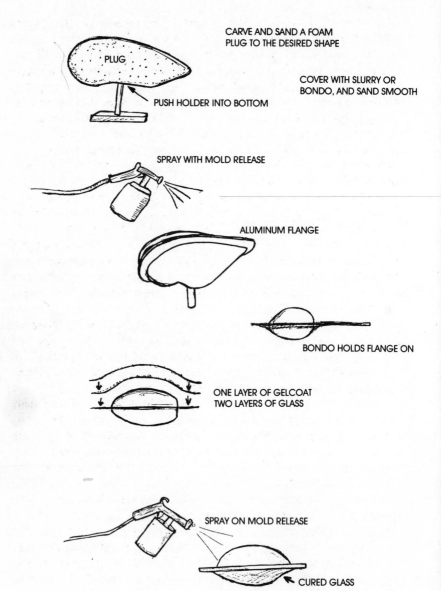

CARVE AND SAND A FOAM
PLUG TO THE DESIRED SHAPE

COVER WITH SLURRY OR
BONDO, AND SAND SMOOTH

PLUG

PUSH HOLDER INTO BOTTOM

SPRAY WITH MOLD RELEASE

ALUMINUM FLANGE

BONDO HOLDS FLANGE ON

ONE LAYER OF GELCOAT
TWO LAYERS OF GLASS

SPRAY ON MOLD RELEASE

CURED GLASS

REMOVE THE ALUMINUM FLANGE

Fig. 4-3. How to make a plug mold.

Long-EZ

This aircraft is one of the highest developments of the canard configuration in the history of aviation. It is an off-shoot of a canard called the VariViggen, which was inspired by a Scandinavian fighter, the Viggen, with a forward horizontal stabilizer. It was made of wood with low aspect ratio wings, and needs a 180 horsepower engine to give acceptable performance. The low aspect ratio wings and limited lift coefficient resulting from the stability needs of a canard are the reason for the high power requirement. The wing must be restricted to a smaller lift coefficient than the canard or it might stall first and cause the aircraft to fall backwards.

There was great interest in the configuration, so another canard airplane called the VariEze was made. It incorporated a higher aspect ratio wing, a Volkswagen engine, and foam cores covered with fiberglass laminate.

At about this time, the movie "Star Wars" appeared in which the fighter "space ships" somewhat resembled the VariEze. It soon caught on as a very desirable plane for homebuilders because of its racy canard design and reputed ease of building. Many people wanted such a radical airplane but, unhappily for some, found they had to build it themselves. Homebuilders bought many hundreds of plans and lots of foam and fiberglass. Dozens now appear at every fly-in. To carry out the fantasy of the Star Wars theme, one owner painted his VariEze black and wore a Darth Vader helmet when he flew.

But aside from its radical and exciting style, how is it as an airplane? With very low frontal area and carefully streamlined details it has a good cruise and top speed. But, it has demonstrated several problems. The prototype used the canard flippers for pitch control. Each side angled differentially when the stick was moved from side to side for rolls. It was like using differential elevator on the back of any lightplane to bank. This didn't work because the plane nosed up or down when the pilot tried to roll into a turn. That problem was cured when ailerons were added to the wings and the canard was used exclusively for pitch.

It also landed very fast, 80 mph on approach, and had a flat angle of climb, again because of the limited lift available in the canard.

Another problem was weight. Too much and too far back. It was partially the fault of homebuilders who couldn't seem to keep the structure light enough, but also because the original engine, derived from the air cooled VW automobile, was deemed unreliable. Some VW airplane engine converters said it was simply overworked in the VariEze and the designers of the airplane had little experience with conversions. The Fournier RF-4, which I have flown for 12 years, has a French converted Rectimo Volkswagen engine that has been particularly reliable. I have never changed the oil or spark plugs and, adjusted the valves only once. There is over 1200 hours on it, and with the exception of its low displacement and therefore low power, I couldn't be more pleased. The 1192 CC four cylinder engine puts out only 28 to 30 hp at the 3200 RPM it must operate at in an airplane, to keep the propeller tip speed low. The auto version, in the Volkswagen, develops about 39 HP as it

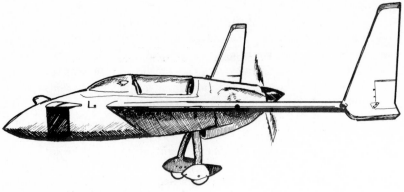

Fig. 4-4. As the artist views the Long-EZ.

can turn 4200 RPM. VariEze designers however, had bad luck with the VW engines they used. Then they recommended a standard airplane engine. So, most builders put in a 100 hp Continental or Lycoming. The result was a much heavier machine that often had the CG too far back.

At an aft CG and high lift coefficients, the wing rocked back and forth as each tip took turns stalling. Instead of going into a spin at slow speed it might go into a rolling dive "auger" maneuver, and go straight down. Recovery could take over 2000 feet.

The VariEze proved the viability of the canard concept, but the designer was not satisfied with its performance. A modification was designed to change the characteristics of the wing. A cuff was added to the leading edge near the outer ends. It stopped tip stall tendencies by creating tiny vortices. The add-on slowed cruising speed by only 4 knots.

Realizing the VariEze was not all that it could be, Rutan designed and built a new airplane that, at a distance, looks the same as the VariEze. Called the Long-EZ, it has a 4 feet 2 inch greater span wing with 50 percent more area and less sweepback. A laminar flow airfoil, computer designed by Eppler of West Germany, is used. It had the needed bigger fin area he called "winglets". It also has larger wing strakes, to hold fuel and baggage and keep this variable weight close to the center of gravity. You can't put fuel in the wing of a canard type plane as is done with most conventional airplanes because it would result in an aft CG. The Long-EZ also accepts the extra power and weight of the Lycoming 235 cubic inch displacement engine with a generator and electrical system.

The Long-EZ has an aspect ratio of 8.3, higher than most other homebuilts. It's equivalent drag area is only 1.9 square feet. The frontal area is much bigger than that, but with it's streamlining, it has the drag of a flat-into-the-wind plate of only about the area of a legal sized sheet of paper. That's clean! It gets twice the miles per gallon of a Cessna 152 or Piper Tomahawk of the same power, due to this high aspect ratio and low frontal area.

The Long-EZ carries a huge 42 gallon load of gas which, combined with its

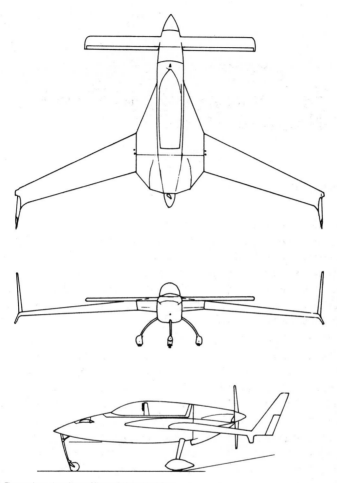

Fig. 4-5. Three-view drawing of the original Vari-Eze.

low drag, gives it a range of 1600 miles at 146 MPH. It can speed at 180 mph full throttle.

The new canard flies very nicely. Its wrist action side-stick control gives a progressive feedback for better pilot awareness of just what is going on. It's a big improvement over the old smaller, but faster Varieze. I felt the controls were unpleasant because of the jerky rudder action but it is something anyone can become accustomed to, and is not dangerous. You can pull the nose up as high as you wish. It will not stall but instead bobs up and down —like most airplanes with forward CG and limited travel elevators, such as the Cessna 210.

The Long-EZ needs a smooth runway because it has small wheels that run over bumps with difficulty and is unable to fly slowly. Such a streamlined airplane with a fast landing speed, eats up runway like a jet. It requires over

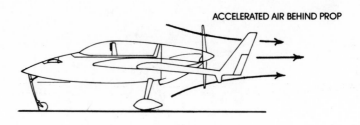

ACCELERATED AIR BEHIND PROP

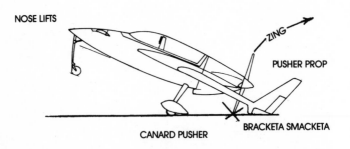

NOSE LIFTS

ZING

PUSHER PROP

CANARD PUSHER

BRACKETA SMACKETA

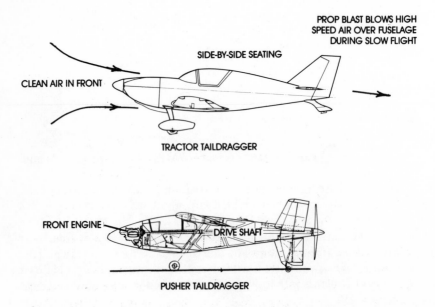

PROP BLAST BLOWS HIGH
SPEED AIR OVER FUSELAGE
DURING SLOW FLIGHT

SIDE-BY-SIDE SEATING

CLEAN AIR IN FRONT

TRACTOR TAILDRAGGER

FRONT ENGINE

DRIVE SHAFT

PUSHER TAILDRAGGER

Fig. 4-6. The advantages and disadvantages of various engine/propeller positions.

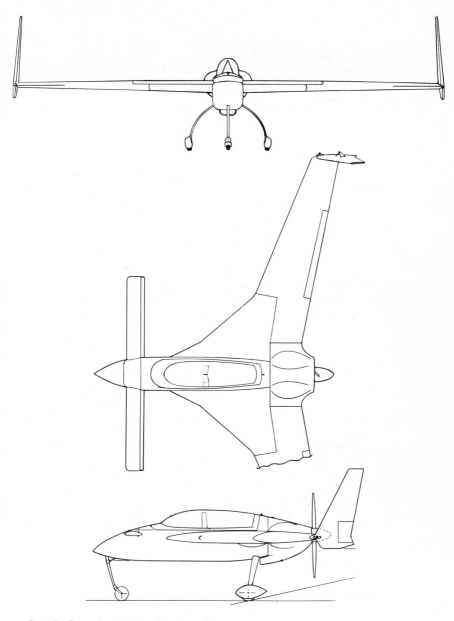

Fig. 4-7a. Three-view drawing of the Long-EZ.

three times more runway than a Cessna 150. That also means it could be
more dangerous in a forced landing, as the crash impact increases with the
square of the striking speed. A plane that can land at 45 mph has one-half the
striking force of one landing at 65 mph. But few of us select an airplane
for its safety in forced landings.

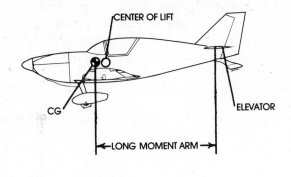

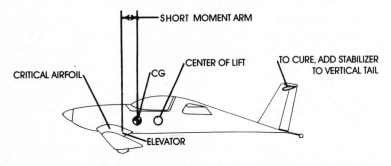

Front wing carries more load per unit area than rear wing, and has an airfoil that is affected by bugs, bumps and rain. The short elevator moment arm means more elevator force is needed to counteract the nosedown force developed by the front wing's reduced lifting power.

Fig. 4-7. Why canards used to nose down in the rain, or experience longer takeoff and landing distances.

Airplanes are intensely emotion provoking machines. When I see a Long-EZ streaking off the runway and sweeping overhead on its V-shaped wings, it is pretty damned exciting. And, that's what airplanes are all about. It is certainly a plane to consider if you love its looks, like fast cruising, and don't need short fields.

Creating a Long-EZ takes over 1000 hours. But how can such a simple structure take so much time? A factory plane, like a Cessna 150 can be assembled in 200 hours. To understand the speed at which airplanes can be made, visit a factory and watch.

I went to the Cessna factory with my brother and a couple of other pilots to pick up some airplanes to fly back to California. We had some spare time, so we spent the day observing the workers riveting the parts together and assembling the neat little trainers.

Two fellows set the ribs and floppy stringers in a big steel frame, called a jig, and began drilling holes and filling them with rivets. The wing assembly got stiffer as the rivers were set with air-driven guns on one side, while bucking bars on the other rattled against the aluminum fasteners.

The men made two wing panels per day. A pair of cute girls assembled, and with some help, put two tailcones a day onto the fuselage center section. Of course, they had the small parts already formed and the big jigs were beyond any homebuilder's concept of "tools for the garage". The speed and ease of assembly of a metal airplane is very impressive and it begins to be easy to understand why factories have not jumped on the composite bandwagon and continue to use aluminum.

Plastic planes have not been made in airplane factories because aluminum is a known and conservatively engineered material. It stays the same size and shape over time and thus lends itself to mass production. The parts made last year will always fit in the jigs. The curing and finishing time of plastic is too long compared to the straightforward joining of metal. The known strength of a rivet is changed to a bond dependent on temperature and precise mixture of catalyst and resin. An equipped Cessna 152 is well over $30,000, so you can guess what a factory made Long-EZ might be, since it takes over five times longer to build.

What the homebuilder can accomplish, revel and enjoy spending time doing perfectly, is often not what happens in factories. Here some people work with little knowledge and care less about airplanes.

Although foam and fiberglass can be very time consuming it is well suited for homebuilders because it's really fun and doesn't require a lot of jigs.

Some Long-EZ builders have devoted 2000 hours to their kit airplane project and are still working. The average time however, is about 1500 hours. A 40 hour week 50 weeks a year is 2000 hours. This is a year's employment for most people. The cost of everything including the $3500 kit, aircraft engine, instruments, and details is $13,500. It's not all that frightening however. The builder buys parts one at a time so the cost is spread out. The airplane takes shape quickly and the basic structure seems to go fast. As with any airplane of composite plastics, about half the time is used in finishing. The details stretch on. Those of us who have built airplanes know it can take longer to mount and plumb a couple of instruments than to make an entire wing. A "simple" canopy latch can use up a weekend of interesting but diligent fitting.

So if you like a different and very efficient airplane for cross country and don't mind always using long, smooth runways, the Long-EZ may be the plane for you.

Specifications

Wingspan	26 ft. 4 in.
Length	16 ft. 8 in.
Height	8 ft. 0 in.
Wing Area	94.8 sq. ft.
Engine Make, Model, HP	Lycoming 0-235, 108 hp
Prop Diameter/Pitch	N.A.
Reduction Ratio	1-to-1
Fuel Capacity/Consumption	52 gal./6.6 gph.

Gross Weight	1425 lbs.
Empty Weight	750 lbs.
Useful Load	625 lbs.
Wing Loading	15.03 psf
Power Loading	13.19 lb/hp
Design Load Factors	N.A.
Construction Time	800-1500 man-hrs
Pricing	$198.50 (plans)

Flight Performance (at gross)

Velocity Never Exceed	N.A.
Top Level Speed	193 mph
Cruise Speed	183 mph @ 75% power
Stall Speed (in free air)	66 mph
Sea Level Climb Rate	1350 fpm
Takeoff Run	830 ft.
Dist. Req'd to clear 50 ft.	N.A.
Landing Roll	680 ft.
Service Ceiling (100 fpm climb)	22,000 ft.
Range at Cruise	1150 mi.
L/D (Glide Ratio)	15.5-to-1

Long-EZ
Rutan Aircraft Factory
Bldg. 13, Mojave Airport, Mojave, CA 93501, (805) 824-2645

Quickie Series

This is a tandem wing bi-plane with no stabilizer or elevator on the tail. The stability principles are the same as for the canard; the front wing carries more than the rear. When it slows, the front wing drops first, and the plane automatically recovers. The prototype was a single seater bi-plane called the Quickie. Several dozen were built and proved to be fast and economical. It used an Onan gasoline engine that was originally intended for powering an electrical generator in a motor home. The little four cycle engine had good longevity at low power but was very heavy. A good VW conversion has over three times the power with less than half the weight. The 18 hp engine was able to pull the Quickie and its pilot over a hundred miles an hour, while using only a gallon of auto gas.

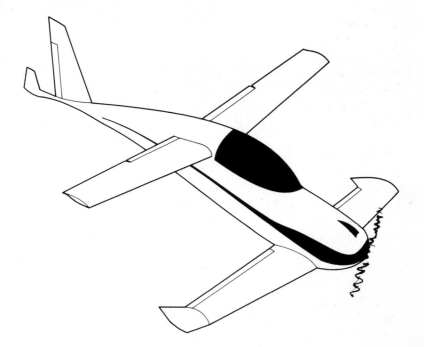

Fig. 4-8. The original Quickie as seen by the artist.

The Quickie group then marketed a similarly shaped but quite different two seater. Called the Quickie Q2, it has outdistanced the single in popularity.

In the first CAFE competition for speed and fuel efficiency, started at the Santa Rosa airport, it won its class. In the second CAFE in 1982 a factory made Mooney 201 four seater won but the Quickie 2 was very close. The Mooney is generally conceded to be the most efficient commercially made plane so you can see the Q-2 is ranked with the very best.

It is very compact and can fit in a garage at home and be trailered to the airport. The fuselage comes in half just behind the rear wing for ease in transport over the road. The plane has only 1.4 square feet of frontal area,

Fig. 4-9. Inboard profile of the single place Quickie.

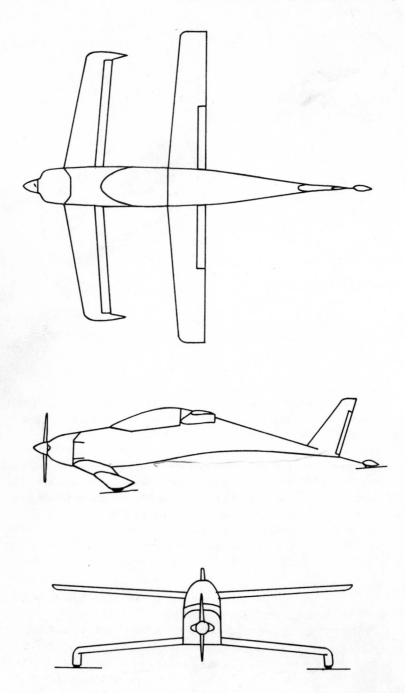

Fig. 4-10. Three-view drawing of the Quickie.

Specifications

Wingspan	16 ft-8 in
Length	17 ft-4 in
Height	4 ft-0 in
Wing Area	53 sq ft
Engine Make, Model, HP	Onan, 18-22 hp
Prop Diameter	42 in
Reduction Ratio	1-to-1
Fuel Capacity/Consumption	7 gal/1 gph.
Gross Weight	520 lbs.
Empty Weight	240 lbs.
Useful Load	280 lbs.
Wing Loading	9.81 psf
Power Loading	29-24 lb/hp
Design Load Factors	NA
Construction Time	400 man-hrs

Flight Performance

Velocity Never Exceed	N.A.
Top Level Speed	140 mph
Cruise Speed	133 mph
Stall Speed (in free air)	53 mph
Sea Level Climb Rate	500 fpm
Takeoff Run	580 ft
Dist. Req'd to clear 50 ft	N.A.
Landing Roll	490 ft
Service Ceiling (100 fpm climb)	12,300 ft
Range at Cruise	525 mi

Quickie
Quickie Aircraft Corp.
Hangar 68, Mojave Airport
Mojave, CA 93501
(805) 824-4313
Sales Manager

even less than the VariEze. It has very brisk controls compared to the Long-EZ and benefits from the engine in front.

Why? The motor in front makes the plane safer in a crash as it can cushion some of the shock and is better than having it come through from behind. It also makes the plane balance more securely as a nose heavy plane is better than a tail heavy machine. One advantage of a puller, or tractor engine and prop, is you can see what's going on out there. If the prop stops, you know it. If any part falls off, even a small nut, it will go into a pusher prop and could knock it off. VariEzes have had exhaust failures that take the propeller off at

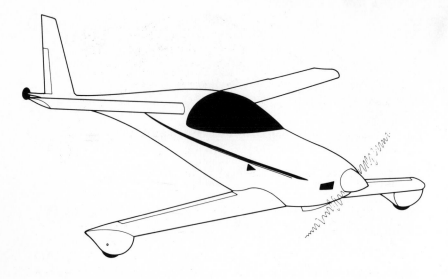

Fig. 4-11. The Quickie Two in perspective.

the same time. Loose parts don't bother a tractor propeller because they fall off with little danger of hitting the blades.

I have flown several different pushers and always had the sensation of not really being sure what was happening back there with the engine.

For example, at Elsinore, CA, I flew a pusher engined Ogar motorglider to take some pictures for a magazine article. While waiting for takeoff the mixture had been set lean by the mechanic, while I wasn't looking, so the Revmaster engine would idle more smoothly. The carburetor poured in too little fuel for full throttle. With the engine in front I would have seen the lack of smoke from the exhaust and pushed the mixture control forward to richen the mixture.

I didn't know why the engine was losing power on takeoff so I pulled back the throttle and opened the air brakes to stop. In the air this could have been dangerous.

Oil leaks are usually seen with a tractor positioned engine right away but this is not so with an engine-behind airplane. All kinds of strange things could be happening without the pilot being aware until all the oil has run out or a part drops into the prop and ends the flight.

In tractor-engined planes the propeller out front in clean air is more efficient. The disadvantage is that the wind from the prop blows back on the fuselage, of course, which should theoretically make more drag, but this is only at slow airplane speeds when the prop blast is high compared to the air over the fuselage. At high speed the slippage is slight so the extra air going over the fuselage is small.

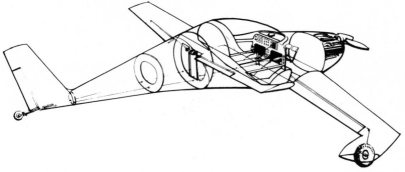

Fig. 4-12. Cutaway of the Quickie Two, showing main components.

A pusher must accelerate the slowed boundary layer air from the fuselage ahead of it. The prop always works in turbulent air, which lowers its "bite".

With a cleanly designed and executed body behind the propeller, drag is surprisingly small. A test of the air movement across the Amsoil Special front wing by coating it with an oil that evaporates in the turbulent part of the boundary layer, showed laminar flow in the supposedly disturbed area behind the propeller!

So, everything considered, the biplane canard with the engine in front is a good solution to the compromise of aerodynamic efficiency and engine-propeller placement.

As you would expect in a small canard, the plane stops flying at 65 to 70 MPH. It cannot make very tight circles because the wings don't lift as much for their size as an airplane with a tail. The front wing must stall first and the nose automatically drops to recover. If the nose is held up and the Quickie 2 is flown at minimum speed the aileron effectiveness is less than the rudder. Due to the dihedral of the back wing it rolls if a slip is generated by using the rudder. That means it can be banked with the rudder better than the ailerons. When slightly tail heavy it will go into the diving auger if the stick is held back and the rudder held to one side. This would look pretty much like a spin and would be equally deadly if a hapless pilot pulled the stick back and tried a turn using the rudder. At low altitude, it could spiral dive into the ground unless the back pressure on the stick is released to allow the canard to start flying again.

It is hard to see forward and down because the very comfortable reclining seats are not matched to the canopy for best visibility. The window sills are too high. This is especially true in the front, side quarters. Exactly where you want to look, the otherwise graceful curve of the canopy blocks the view during taxi and takeoff. Lowered sills and higher seats and canopy would improve visibility.

Quickie 2 uses the Revmaster engine derived from the ubquitous Volkswagen with specially made custom parts. A couple years ago, in a motorglider, I flew behind a Revmaster 8000 miles, from California, south to Peru across the Andes and over the jungles to Asuncion, Paraguay. I can

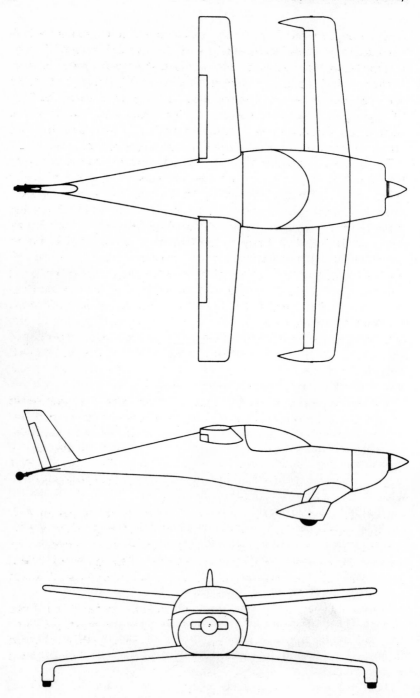

Fig. 4-13. Three-view drawing of the Quickie Two.

verify the engine is certainly reliable. I didn't want to be let down in the high mountains or trackless jungles and the Revmaster purred happily all the way. It burned so little oil I donated my spare cans to the flyers in LaPaz, Bolivia.

The powerful engine very quickly accelerates the Q-2 past the 65 to 69 MPH lightweight stall speed, so the plane can take off in 500 feet. The 2100 CC engine pulls it up 800 feet per minute. With two on board, the takeoff and climb is considerably slower, as is true with all the small homebuilts. This occurs because the pilot weight is such a large proportion of the total.

To find what an airplane will carry at claimed minimum speed, is easy to work out. Multiply the wing area by the lift coefficient times the minimum speed squared, then divide all that by 391. Lets do it: 67 sq. ft. wing area, times the estimated lift coefficient of about 1.2 equals 80.4. Multiply that times the speed squared. 61 times 61 times 80.4 is 2991668.4. Divide that by 391, a number that represents standard air pressure. The result? At a lift coefficient of 1.2 the plane will lift 765 pounds at 61 mph. So the lift coefficient must be a little less than 1.2. Now let's see how much the plane will lift at 64 mph. It works out to 1010 lbs. Flight tests, however give a minimum speed of 65 to 69 mph which would give a lift coefficient of only 1.05! This is very low. A standard airplane like a Cessna has a lift coefficient of 1.5 and with flaps can go to a C_l of 1.8. That's over 40 percent more lift per unit of wing, compared to the Quickie. The designer of the VariEze and Long-EZ was also the consultant on the original Quickie. He told me he was dissappointed in the low lift coefficient of the plane.

Another phenomena peculiar to tandems and canards is the change in trim when bug remains, rain, or paint strips cover the surface — the lift coefficient is lowered. The plane is supposed to pitch down whenever the canard loses lift. If a canard flies into a passing condition that reduces lift, such as rain or snow, the front wing will lose relatively more lift than the back and drop, thus making the plane dive since it carries a higher load than the rear wing. The plane should not stall because it corrects itself.

One problem. All airplane wings lose lift when the air flow passing their surfaces becomes turbulent. Why don't rain and bugs affect regular airplanes? They do, but the reduced lift of the wing on a conventional plane does not change the trim. Its tail carries only a little down load. So a conventional airplane that gets a wet, icy or bug splattered wing will still be trimmed the same despite the reduced lift.

A horizontal stabilizer and elevator on the Quickie was the solution. Since it already has a tail with a fin and rudder, it would seem obvious to put a little stabilizer back there. With a downforce on the tail the better the lift obtained from the wing by flying only 8 mph slower. I recommended a tail for the Quickie several years ago, to the baleful look of Tom Jewitt.

Ah yes! It is so wonderful to be right first.

Gary LeGarre, the Quickie designer, is now marketing a tiny stabilizer to be retrofitted on Quickies. Although still inferior to performance expected from a standard sized stabilizer, it is a step in the right direction. As a matter of interest, the Amsoil Racer, which looks pretty much like the Quickie, does have a horizontal stabilizer to increase the lift in turns as it sweeps around a race course.

The Quickie One was the first of the tandem wing designs. It is not as popular as the two place Q-2, but may be just the little plane for you. It is an all foam and composite airplane half the cost of the Q-2. It is, however, a fast machine on only 18 HP, furnished by an Onan RV generator motor modified for turning a prop. A suped-up version can put out 22 hp. The airplane gets over 65 MPG flying at a hundred and seven miles an hour. The takeoff run, by most pilot reports, is around 1500 feet — although the designers claim 650 feet. Empty weight for the tiny biplane is only 240 lbs. This is below the FAA's Ultralight classification, but its high landing and takeoff speed makes it an Experimental. A student pilot license and aircraft certification is needed. The prospective Quickie pilot should have some experience in sensitive planes like the Grumman American "Yankee" trainer.

It won the 1978 EAA Oustanding Design award and has had great plan and kit sales. The kit is about $5000 complete with engine, prop, and all metal parts finished.

The Q-2 is a two seater version that was designed by Gary LaGare, a Quickie dealer in Canada, and sold to the Quickie Aircraft Corporation for final development and marketing. Price is $3,595 for the plans and fuselage which includes the Quickie Newsletter, wheels, molded canopy, pre-molded shell of its elegant "porpoise" shape, machined and drilled parts and all the rest of the material for the fuselage. $2455 is the cost of the wing kits. The Revmaster engine is $3243 including the generator and starter; $1850 for the propeller, exhaust, engine cowling and instruments complete the power package. The complete kit is $11,143.

Time to build, at 600 to 1200 hours, is about half that of the Long-EZ. Again the details and finishing take as much time as the structure.

The Continental 100 HP, 0-200 engine is now being put in the latest Q-2. With a new front wing and airfoil to carry the extra weight, the aircraft is reported to go over 200 mph. Cost of the 0-200 engine is $3000.00 more than a new Rev-Master. Get plans and latest information from Quickie Aircraft Corporation, Hangar 68, Mojave Airport, Mojave, CA 93501 (805) 824-4313. A newsletter for Quickie Builders Association is published by Robert Herd, 2306 9th St., Lubbock, TX 79401.

Specifications

Wingspan	16 ft-8 in
Length	19 ft-7 in
Height	3 ft-0 in
Wing Area	67 sq ft
Engine Make, Model, HP	Revmaster 2100 DQ, 64 hp
Prop Diameter	56 in
Reduction Ratio	1-to-1

Fuel Capacity/Consumption	20 gal.
Gross Weight	1000 lbs.
Empty Weight	475 lbs.
Useful Load	525 lbs.
Wing Loading	14.93 psf
Power Loading	15.62 lb/hp
Design Load Factors	N.A.
Construction Time	500 man-hrs

Flight Performance

Velocity Never Exceed	N.A.
Top Level Speed	180 mph
Cruise Speed	172 mph @ 75% power
Stall Speed (in free air)	64 mph
Sea Level Climb Rate	800 fpm
Takeoff Run	610 ft
Dist. Req'd to clear 50 ft.	N.A.
Landing Roll	1000 ft
Service Ceiling (100 fpm climb)	15,000 ft
Range at Cruise	682 mi
L/D (Glide Ratio)	11.5-to-1

Quickie Q-2
Quickie Aircraft Corp.
Hangar 68, Mojave Airport
Mojave, CA 93501
(805) 824-4313
Sales Manager

The Viking Dragonfly

Another airplane that looks like the Q-2 is the Dragonfly. It came out before the Q-2 was unveiled and there has been no knowledgeable accusation that it was a copy because it is remarkably different. It has bigger wings, (97 compared to 67 sq. ft.) and a 30 percent lower wing loading. It uses the HAPI VW conversion of less displacement and power than the Revmaster Q-2 has up front. The creator is Bob Walters, an ex-navy airplane pilot. He designed the plane as an "interesting exercise" and is quite aware of the lift to be gained with a tail-in-back design and the controversy of putting wheels on the wing tips of the forward wing. With his longer forward wing, or canard, the spar had to be made of that very stiff material, carbon fiber. The point load of the landing gear is far out so the bending moment arm is very great.

"Why not put the wheels in closer as in a normal plane?" I asked Bob Walters. "Looks, and perhaps less drag, because you would have to have longer gear legs if you moved them in. Also the front wing has a down slant, or "anhedral", and the rear wing bends up, called "dihedral".

Walters says, "No one has ever tested this idea in a wind tunnel but keeping

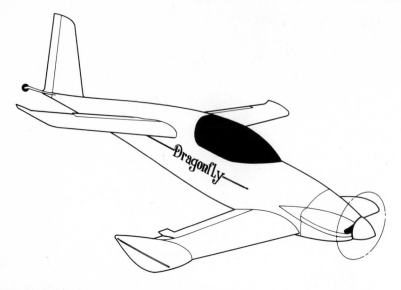

Fig. 4-14. The Viking Dragonfly is larger than the Quickie Two.

the wing tips separated may reduce the interference drag. So, it might be a good idea to keep the front wing anhedral. Since it's so low already, why not put wheels on the ends? Despite the point load so far out it does eliminate the gear legs."

The 800 plus sets of plans that have been sold for $175 will be made into Dragonfly clones after 1200 hours of part time work and $9000. A more complete kit with molded parts is expected from TASK research of Santa Paula, CA.

If the pilot is experienced in taildragger airplanes there should be little problem flying the slick machine. It takes off about 10 miles an hour slower than the Q-2 look-a-like because of the larger wing area. The speed and climb rate are the same because the engine, at 60 hp, has less pull than the 64 HP Revmaster. It uses the side stick as do the Long-EZ and Quickies. The light touch makes for easy flying and the airplane is steady in the air.

I prefer lower sills for better downward visibility. I have the same complaint for the Q-2. The wing tip wheels can make for huge groundloops, "broadies", or whatever, if one of them goes off the edge of the runway or is stuck in a rut. They are 20 feet apart so the moment arm is far away from the aircraft's center of gravity. The brake system is therefore designed to hold both wheels equally, as a safety measure. If a flyer inadvertantly put a slight touch more on one brake than the other, the stopped wheel could whip the plane around.

With all the canards, a certain difference in technique is necessary for landing. The airplane should be flown onto the runway, not slowed and stalled on, as can be done with a standard airplane. Here's why. A conventional airplane stalls, with the wing, not the control surface. The tail

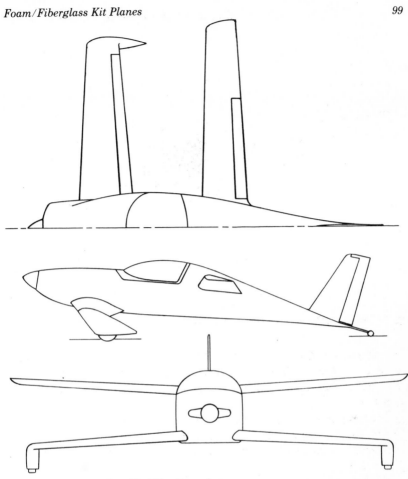

Fig. 4-15. Three-view drawing of the Viking Dragonfly.

conventional airplane stalls with the wing, not the control surface. The tail can continue to hold the wing up into the wind. If a pilot gets too slow upon landing and the wing stalls the elevator control can still be held back to keep the wing lifting. Most wings have considerable lift past the stall. Sure the air is separated but there is a good deal being pushed and pulled downward so there is a lot of lift. If a flyer stalls at five feet above the runway the plane can still make a fairly good landing by holding the control back and letting the plane settle with a nice thump. I have been surprised how often it makes a good landing from a slightly high stall. The pilot adds power and recovers, or, if the stall is high enough to recover, puts the nose down, picks up speed, then eases it back again for the touchdown.

Sometimes, there is not enough space to recover. If the pilot puts the nose down the airplane might hit the runway before recovery. Bump! The decision is up to the pilot and past experience whether to try a recovery or hold the nose up for a stalled on landing.

Not so with these canards, particularly the Dragonfly and Quickies. The front wing carries much more of the plane than the rear wing. In all canards the forward wing itself loses lift well before the rear wing, so the nose drops no matter what the pilot wants to do. A canard can drop nose down if slowed too much. The long "springboard" front wing bounces the plane back into the air for embarrassing bounds along the runway. It's best to add power, go around and try it again. Canards should be flown onto the runway without attempting to set down at minimum flying speed.

The Dragonfly lands and takes off at slower speeds than the Quickie. Its large rudder gives good control at these slower speeds.

The first Dragonfly has one of the most beautiful finishes I have ever seen. Al Nelson was one of the important builders of the plane and has vast experience making surfboards.

Dragonfly was given the "Outstanding New Design" Award at the 1980 Oshkosh Experimental Aircraft Association Convention. The prototype fuselage used a pre-scored clark foam as the basic shape instead of molded parts, but more about that later.

If you prefer a slower landing and takeoff canard, the very efficient and compact tandem bi-plane called the Dragonfly is the answer. Plans and kits are from Viking Aircraft at R.1 Box 1000V, Eloy, AZ 85231.

Specifications

Wingspan	22 ft. 0 in.
Length	19 ft. 7 in.
Height	4 ft. 5 in.
Wing Area	97 sq. ft.
Engine Make, Model, HP	HAPI, 1835cc
Prop Diameter/Pitch	52 in./42 in.
Reduction Ratio	1-to-1
Fuel Capacity/Consumption	15 gal./3¼ gph.
Gross Weight	1075 lbs.
Empty Weight	590 lbs.
Useful Load	485 lbs.
Wing Loading	11 psf
Power Loading	23.9 lb/hp
Design Load Factors	+4.4, -2.0
Construction Time	750 man-hrs
Pricing	$175 (plans)

Flight Performance

Velocity Never Exceed	N.A.
Top Level Speed	180 mph
Cruise Speed	155 mph @ 75% power
Stall Speed (in free air)	45 mph
Sea Level Climb Rate	600 fpm
Takeoff Run	450 ft.

Dist. Req'd to clear 50 ft.   N.A.
Landing Roll   N.A.
Service Ceiling (100 fpm climb)   17,000 ft.
Range at Cruise   500 mi.
L/D (Glide Ratio)   14.5-to-1

Dragonfly
Viking Aircraft
Eloy Municipal Airport, R.R.1, Box 1000V, Eloy, AZ 85231, (602) 466-7538, Rex Taylor

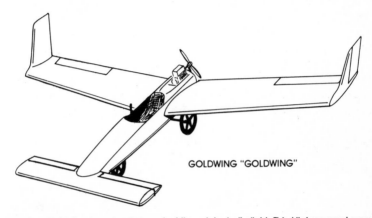

GOLDWING "GOLDWING"

Fig. 4-16. The Goldwing is a development of the original ultralight. This kitplane must now be registered as amateur-built, because it exceeds the ultralight weight and speed limits.

Goldwing
This is the lightweight end of the composite canard airplanes. Although it weighs the same as the Quickie One it is the largest of the canards with its 30 foot span and 128 square feet of wing area. But it only weighs 500 lbs with the pilot ready to fly. It takes off and lands around 32 and cruises 55 to 60 mph. It can take off in 150 feet with a slight breeze and burns only one gallon and a half an hour.

Classed as an ultralight it doesn't need to be licensed by the Federal Aviation Administration nor does its pilot need a certificate or physical exam. An ultralight is any airplane weighing less than 254 lbs. empty, stalls less than 27.6 mph with a top speed of no more than 63.25 mph. Fuel is limited to 5 gallons.

The designer had some trouble with the first versions. The wing spar was too weak. I stood on the ultralight runway at Elsinore, CA. watching the various machines being demonstrated by the manufacturer. The Goldwing came by bobbling as the pilot, a foreman at the Goldwing plant, countered the gusts with movements of the canard. He pulled up over the center of the field, and with a crunching bang, the wing folded. The pilot carried no

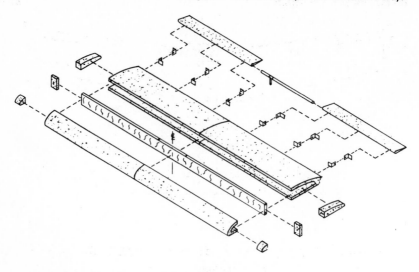

Fig. 4-17. Some details of the Goldwing's composite construction.

parachute. The plane fell to the hard packed sand. Although unconcious but moving when the medics picked him up I could see his head swelling with the terrible shock of the fall and I sadly realized he would not survive. He died shortly thereafter.

Parachutes attached to the airframe are available. Some versions, using a spring or powder charge, can shoot out and open almost instantly letting an ultralight down safely, so the pilot doesn't even have to get out of his seat. Competition hang glider pilots are 100 percent equipped with parachutes but it is trickling down to the powered ultralights somewhat slowly, for no good reason I can think of.

The factory said a wing scrape with the ground a week before, resulting in unseen damage, was the cause of the failure. They could not, however, duplicate it at the factory.

Months later, on another writing project, I happened to talk to Marty Hollmann, a professional structures engineer for one of the major aircraft manufacturers. He said he was visiting Goldwing and asked what G loading the spar would take. The designer told him 6 g's. That's easy enough to check, as Marty proceeded to measure the spar tubing and fittings. The Goldwing designer walked off but another employee of Goldwing stayed to watch. His calculated result was that the spar would take only one-and-a-half "G" design load!

After the tragic wing failure the designer strengthened the spar over that which collapsed the earlier model. The Company claim is now for a 3.4 positive and 1.7 G negative design load for the wing.

Because of its composite plastic construction the Goldwing has very smooth surfaces and is quite advanced aerodynamically, compared to other

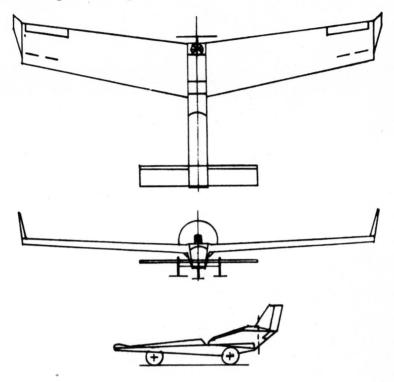

Fig. 4-18. Three-view drawing of the Goldwing.

ultralights. The plane takes off at a little over 30 mph, pushed by a Cuyuna two cycle engine. It has won most speed events in its class easily and has been flown, with a couple of daily stops, across the USA from Jackson, CA. to Jacksonville, Florida. A single seater, it has stick and rudder controls so the average airplane pilot can readily learn to operate it. After a few runs along the field and another hour of low hops, the pilot can take it up to go around the pattern. It has been compared by inexperienced pilots to the Cessna 150 in flying ease.

The kit is $7,595 including the engine and prop. Plans alone, are also for sale. The production kit has the wing and canard spars, along with ready cut foam parts, and a pre-jigged fuselage that needs only the foam and glass applied to finish the basic shape. The Goldwing requires about 400 hrs. to build, complete with finishing. The basic structure can be done in 100 to 200 hours because the foam cores are hot wire cut and ready for spar installation and fiberglassing.

*Ed. Note. The original Goldwing is marketed as an amateur-built kit, since it weighs in excess of 254 pounds. The Goldwing UL however, is marketed as an ultralight, and is factory-built.

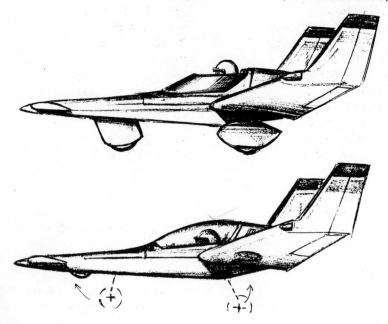

Fig. 4-19. Designer's sketches of future Goldwings.

Specifications   *Goldwing - ST*

Wingspan	30 ft.
Length	12 ft.
Height	5 ft.
Wing Area	140 sq ft
Engine Make, Model HP	Cuyuna 430, 30 hp
Prop Diameter/Pitch	36 x 16
Reduction Ratio Direct Drive	1-to-1
(Optional 2:1 Reduction Unit)	
Fuel Capacity/Consumption	6 gal./2 gph.
Gross Weight	540 lbs.
Empty Weight	280 lbs.
Useful Load	260 lbs.
Wing Loading	3.8 psf
Power Loading	18 lb/hp
Design Load Factors	+3.8, -1.8
Construction Time	100-200 man-hrs
Field Assembly Time	15 min
Pricing	$5295.00

Flight Performance

Velocity Never Exceed	70 mph
Top Level Speed	70 mph

Cruise Speed	60 mph @ 75% power
Stall Speed (in free air)	26 mph (canard)
Sea Level Climb Rate	800 fpm @ 45 mph
Takeoff Run	150 ft
Dist. Req'd to clear 50 ft	N.A.
Landing Roll	200 ft
Service Ceiling (100 fpm climb)	16,000 ft +
Range at Cruise	200 mi
L/D (Glide Ratio)	16-to-1 @ 42 mph
Minimum Sink Rate	325 fpm @ 35 mph

Goldwing
Goldwing, Ltd.
Amador County Airport, POB 1123 Dept CC, Jackson, CA 95642.

Summary
- The popular foam-fiberglass kit airplanes are canards because of acceptance of the original VariEze and the follow on projects which used similar construction.
- Finishing the laminate after it is applied over the foam core is the most time consuming part of the moldless airplane.
- Canards minimum speeds are not as slow as similar aircraft with the rear tail.

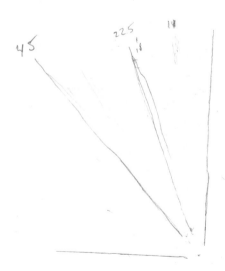

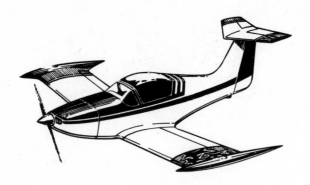

5

Paper/Fiberglass Kit Planes

When we were in school everyone made paper airplanes, the kind you fold into a dart or a tailless glider. Perhaps I made more than my share. I remember, more than once, the imperturbable Father Podesta snatching them from the quiet mid-air of study hall, deftly balling and flipping them into the wastebasket. Using paper to make things is easy. When combined with fiberglass, it becomes a very inexpensive alternative material for amateur airplane building.

Paper construction has been used for parts of airplanes since the 1920's. The Bowlus Albatross sailplane of many record endurance flights in the 1930's, used paper ribs reinforced with strips of wood. In 1960, I made fairings for my Fauvel flying wing by taping bond paper fillets between the wing and fuselage. I fiberglassed over the paper and left it a permanent and trouble free part of the structure that improved the airflow in this important intersection.

Up in the logging and paper country of Oregon and Washington, two homebuilt enthusiasts, Molt Taylor and Jerry Holcomb, began experiments making aircraft parts of Kraft paper and fiberglass. This chapter will tell

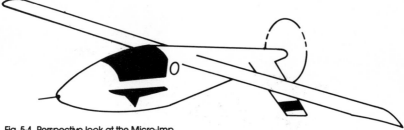

Fig. 5-1. Perspective look at the Micro-Imp.

about their process, as well as the MICRO-IMP and BULLET kit airplanes using this material.

Molt Taylor is one of the grand old names in original airplane design. He made a roadable flying machine that is certificated and licensed as an auto and airplane. His Coot amphibian and all metal Mini-Imp, with a mid-engine and pusher prop, are popular with flyers who like high performance on low power. Molt Taylor was one of the designers who greatly influenced the late Bill Lear in the development of the new pusher, inverted tail, LearAvia turboprop executive transport. He knows what he is doing.

Molt's latest contribution is the TPG (Taylor-Paper-Glass) method of construction for his Micro-Imp very light plane. It can be used for anything suitable, of course, and is probably the most inexpensive of all composite airplane building methods. The greatest cost in an airplane is still the engine and your time. Airplane building is, of course, an enjoyable hobby so we shouldn't have to count our time. The next greatest expenditures are for the radio, instruments, wheels, fittings for controls, fuel tanks and lines retraction mechanisms, canopy and cockpit equipment. By using paper, the cost of the basic structure is minimal.

I landed my motorglider at Longview, Washington to visit Molt Taylor's shop one cloudy Sunday. He drove me to his design and prototype factory where I delighted in his very aerodynamically clan and unique pusher airplanes.

"Here's our newest idea, Jack", he said, and showed me an elevator, and the pitch control surface he had made of paper for his Micro-Imp. "This cost only a dollar for materials." It seemed featherweight in my hand.

"Yes, but how strong is it?" I asked. He grabbed one end, offered the other to me and held tightly. I twisted it as hard as I could. It did not flex.

"Is that stiff enough for you?" grinned Molt. The piece deformed not at all with our powerful wrenching.

After Molt explained the details of how it is made I was sold on TPG as another superb method of composite construction for homebuilding airplanes. The idea is to use paper known as "Kraft liner pulpboard" with a layer of fiberglass cloth and resin on each side. The builder draws a part on the paper, applies resin and, after it hardens, covers each side with a layer of resin impregnated fiberglass cloth.

The resulting sandwich part, which is as strong as $50 a foot aircraft plywood, can be sawn, drilled and have metal fittings attached. One of its greatest advantages is health safety. It does not turn into dangerously breathable dust when worked, as do some of the foams, nor does it have to be handled carefully, as do aluminum sheets, to keep from cutting fingers. It is convenient for homebuilders who are making custom parts because any markings on the paper can be seen through the relatively clear fiberglass, so holes or cuts can be made on the lines. It is stiff for the same reasons as all composites, tensionally strong fiber outside with compressionally strong material in between.

Fiberglass cloth, made from wovenfine strands of glass, by itself has little ability to resist pushing forces. It's floppy like a piece of string with low compressive (pushing-crushing) but high tensile (pulling) strength. Fiberglass gains its compressive strength by combining with a material that can resist crushing. This is the job for the paper and resin. By imbedding it in a plastic resin, the strength is raised because the glass fibers are held from bending. With paper resined to the fiberglass, it adds even more compression strength. The thickness of the paper makes the part stiffer by keeping the glass layers farther apart. Remember, doubling the thickness of something makes it eight times stiffer.

The Taylor Micro-Imp

The first airplane built with this method, called the Micro-Imp, will be furnished as a kit with the parts printed full size on the paper. The builder first cuts the parts out with a knife and straightedge. They are then resined, glassed, and assembled with triangular wood corner strips and staples. It is covered with stabilized Dacron fabric requiring no dope or paint.

Although the Micro is in the class of ultralight airplanes (under 254 lbs.) it has advances common to regular planes, such as retractable tricycle gear and the special General Aviation Airfoil developed by NASA. The thick airfoil allows the long wing to be made without external bracing, yet still be strong and light.

Molt has also included flaps to give it a wider range of lift coefficients, another sophistication not found in such small homebuilts. For landing, the full span flaps can extend down, for greatly increased lift and drag, and short easy landings. I especially like flaps for landing at strange fields because all I have to do is put them down and aim at the edge of the runway. Their drag will keep the plane from speeding up if I'm too high. It is better to approach a little high for safety anyhow. If the engine stops, or a downdraft or gust from behind occurs, the airplane may need the extra height. These flaps also serve as the ailerons. They are actuated by a conventional control stick, varying the lift on each wing to bank and turn. Another lever moves them down or up as well. The large wing is not necessary for the lift needed at cruise since the airplane is going so fast. By setting the flap to negative or "up" the lift coefficient of the airfoil is reduced. The lower lift of the airfoil gives it slightly less drag, enabling the Micro-Imp to go faster more efficiently.

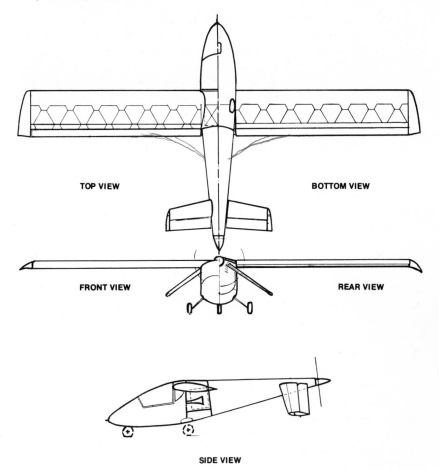

TOP VIEW   **BOTTOM VIEW**

FRONT VIEW   **REAR VIEW**

SIDE VIEW

Fig. 5-2. Three-view drawing of the Micro-Imp.

Another feature making for good flying qualities is the inverted tail. This kind of rear vertical surface will roll the airplane out of the skid caused by a gust or uncoordinated control movements. The sidewind hitting the tail pushes the nose into the relative wind as well as tilting the wing down, on the windward side, thus instantly stopping the skid. (An airplane with the vertical tail on top tends to aggravate the sideslip because it rolls away from gusts as it weathervanes and straightens out). The Micro-Imp propeller is at the rear and must be protected. Having the low vertical tail is a good way to do it since any over-rotation will result in the tail tips rubbing the ground, protecting the prop blades.

The pilot is the main balancing weight for this little flying machine. As the flyer climbs out, the aircraft will rock back, obviating yet another purpose for the inverted tail. The airplane sits nicely on the tips of the inverted V tail.

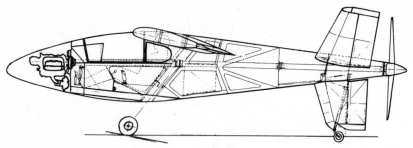

Fig. 5-3. Inboard profile of the Bullet.

The Micro-Imp has an adjustable pitch prop in the tail. This puts the high-speed turbulent air and noise it produces, behind the airplane. This saves drag, instead of making all that tortured air flow along the fuselage disturbing the airflow.

The drive shaft incorporates a unique "fluid" coupling device consisting of two wavy-disk-like members, one joined to the prop and the other to the shaft. Torque is transmitted from one plate to the other by thousands of tiny steel balls. This result is something like a hydraulic coupling. This device, called the Flexidyne, remarkably balances out all the surges of the piston accelerations on the drive shaft. This allows mounting the engine in the center near the CG of the airplane, while the prop can be located at the tail end of the fuselage.

The powerplant is a French Citroen 2CV, air cooled two cylinder, four-cycle, auto engine of 25HP, modified by Revmaster aero engines at Chino Airport, California. It gets suitable power at only 3600 RPM, making a direct drive acceptable. Cooling is assisted by a fan to move air in and out of the engine compartment behind the pilot. The fuel tank is part of the airplane, again near the CG, so varying amounts of fuel won't upset the flying trim.

The fuselage, tailcone, wings and empennage (tail) have been tested under actual loads, instead of calculated, to be sure something made of such a different material is strong enough. (This is true of almost all composite construction. Any airplane made of plastic should have the major parts tested to failure to be certain they will take the loadings the designers and aerodynamicists say they should.) Molt found, as have most composite designers, that plastic is just that. It may cold flow under point loads so he uses metal hinges, fittings, bolts and positive metal connections at all critical points.

I sat in one of Molt's airplanes at Longview and was impressed with the comfort and wonderful view. It's the same as a jet fighter with the wings and engine behind. It was easy to picture myself flying around using auto gas at only one and a half gallons an hour while cruising close to 100 mph. The Micro-Imp will fly along with a Cessna 152 of 100HP in every performance category yet it requires only 25 hp. The wings can be removed in a few

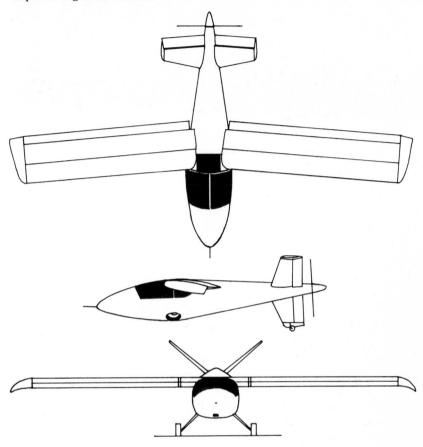

Fig. 5-4. Three-view drawing of the Bullet.

minutes and easily handled by one person, so a great saving in tiedown and
hangarage is possible. My Fournier costs over $1400 a year to hangar at
Chino, CA. airport. In only five years, hangar rent savings could cover the
cost of a Micro kit.

As an option, the 2CV engine may be turbo-charged. This will increase
power from the present 25 to over 35 hp and allow high altitude flying where
the thin air would make an ordinary engine too starved for oxygen. Extra
fuel, beyond the present 9 gallons, can be added with proposed tip tanks to
make it a long range cross-country machine. So, if a very advanced
featherweight airplane interests you, the Micro-Imp could be your top
choice.

Bullet

This two seater is similar to the Micro-Imp in aerodynamics. It has a
slightly wider fuselage to accommodate a side by side crew, swept foward
wings and a "Y" tail. Power comes from the big Revmaster 2100D 65 HP

custom VW aircraft engine in the nose, driving a Maloof adjustable pitch propeller in the tail via a rather long shaft. The wings fold and the airplane can be towed on its wheels to be kept at home.

A motor-in-the-nose/prop-in-the-tail seems unusual, and for an airplane it is. However, it solves a host of problems if you insist on a pusher. With a "conventional" pusher, the engine is usually in the rear. The pilot is therefore the balancing mass and when the cockpit is empty the tendency is for a tricycle geared plane to sit on its tail. Pilots vary in weight which may change the trim. The Goldwing uses weights to achieve proper balance for each individual pilot. The Vari-Eze must be parked with the nose wheel folded so it kneels on its nose. The Bullet pilot and passenger are on the center of gravity, so the airplane can be flown single or double with no change in trim. The engine in front is the main balancing weight, putting the CG at the seats.

The shaft from engine to prop runs between the pilots under the arm rest. The Bullet's shaft is in three sections with bearings and a Flexidyne coupler on the propeller to eliminate shaft whip and vibrations.

The Bullet is a taildragger with two retractable wheels in front and a tailwheel at the bottom of the inverted rudder. With its nose-up ground angle and flapperons, it should have spectacularly short takeoff and landing performance. The turbo-Revmaster can be put in the Bullet to give it a very fast true airspeed at high altitudes. The stall at 50 mph and top speed of 150 mph, combined with an empty weight of only 550 lbs puts it in the high performance category, in competition with the other composite aircraft.

Cost will be almost twice the Micro-Imp. But, for a plane with such a slow takeoff speed, high top speed, and two seats, it may just be the adventure machine for the builder who enjoys new construction methods coupled with a worthwhile goal.

To demonstrate how paper planes are made, try a small part using most of the techniques so you can see how it works. Do a control or flap like the one I saw at Molt Taylor's. Four feet long and a foot wide is a realistic size.

Specifications

Wingspan	31 ft. 0 in.
Length	18 ft. 9 in.
Height	6 ft. 0 in.
Wing Area	120 sq. ft.
Engine Make, Model, HP	Revmaster 2100D, 65 hp
Prop Diameter/Pitch	54 in.
Reduction Ratio	1-to-1
Fuel Capacity/Consumption	18 gal./3.8 gph.
Gross Weight	1100 lbs.
Empty Weight	550 lbs.
Useful Load	550 lbs.
Wing Loading	10.9 psf
Power Loading	16.9 lb/hp

Design Load Factors	N.A.
Construction Time	N.A.
Field Assembly Time	N.A.
Pricing	N.A.

Flight Performance

Velocity Never Exceed	N.A.
Top Level Speed	150 mph
Cruise Speed	N.A.
Stall Speed (in free air)	50 mph
Sea Level Climb Rate	750 fpm
Takeoff Run	N.A.
Dist. Req'd. to clear 50 ft	N.A.
Landing Roll	N.A.
Service Ceiling (100 fpm climb)	N.A.
Range at Cruise	500 mi
L/D (Glide Ratio)	N.A.

Bullet
Taylor, M.B. (Molt)
P.O. Box 1171, Longview, WA 98632, (206) 423-8260, Molt Taylor

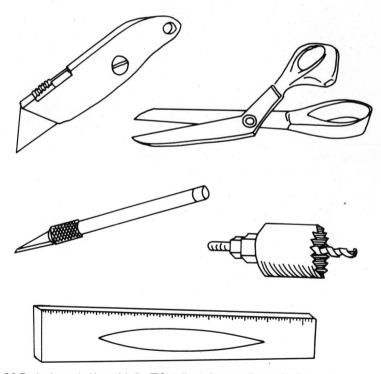

Fig. 5-5. The tools needed to work in the TPG method of composite construction.

The Paper

Perhaps you can get good practice paper nearby. Many paper suppliers are in every city. Ordinary cardboard can be used for practice but it has too much silicon and clay in it, which when combined with the resin will make it too heavy.

Wicks Aircraft Supply, 410 Pine St. in Highland, Illinois, handles Kraft paper. Another vendor is Multi-Enterprises, POB 891 Mercer Island, WA 98040. Both sell the same Kraft paper Molt Taylor uses on his Micro-Imp and Bullet. So, why not write directly to them.

There are several types of Kraft that can be used. The bags you carry your groceries in are made of the same Kraft paper I'm talking about but it is too thin for most airplane use. The 90 POUND LINER BOARD is good for making curved parts and it comes on a roll. LAMINATED CONTAINER BOARD is made of multi layers of the 90 pound. It is quite stiff, so it must be stored flat. It cannot be curved unless it is first scored.

The specifications of Kraft #90 PULPBOARD are: .027 in. and 1.44 oz/sq ft. For .050 LAMINATED, made of a sheet of 42 pound combined with two of the 69 pound, is 2.9 oz/sq ft and, of course, it's .050 in. thick. The "90 pound" or "69 pound", refers to the weight for each 5 feet wide by 200 feet long (thousand square feet) sheet of paper.

Making A Part

For our try-out piece we'll use the Laminated .050 Kraft paper. Work on a table you don't mind scratching. Or, cover it with cardboard and wax, to prevent resined parts from sticking to the table.

Draw the ribs, with pencil or pen, right on the paper. Using a utility knife, such as the Stanley, Exacto or heavy scissors, cut out the parts. Next, draw the top and bottom sections. Cut the straight lines with your knife and a straight edge. Tape the pieces together with bits of masking tape to check how it's going to fit. (Paper is so easy to use and so cheap, you can skip this trial assembly if you're confident.) Lay the parts on the table for resining. The top piece is scored (cut halfway through) with your knife and carefully bent over the table edge for making the curve in the front.

Resin Sealing

Epoxy and Polyester are syrupy, clear fluids made from petroleum. Mixed with a small amount of catalyst, they cure into a hard plastic used to give form to the fiberglass. Epoxy made laminates are about 37% stronger in compression and 13% stronger in tension than the Polyesters. Epoxy retails for $44 a gallon compared to only $20 for the polyester. Since the compression is so much enhanced by the paper center it is not cost effective to use the 55% more costly Epoxy. The shop temperature for working with Epoxy should be 77° F and the resin warmed to 85° F. Also, the problems of breathing Epoxy fumes or getting it on the skin are so serious for most people, it doesn't seem wise or necessary to use anything but Polyester when making a paper airplane. On the other hand, if you're not bothered by

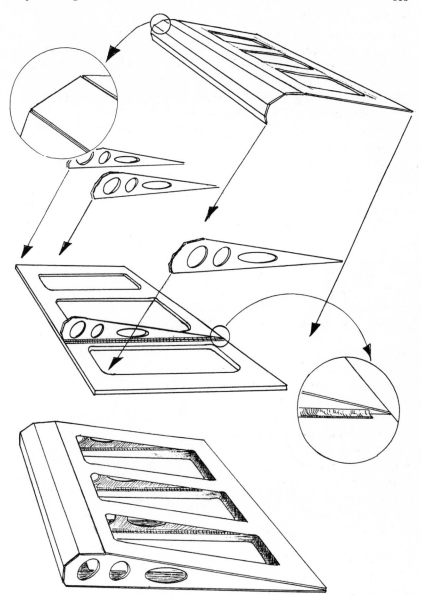

Fig. 5-6. The sequence used in assembling a "paper" flap.

Epoxy, have a temperature controlled shop, and don't mind the extra cost, there is no reason not to pick up a little extra strength by using Epoxy resins.

Thoroughly mix a cup of Polyester resin thinned 50 percent with styrene, then add the specified MEK catalyst, stir, and paint it on both sides of the paper parts. Use brush or a small 3 in. short-nap paint roller. Clean the pan and brush immediately with solvent. I never clean, but use lots of cheap rollers and small boxes for the "pan". Cut up the 9 inch roller into three 3 inch

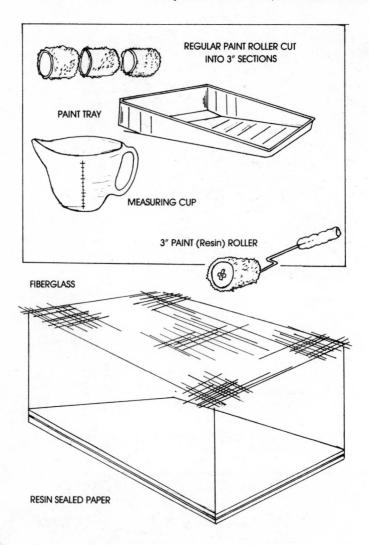

REGULAR PAINT ROLLER CUT
INTO 3" SECTIONS

PAINT TRAY

MEASURING CUP

3" PAINT (Resin) ROLLER

FIBERGLASS

RESIN SEALED PAPER

Fig. 5-7. How to resin seal a part.

sections to save money. Throw the roller in the trash can when the resin goes off.

With various temperature experiences you can learn to make the right amount of resin and catalyst to cover your parts and have enough working time before the resin hardens. The time it takes resin to cure depends on the amount of MEK (ketone) catalyst and your shop temperature. The hotter your shop the smaller amount of catalyst needed. If it is very hot in the shop, and you mix a big cup of resin with the right amount of catalyst for a small batch on a cooler day, you may be in for a surprise! The resin will "go off" so quickly, there will be no time to use it before it starts to gel.

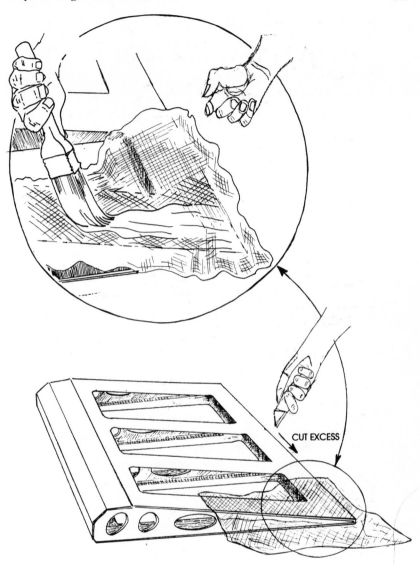

Fig. 5-8. Laying on the fiberglass cloth and trimming when the resin first cures.

It is important that the 50 percent Styrene be added to the resin so it will spread more easily, soak into the paper, encapsule the wood fibers and make a water and humidity proof part.

Although Polyester resin is far less irritating to most builders than Epoxy, it is still a good idea to wear rubber kitchen-type gloves when working with the gooey stuff. Molt uses Koppers Dion 6692T Fire Retardant Resin with a strength in tension of 10,350 lbs/sq in, which is about as good as any. Some resins may be stronger, but more brittle. The resin you use should be flexible enough to take sudden loads and vibrations. Get enough parts ready to resin

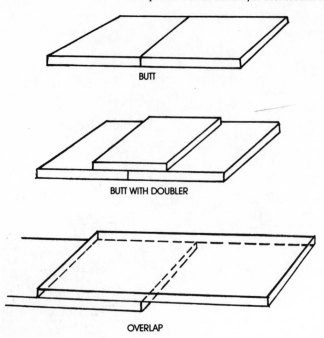

Fig. 5-9. The basic types of joints between two surfaces.

coat so you won't waste any if you mixed too much. Or simply make small batches at a time.

Wipe off dirt or dust from the paper and roll on the resin from your paint pan. You will see the tan paper turn brown. This means the resin is soaking in nicely. If the color change is not even you may have wax, oil, or dirt on or in the paper. Use a squeegee to wipe off extra resin to keep the part light.

Examine any section that has repelled the resin. It might mean you didn't roll the paper evenly and some part is too dry. A simple matter. Go over it with the roller and add more resin. If the reason for the resin not soaking in properly is oil or wax on the paper, you should throw it away because it will never take up the resin properly.

If part of the paper has gotten scuffed or roughened, it may soak up more resin and appear darker brown. That's alright. It is strong enough, but may be a little heavier because of the extra resin. Go ahead and use it.

Look at the piece after the resin starts to harden. For a while it is very easy to cut. Use scissors or shears to trim any drips along the edges and a knife to scrape smooth any drops or bugs that might have tried to preserve themselves in the resin. If it is not a part that will be seen or exposed to the airflow you may leave any critters for posterity as it makes little difference in the strength.

After it cures enough not to be tacky, turn it over and resin the other side. You must mix another batch of resin because your first will have hardened long before the thin layer on the paper.

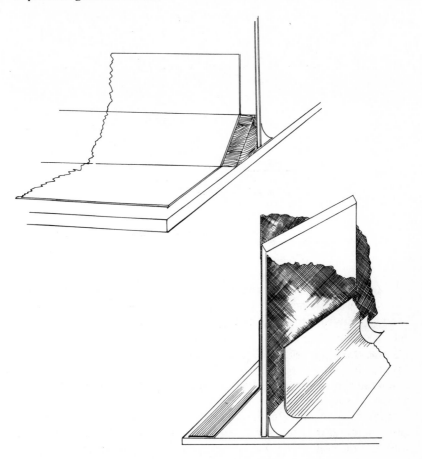

Fig. 5-10. A corner joint is reinforced with triangular sectioned strips of spruce fiberglassed, resined and stapled in place.

Both sides should be done at the same sitting, or the paper may warp from shrinking of the resin on the treated side or, from a dry day evaporating water content on the untreated side. By surrounding the paper with resin it will cure evenly and stay flat.

Glassing

Any glass will do for practice parts but, for aircraft, you want the lightest and strongest construction. Use a very tight weave fiberglass, grade 1528 or 7528 (Burlington Mills), which is the same as style 143 and 181 (Hexicell Corp.). A tight dense fiberglass does not allow a lot of extra resin to puddle in between the weave as it would on a looser weave.

Apply another light coat of resin on the paper, lay on a slightly oversize piece of fiberglass cloth and keep rolling to force the resin up through the weave. You can also bring up the resin from the paper into the glass cloth by

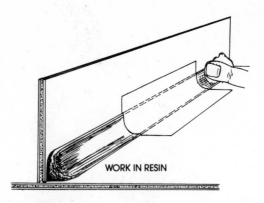

WORK IN RESIN

Fig. 5-11. The micro-balloon method of reinforcing corner joints.

using a stiff inexpensive brush and poking. This method is called "stippling".

Another way is to put the glass on the paper and roll the resin down into it. If you do it this way, the roller may pick up the glass cloth until it is saturated and sticks to the paper. Whatever way works for you, uses minimum resin, yet completely wets the fiberglass cloth, is best.

As the resin starts to cure, leave it alone. The thickening mixture won't soak into the glass anymore. If you continue to roll or brush the glass, you may pull it up from the paper, ruining the part.

Examine your work after it has cured, looking for even color. If there is a lighter section of the cloth, it may show where the resin soaked away from the cloth into the paper. This would happen if the paper were not sealed well during the first roll-on of resin. You can save this piece by going over that section, but your part may be a little bit heavier. If this is a problem in your paper sealing it might be better to resin the paper twice. This will insure sealing for a lot less resin weight than going over the glass to fill in dry spots on the paper below.

The perfect time for trimming is when the glass first cures, here, it is rubbery and can easily be trimmed to the paper's edge by using a utility knife or shears. Turn it over and inspect the other side for drips that may have run through, or bits of resin that have stuck on.

Roll on more resin. Apply the cloth and roll or stipple until the second side is fiberglassed. The most common problem is using too much resin. You don't want a shiny slick surface. It should show the weave of the glass cloth. In the event you do get too much resin puddling over the glass, use a squeegee or stiff bit of cardboard to take off the excess. The drier it is the lighter the part will be with no decrease in strength.

When the side has "rubbery" cured you again trim to perfection and, there you have the bottom part of the aileron. When you have all the parts finished, strong, and light, they will be ready to be joined with the top section and ribs.

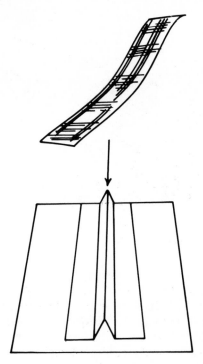

Fig. 5-12. Large, unsupported areas can be stiffened by adding triangular strips of paper, covered with fiberglass and resin.

Joining Parts

There are several joining techniques, depending on the kind of joint and its use.

First let's look at joining the paper compression layers. There are times when the part may be too long to do with just one piece of paper. A couple of paper sections must be used.

A plain butt joint has no strength except the glue itself, so consider it only a very temporary joint.

A lap joint is strongest but if it is on the outside of the airplane it might look better to do a butt joint with a doubler plate on the inside. The twelve-to-one scarf joint was required for aircraft plywood seams, and doublers should be also twelve times the thickness of the paper. That means that if the paper is 1/8 inch thick the overlap should be 12 times that, or an-inch-and-a-half wide.

In putting together the shear web for a wing spar, the paper can be cut at four to one, edge to edge, and glued alternately.

Corner Joints

Straight edged, 90 degree corners can be put together using strips of wood and staples. Use a one inch board sawn along the grain into triangular strips. For small parts, you can use a half inch to one inch piece. Next, cut these

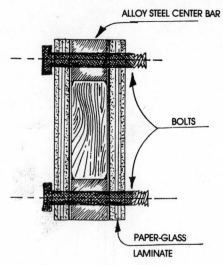

Fig. 5-13. Concentrated loads are handled by metal bolts. These are known as hard points.

triangles to the length of your joint. Brush a layer of resin along the edge, then push the wood into the resin and staple in place. A strip of fiberglass cloth is laid over the wood and paper and resined in place for an almost indestructable bond. This should be done along the edges of each rib.

But what kind of wood should you use for bonding strips? Spruce, is the standard for aircraft because it is the strongest wood for its weight. It is very expensive for aircraft grades and impossible to get except from aircraft supply houses.

A substitute is straight grained, kiln dried, Douglas Fir. It is only a tenth the cost of comparable Spruce. I still like Spruce, although Fir is stronger and stiffer by about 30 percent. But Douglas Fir, compared to Spruce, is also splitty and 26% heavier. The main reason I prefer Spruce is that it is far less liable to splitting when you drive staples. You can select Spruce from less than perfect pieces at the lumber yard and cut around the knots or crooked grain sections. Aircraft Spruce used for spars must be flawless and can cost hundreds of dollars a piece. But, the short little bits you need for reinforcing and bonding corners can be obtained from scraps at a box factory or lumber yard for very little or nothing.

As an alternative to the wood batten method, corners can also be strengthened with microballoons or chopped fiberglass and resin. Mix the resin with these fillers until it is thick enough not to droop. Then, putty it into the joint to make a fillet. When it hardens, cover it with a layer of fiberglass tape and resin.

Sometimes a large area is unsupported and the paper fiberglass will flex too much. For stiffening panels a "V" shaped ridge can be formed by scribing and scoring a narrow piece of paper glued across the area you want strengthened and covered with a strip fiberglass.

Fastening

A composite paper laminate by itself is too easily frayed or crushed by concentrated loads. The idea is to spread the pressures over a wider area so there is less force at any one point. Alloy plates attached to the laminate with nuts and bolts or rivets are used to distribute point loads.

Aluminum angles fastened by rivets and bolts are a good way to attach fittings to the paper composite. Hinges for controls, landing gear attach points, and engine mounts can thus be reliably put together to transfer their loads to the laminate structures.

Use big washers and the largest head pop rivets you can find. It is important to use bolts and rivets that are long enough to hold the parts, layers and washers together with a few threads showing for security.

Drilling holes to mount the metal parts can be done with a common high speed drill or hole cutter. An extra layer of paper and glass can also be used to spread loads more gradually to the paper-glass laminate.

For making something as important and as stressed as spars, aluminum or steel for the attach fittings are held together by nuts and bolts to the spar caps and paper-laminate shear webs.

As can be surmised, the Micro-Imp spar uses the best of each material. Metal to take the concentrated loads of the fittings, with wood used for the spar caps. The shear loads between the caps are taken care of by paper and glass.

Curved Parts

A holder for the paper sheets is used in making the tailcone or other parts. This is not a mold, but a simple jigging fixture. The scoring technique, partial cuts parallel to the center of the curve, makes nice bends but the process can also be done by wetting the inside of the paper curve with water and ammonia. This softens the inside layer allowing it to take a smooth bend. The water method, with the paper bent over the pipe, can result in remarkably sharp curves. After it dries, the paper is resined and glassed on both sides, after which the curve is permanent.

Another way to make bends is to seal and glass only one side of the paper. The Fiberglass shrinks slightly as it hardens putting a curve permanently in the paper. It has the advantage of eliminating the watering and drying step, but if the curve isn't the way you want it you have wasted a lot of more expensive material than just the paper and a little water of the other technique.

You have a problem if the laminate must be cut after it has cured. The glass gets so hard you must use a straightedge to keep the blade from sliding off the mark. Keep going over and over the lines until you cut through the laminate.

You can cut curves the same way. Make a careful cut along the curve. Once a little groove is set keep going over it until it is cut through. It may need a light sanding to smooth the slightly jagged edges that result from the tearing action of a saw or hole cutter.

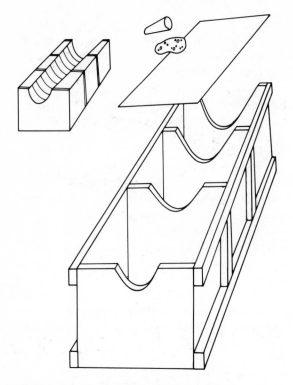

Fig. 5-14. A simple jigging fixture is needed to make curved parts.

Painting

Silver paint is used to protect the structure from sunshine. The sun's radiation will eventually degrade the fiberglass but the aluminum particles in silver paint block out this action. For finishing, the usual procedures of any such project are recommended: fill with several coats of primer; wet sand and apply a final high quality paint of a light color, to keep the glass cooler.

Summary

- Use Kraft linerboard sized to your strength needs
- Cut out your parts with a sharp utility knife
- Seal both sides with resin
- After curing, cover parts with tight weave fiberglass
- Use just enough resin to saturate the weave
- Trim edges and glops while layup is still rubbery
- Join parts using wood strips stapled and covered with fiberglass tape
- Spread concentrated loads with metal fittings or wood stiffeners in combination.
- Protect the fiberglass with opaque paint silver undercoat.
- Make sample pieces for destructive testing to insure strength of original design parts.

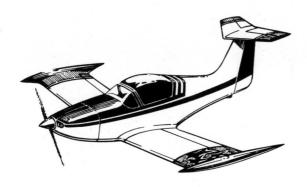

6

Pre-Molded Composite Kit Planes

After the foam structure, glass covered planes came out, a lot of builders struggled mightily. They had to develop the patience and/or skills to do the fine surface contours required for good aerodynamics.

But why should each builder have to create what can be thought of as the "plug" for a female mold and fly it around? It was obvious to just as many that once a superb plane was finished, it would be a great idea to make a mold using the completed plane. It became increasingly clear that if a plane were popular enough it would be cost effective to spend the time to make perfect molds. Then parts could be made in the molds at the factory. Kits could be furnished with the parts ready to put together.

The kit buyer then glues the sections together, like a plastic model, to create a beautifully surfaced machine. Because the parts were already accurately made in a mold, quality control can be high and the precise amount of glass and resin would make a lighter, stronger airplane. If the great effort that goes into a mold is spread over dozens or hundreds of airplanes, it could be inexpensive, especially when considering the homebuilder's time.

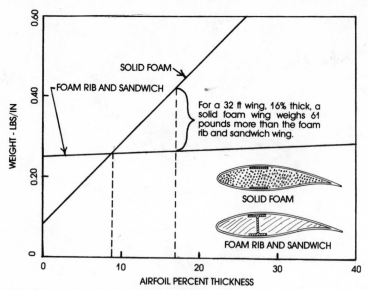

Fig. 6-1. The weight advantages of pre-molded wings.

Even earlier foam structure airplanes, like the Long-EZ have complete sections that can be bought from vendors, ready to bond. I visited TASK Corporation at the Santa Paula, CA. Airport to watch them make such parts. They had a superb mold for the Long-EZ engine cowling. Kevlar, lighter because it's very much stronger than glass, was laid in and regular fiberglass put in around the edges. The fiberglass, although it must be thicker, is much easier to cut without using the special drills necessary for Kevlar.

I was lucky to be there at the right time to see another interesting process. They had one of the original Dragonfly tandem wingers in one of their shops being copied, so they could make molds to produce parts. The three workers taped plastic sheeting over the plane. Then, they laid strips of masking tape along the lines they thought would be logical part separations. One man mixed plaster while another pulled hemp (rope) apart to put in the white gooey plaster. The third man spread it over the sections to be molded. A stick was laid in at about every foot, to stiffen the mold and allow it to be picked up. These plaster molds were used just as a start. Fiberglass is laid in and a glass mold is made with great care. The parts made from that are checked for any changes needed to make a perfect fit before production starts.

With the molds for its cloning taken, the Dragonfly itself would fly home to its base in Eloy, Arizona in a few days, none the worse.

No question this method of factory laid parts will be the dominant method of making composite aircraft kits for homebuilders. The TASK workers were already making up the molds and parts for the Solitaire canard, powered, self-launched sailplane. It will soon be offered as a pre-molded kit. Let's take a quick look and analysis of the airplanes out now with pre-molded parts.

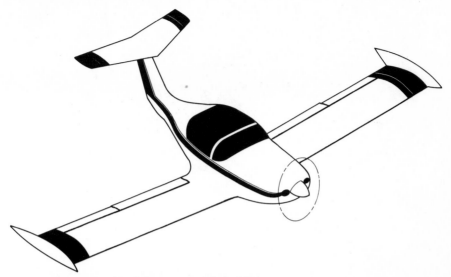

Fig. 6-2. Artist's sketch of the Polliwagen reveals its sleek lines.

Polliwagen

My friend Jose Alvarez, a tall, enthusiastic, confident ex-Argentinian, decided in 1973 that a fast two seater should be developed for homebuilders. Being an accomplished radio control airplane maker, he built a large model for preliminary testing. It worked beautifully. The fuselage aft of the wing model was short with a sharply pulled in waist. Fellow gliding enthusiast of countless years, Herman Stiglmeier, thought it looked like a pollywog (a frog before it grows its legs). Since it was to use a Volkswagen-derived engine, he dubbed it "Polliwagen", an apt name, as cute as it is descriptive.

The full sized airplane was flown in 1980 by Phil Paul. At first, he had some trouble getting the nose up to make a quick takeoff. Typical of "T" tailed airplanes, there is little wind blowing back from the prop on the stabilizer because it is up so high. It therefore did not develop enough down force to rotate the nose up until it was near 58 mph.

Phil gave me a "once-around" check ride in the machine and Joe had me fly it for several passenger flights. The Revmaster engine had a turbocharger which gave it plenty of acceleration. It bobbled up and down after lift off. This occurs because you are pulling back on the stick to rotate and when it finally does, it leaps into the air so steeply you immediately nose down. I found, after four takeoffs, the problem was greatly lessened by not trying to pull it off but simply letting the Polliwagen rise by itself. Becoming accustomed to the control inputs and holding the stick steady, also helped.

With the gear extended, we got up to 145.6 mph true airspeed at 2000 feet. Normal cruise, gear up, is 168 mph at 8500 feet. The ailerons were crisp and quick acting. Rolls and turns could be made "on-a-dime." Adverse yaw was handled by appropriate rudder. Later revisions of the aileron linkages resulted in a reduced need to use the rudder in normal flying. In 1980, the

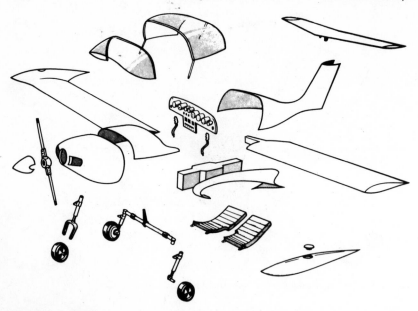

Fig. 6-3. An exploded drawings showing the various pre-molded components of the Polliwagen.

rudder area was increased over that of the prototype's.

Landings are different from the conventional because the tail is high and out of the ground effect when the wing is low to the runway. At an 80 MPH approach, there is plenty of speed over the stall of about 51 MPH, but it will not balloon or float for a stalled touchdown if held within three feet of the ground. Instead, it plants itself on the runway, no matter how much you try to level the glide to let it ease on. However at 15 feet up when the stick is pulled back, the nose will go up and the plane will slow and quickly settle. It seems to be that T tail effect again, same as on takeoff, where it loses its force close to the ground.

The Polliwagen should be considered a high performance machine. Aspiring pilots of this aircraft should have experience in a Cherokee, 172, or Cheetah before moving up to its performance level. Even so, 152 pilots have been known to handle the aircraft. It is surprising how well one can get used to the little ship and make fine takeoffs, landings, and rapid turns.

Since the completion of engineering drawings for the use of the Continental 0-200, Lycoming 0-235, 0-290, and 0-320, the vast majority of builders have opted for these certified aircraft engines. The Polliwagen folks also announced recently that the fuselage is now fully prefabricated in three sections. Furthermore, the width at hip level has been increased to 44 inches. A fixed tricycle gear version of the aircraft is available, as well.

Polliwagen's dealer in Switzerland recently had his aircraft tested and certified by the Swiss government. After completion of testing, it was issued a Swiss Type Certificate, one of two homebuilts to share this honor.

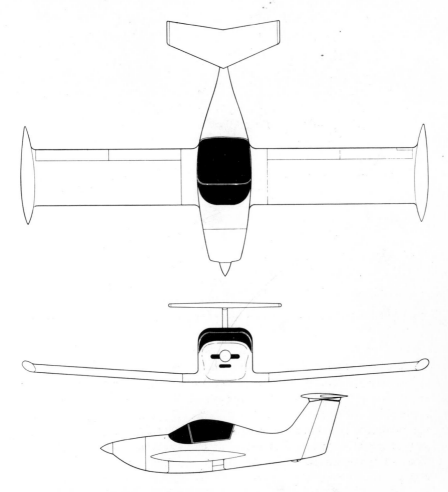

Fig. 6-4. Three-view drawing of the Polliwagen.

The plane can be transported to or from the airport and kept at home by detaching the wings and putting it on a modified trailer. Two ¾′ 4130 steel pins on each side hold the main spar. The wing fuel tanks have quick disconnects on the lines and the ailerons have 3/ 16″ nuts to quickly attach the controls. The trailer is a standard 750 lb. boat type that comes in a kit from any local boat dealer. With a couple of helpers, the airplane can be ready to go on the trailer in fifteen minutes.

The kit is beautifully done with all main composite structural parts molded. Plywood blocks for attachments are imbedded where needed and all fittings, rudder pedals, the control stick, engine mounts, canopy and latch parts, flaps and landing gear are furnished. There is no drilling, cutting or welding needed. The stabilator, for example, can be assembled and bonded in a few hours. The builder attaches the spar and fittings to one of the skins then bonds the other one over.

Joe Alvarez and his wife Lucy, have builders workshops throughout the country as well as Saturday seminars at their shop. They have a video cassette of every step for $75. The 200 page plans are $120, and updated free. A newsletter is mailed periodically to all Polliwagen builders.

Fig. 6-11. The Polliwagen features dual controls and a panel large enough for almost any instrumentation.

They say the airplane can be made in 500 hours. However, it has been my experience in talking to homebuilders that, whatever the maker says should be multiplied by about 1.5 before the airplane will be fully complete. That would be some 750 hours for a Polliwagen, still only about half the time of a Long-EZ.

Price of the kit is $10,000. This doesn't include paint, instruments, etc., so you could add a couple thousand to that. The complete expense would be something around $12,000.

Specifications

Wingspan	26 ft. 0 in.
Length	16 ft. 0 in.
Height	5 ft. 7 in.
Wing Area	90 sq. ft.
Engine Make, Model, HP	Revmaster R-2100 D, or (Cont O-200, Lyc. 0-235, 0-290, or 0-320)
Prop Diameter/Pitch	59 in. dia Maloof Constant Speed
Reduction Ratio	1-to-1
Fuel Capacity/Consumption	35 gal./3.3 gph. (Revmaster)
Gross Weight	1250-1500 lbs.
Empty Weight	650-750 lbs. (depending on engine)
Useful Load	600-750 lbs. (depending on engine)
Wing Loading	14-16.67 psf
Power Loading	10-19 lb/hp (depending on engine)

Design Load Factors	+9, -6
Construction Time	500 man-hrs
Pricing	$10,000

Flight Performance (Revmaster)

Velocity Never Exceed	255 mph
Top Level Speed	185 mph @ 15,500 ft.
Cruise Speed	168 mph @ 8500 ft.
Stall Speed (in free air)	51 mph
Sea Level Climb Rate	900+ fpm
Takeoff Run	500 ft.
Dist. Req'd to clear 50 ft.	1,000 ft.
Landing Roll	500 ft.
Service Ceiling (100 fpm climb)	19,000 ft.
Range at Cruise	1520 mi.
L/D (Glide Ratio)	17-to-1 @ idle

Polliwagen
Polliwagen, Inc.
P.O. Box 860, Murrieta, CA 92362, Joe Alvarez

Glassair

This machine was responsible for an almost frantic interest at the Oshkosh homebuilders convention in 1979.

The grass around the prototype was mercilessly trampled by excited homebuilders. It was another pre-molded, side by side, sleek little airplane. But, using a big engine they get truly high performance. The latest version has a retractable tricycle gear. It carries two people 231 mph on a fuel consumption of only 6.2 gallons per hour (32 mpg) for its 160 hp engine. The plane has phenomenal short field performance and rather straightforward control characteristics. It weighs a thousand pounds and carries 600, not a lot, but very adequate. The first version of the Glassair had beautifully streamlined, fixed taildragger gear that brings the weight down about 80 lbs., compared to the retractable version.

The kit comes with pre-molded composite shells already gelcoated. The spar is bonded into the bottom half of the wing as delivered. Canopies, engine mount, gear, and cowling, are included. The controls are pre-welded and the metal parts are stamped out. Axles, nuts and spacers, wheels brakes, tires and tubes, master cylinders, brake lines, prop extension, exhaust pipes, engine mount rubbers, instrument panel, engine ducting seats and belts, canopy hardware and, whatever else you can think of, is also included. Builders must install their own engines and instruments. The taildragger kit is $12,500 and the retractable tricycle gear version is $3600 more at $16,100. Another $5000 for engine and $3000 for radio and basic instruments plus perhaps $2000 for incidentals, will put the completed airplane at $26,100.

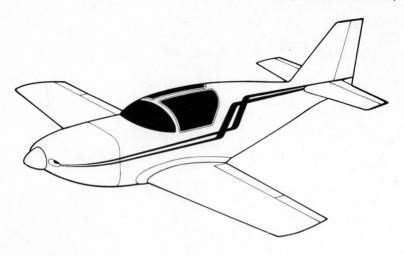

Fig. 6-5. The Glassair RG offers high performance on 160 HP.

But what a plane! This is an outstanding kit buy for a high performance airplane with such great economy. It handles mild aerobatics, such as rolls, easily. Because of its power, the ability to get out of small fields is superb. The 160 hp hauls it up to speed and into the air, in seconds. The stall with full flaps comes at 58 mph, which means it can stop quickly once down, and the brakes are put on.

The designer, Tom Hamilton, would like you to send $10 for more detailed information. His address is 18701 58th Ave. NE Arlington, WA 98223.

Specifications	**R.G.**	**T.D.**
Wingspan	23 ft. 3 in.	23 ft. 3 in.
Length	18 ft. 7 in.	18 ft. 7 in.
Height	6 ft. 8 in.	7 ft. 3 in.
Wing Area	81.2 sq. ft.	81.2 sq. ft.
Engine Make, Model, HP	Lyc. 0-320/160 hp	Lyc. 0-320/160 hp
Prop Diameter/Pitch	72 in/in constant speed	68/78
Reduction Ratio	1-to-1	1-to-1
Fuel Capacity/Consumption	42 gal./8 gph.	36/8
Gross Weight	1800 lbs.	1500 lbs.
Empty Weight	1100 lbs.	925 lbs.
Useful Load	700 lbs.	575 lbs.
Wing Loading	22 psf	18 psf
Power Loading	11.25 lb/hp	9.375 lb/hp
Design Load Factors	+9, -6 G's	+9, -6 G's
Construction Time	1200 man-hrs	1200 man-hrs
Field Assembly Time	N.A.	N.A.
Pricing	$17,500	$12,500

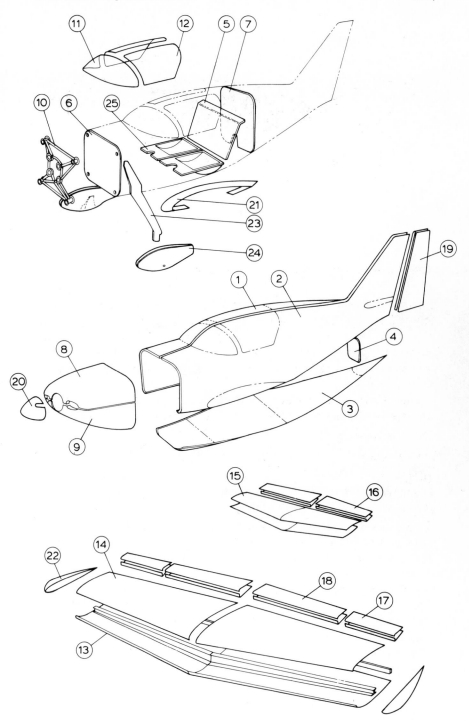

Fig. 6-6. The Glassair's pre-molded parts somewhat resemble a plastic model airplane's parts.

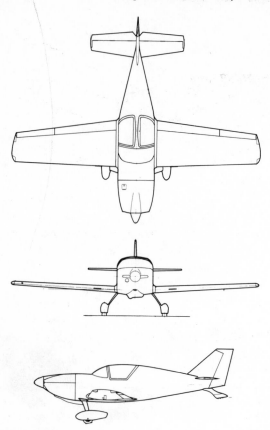

Fig. 6-7. Three-view drawing of the Glassair RG.

Flight Performance

Velocity Never Exceed	250 mph	240 mph
Top Level Speed	241 mph	230 mph
Cruise Speed	234 mph @ 75% power	224 mph @ 75%
Stall Speed (in free air)	60 mph	57 mph
Sea Level Climb Rate	2300 fpm @ 100 mph	1900 fpm @ 130 mph
Takeoff Run	380 ft.	390 ft.
Dist. Req'd to clear 50 ft.	900 ft.	900 ft.
Landing Roll	500 ft.	500 ft.
Service Ceiling (100 fpm climb)	19,000 ft.	19,000 ft.
Range at Cruise	1150 mi.	1000 mi.
L/D (Glide Ratio)	14-to-1 @ 95 mph	14-to-1 @ 85 mph

Glasair SH-2
Stoddard Hamilton Aircraft
18701 58th Ave. NE, Arlington, WA 98223, (206) 435-8533, Mike Currieri

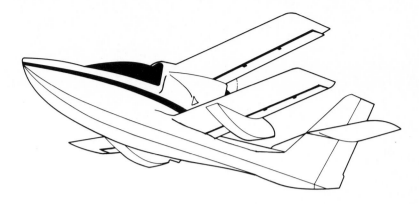

Fig. 6-8. The Sea Hawk is an amphibious, cantilever biplane with retractable landing gear.

Seahawk

Gary LeGare, the Quickie-Two designer and builder, left his native Canada and came to the "Mecca of Glass", Mojave Airport in the Southern California desert, to set up shop. He makes a little horizontal stabilizer, in the back where it belongs, for Quickies. This fix is to pull the nose up and reduce its tendency to dive when the front wing gets wet.

Gary sells the add-on tail to keep the Quickie from diving when the front wing gets water or bugs on the airfoil. But another exciting product is his new design, the SEA HAWK. It is a bi-plane amphibian. And get this, it is a cantilever biplane!

"Why make a biplane when its main feature, lighter structure by wire and strut crossbracing is not used?" I asked. "For no reason", honestly admits LeGare, "except I wanted to."

The land and sea plane can use a 70HP Revmaster on up to a 150 HP certified airplane engine. The big engine would give it a cruise of 160 MPH instead of the 115 MPH of the little 70 HP Revmaster. Most startling, is the claim of a 37 MPH stall at 1320 lbs gross on the prototype's 108 square feet of wing area. (Production version has 118 square feet) This works out to a lift coefficient of 3.5! This would earn the "Von Karman" prize as the highest lift in the history of plain flapped airplanes. For comparison, the competing Osprey 2 amphibian of wood and foam construction has a slightly lower wing loading but stalls at 63 MPH. I figure stall on the Sea Hawk should be about 47 MPH with the flaps down. The full span ailerons on the top wing go down when the flaps on the bottom wing are in landing position, increasing the lift so the plane can fly more slowly.

I sat in the cockpit. It is comfortable and visibility seems unhindered, since the engine and wings are behind. The airplane is a flying boat, riding in the water on its fuselage. The pusher propeller is behind the top wing to protect it from the water spray which would otherwise quickly erode the propeller.

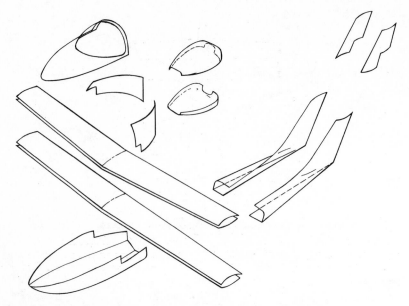

Fig. 6-9. Exploded drawing showing the various pre-molded parts of the Sea Hawk.

The parts I saw were beautifully smooth. LeGare even had an experimental wing of carbon fiber and Kevlar at his factory. The problem of drilling or cutting Kevlar was considered too much for homebuilders, so production wing layups will be made of fiberglass with carbon fiber inlays for spar strength. Incidentally, plastic seaplane will not rust or corrode.

The Sea Hawk has a long wheelbase, a wide tread and the increasingly popular simple free castering nosewheel. This allows swinging in its own length when one of the independent brakes on the side gear is set. With its large tail in the slipstream, the plane handles easily. With its lower center of gravity, water landings and takeoffs, compared to other float planes, are easy and fun.

More complex than a land plane, the Sea Hawk is a boat as well as an airplane. Fortunately however, much of the really time consuming details are done at the factory. The canopy, for example, is glued in and the rear bulkhead is fitted and bonded. The vertical fin is on the fuselage and all metal parts welded and cadmium plated. The kit is $11,000 with everything but the engine, instruments, and wiring. It can be divided into three packages: fuselage, wings, landing gear and engine installation. With a used airplane engine of 150 HP, it would be near $18,000 completed.

This is the very latest of the pre-molded composite kit planes, so I expect there will be some changes in specifications. They are already talking about 2+2 and a four place Sea Hawk.

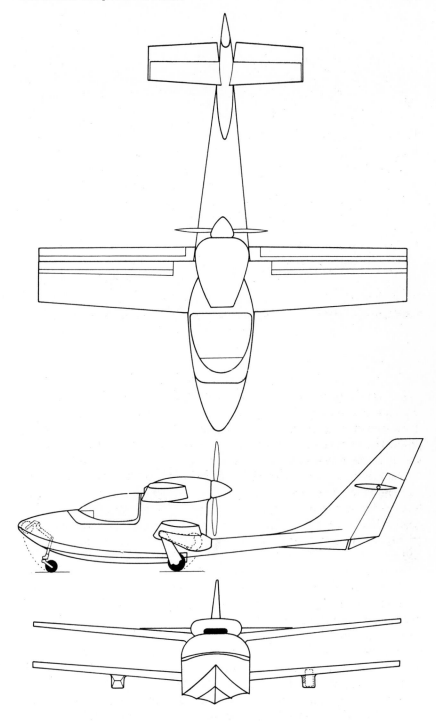

Fig. 6-10. Three-view drawing of the Sea Hawk shows the "reinvented" biplane concept.

Specifications

Wingspan	24 ft. 0 in.
Length	21 ft. 0 in.
Height	6 ft. 9 in.
Wing Area	118 sq. ft.
Engine Make, Model, HP	100-160 hp
Prop Diameter/Pitch	64 in/64 in
Reduction Ratio	1-to-1
Fuel Capacity/Consumption	70 gal./8.5 gph.
Gross Weight	1600 lbs.
Empty Weight	850 lbs.
Useful Load	750 lbs.
Wing Loading	12.72 psf
Power Loading	9.4-15 lb/hp
Design Load Factors	+5, -3
Construction Time	1000 man-hrs
Pricing	$11,950 (kit less engine)

Flight Performance

Velocity Never Exceed	180 mph
Top Level Speed	165 mph
Cruise Speed	155 mph @ 75% power
Stall Speed (in free air)	42 mph
Sea Level Climb Rate	1000 fpm
Takeoff Run	400 ft.
Dist. Req'd to clear 50 ft.	1800 ft.
Landing Roll	1200 ft.
Service Ceiling (100 fpm climb)	18,000 ft.
Range at Cruise	1320 mi.
L/D (Glide Ratio)	10-to-1 @ 80 mph

Sea Hawk
Aero Gare, Inc.
Bldg. 105, Mojave Airport, Mojave, CA 93501, (805) 824-2041, Garry LeGare

Summary
- Pre-molded kits seem to be the future of composite homebuilt planes. Cost is higher, but much time is saved.
- Previous kits using hot wire foam cutting and careful layups are now offered with many pre-mold parts as an option.
- Quality is assured and parts are light because of resin control, with a geometrically smooth finish for good aerodynamics.
- Engineering and planning by the designers and kit makers is more extensive, which insures building that is simpler and more foolproof.

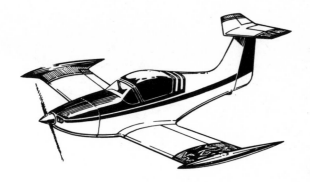

7
Foam Over Structure
& Moldless Composites

A few years ago Ken Rand, a compact, dynamic Southern California flying enthusiast, showed up at a homebuilders "fly-in" with an airplane that looked like an oversized model. He called it the KR-1. I tried sitting in it but the cockpit was too small — Ken built it to fit him. Most interesting was its construction, which was very different from other little planes at that time.

Beneath its curvy outer shape was a simple, boxy, wooden airplane. Its basic structure was covered with urethane foam blocks, carved and sanded to shape then covered with Dynel cloth and resin.

The tiny plane caught the fancy of many homebuilders. Over 10,000 sets of plans, as well as hundreds of kits have been sold. Some of the kit builders shaped their foam to make the fuselage look like a P-51 or Spitfire. Minor changes were easy with the foam because it was non-structural. It was possible for every builder to have a custom looking airplane.

The first versions used a cloth called Dynel. It is not made in small lots anymore, so almost all the airplanes using this type of construction now use fiberglass instead. The Dynel synthetic cloth is laid up much the same as any composite foam and glass airplane. That is, the resin is rolled into the foam and the cloth laid over, with more resin brushed or rolled on.

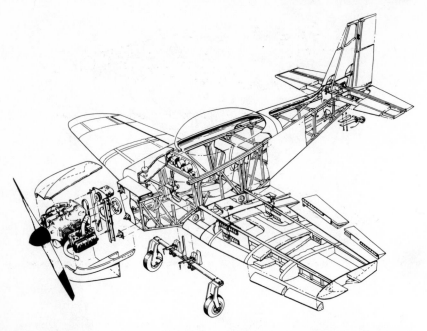

Fig. 7-1. Cutaway of the diminutive KR-1 shows the essence of the foam-over-structure construction technique.

There is a big difference however. With foam and Dynel over the structure, there needs to be only one layer of cloth and the parts are not really critically stressed since the airplane has its structural components made of wood or steel tubing.

Dynel is fun and easy. It clings like that plastic you use to wrap sandwiches with, or cover left overs. It has a big open weave and can go around all kinds of curves, including two directional, without wrinkling. The open weave takes up a lot of resin so the parts may be heavier than for a fiberglass surface. Thus, fiberglass can be stronger for its weight because of the tighter weave and less of a requirement for resin to fill it. The joy of foam and Dynel is the ease of working and boundless freedom in shaping by hobby class workers. Unfortunately, it is hard to find, so most builders have substituted glass cloth.

Pilots like the purposefulness of warplanes. That they were used to destroy and kill is lost in the image of macho romance of men against men with aircraft. Remember, airplanes are emotional machines. Flying around in your own authentic looking little fighter without the expense of a real one, is a greatly intriguing idea. A real fighter, running a big V-12 Rolls Royce engine, such as is used in the P-51, can burn over a hundred gallons of high octane fuel per hour. With the terrific interest in warplanes, the foam and Dynel technique was quickly picked up as a way to make inexpensive scale replicas of any fighterplane.

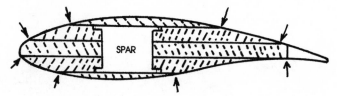

POOR METHOD. Feather Edges Of Foam And Glue Lines Are Difficult To Sand.

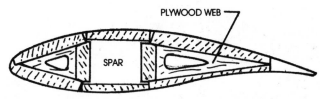

GOOD METHOD. Uses 40 Millimeter Blocks of Urethane, With Only The Outside Glass Covered.

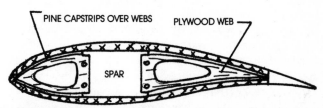

BEST METHOD. Sheet Foam Is Bent Over Plywood Ribs. One Layer Of Glass Is Placed On The Inside Of The Foam Before Assembly, And On The Outside After Assembly.

Fig. 7-2. The three primary approaches to foam-over-structure construction technique.

War Aircraft Replicas

One day, four of us in our motor gliders were coming down from the Watsonville air show. Charlie Webber and I spent an hour soaring the last 25 miles and glided in for landings. It is a short, smoothly paved airport surrounded by neatly kept hangars. (Note: When you're talking about the kind that you put airplanes in it is spelled "hangar", "not hanger", which is the kind you use for putting away sport coats in the closet.) At any rate, we walked around looking at some unique machines. A European biplane called a Stampe from the 1930's, a Bell Airacobra fighter in Mira Slovak's hangar. Clete Roberts, the TV reporter, was working on a restoration.

In one hangar sat a perfect FW 190, scourge of the skies for the B-17 pilots over Germany. I moved closer to inspect this incredible find. It seemed small for some reason. It was a replica! Three inventive flyers, Jim Kern, Warren Eberspacher and Ken Thoms had used Rand's idea to make a basic frame covered with foam to duplicate the fighter at half-scale size. Even the fabric covered rudder of the original was duplicated with gentle dips reproducing

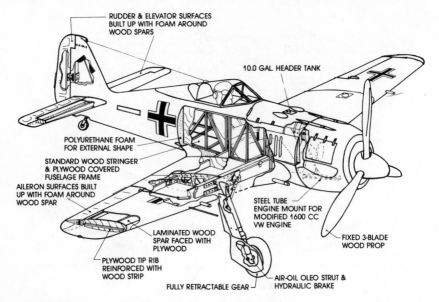

RUDDER & ELEVATOR SURFACES
BUILT UP WITH FOAM AROUND
WOOD SPARS

10.0 GAL. HEADER TANK

POLYURETHANE FOAM
FOR EXTERNAL SHAPE

STANDARD WOOD STRINGER
& PLYWOOD COVERED
FUSELAGE FRAME

AILERON SURFACES BUILT
UP WITH FOAM AROUND
WOOD SPAR

STEEL TUBE
ENGINE MOUNT FOR
MODIFIED 1600 CC
VW ENGINE

LAMINATED WOOD
SPAR FACED WITH
PLYWOOD

FIXED 3-BLADE
WOOD PROP

PLYWOOD TIP RIB
REINFORCED WITH
WOOD STRIP

AIR-OIL OLEO STRUT &
HYDRAULIC BRAKE

FULLY RETRACTABLE GEAR

Fig. 7-3. Cutaway of W.A.R. FW-190 reveals the inner secrets of the foam-over-structure method.

the "fabric tension" between the ribs. Inspection covers, bulges for the wing guns, scoops and skin joints were all in the precise positions of the original. They designed a structure that could be used for almost any radial engine fighter of WW 2 that could be filled out with foam for the outside contours. The same structure combined with their patterns and foam can be used to make the FW 190, F4U Corsair, Japanese Zero, Hawker Sea Fury, F85 Bearcat, Republic P-47, F6f Hellcat, Curtiss Hawk 75A, and the Russian Lavochkin. It is surprising how similar the fighters of those days appeared, especially their wings.

Airplane spotting was an art in WW2 because of the similar appearances of the competing nations' airplanes. This all worked out well for the Santa Paula gang. The fuselage of each plane is where the differences show up. The many details and two way curves would be a nightmare for any other kind of material but easily made of wood with Dynel covering. The first replica they made was a Focke Wulf 190 powered by a Volkswagen engine. A half scale copy of the US Navy Corsair fighter is now flying, as well.

Like any airplane, it takes a long time to make these replicas. This is not to say the foam-Dynel method is difficult, it's just that the many detail parts in a replica require a lot of time. The landing gear retract mechanisms, wing and canopy fittings, instruments, controls and engine installation, gasoline tank, pumps, and trim tabs, plus the electrical and fuel systems, and controls for everything, such as the throttle, primer mixture, etc., are what makes up the 1500 to 2000 hours building time. This is a couple years of full spare time hobby effort. The W.A.R. Aircraft Replica Company is at 348 South Eighth St., Santa Paula, CA 93023. If you want an inexpensive two seater, however the KR-2 might be the better choice as it is very simple.

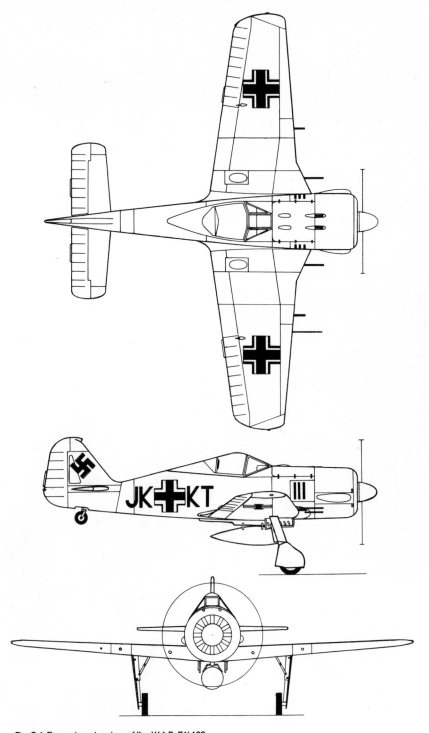

Fig. 7-4. Three-view drawing of the W.A.R. FW-190.

Specifications

Wingspan	20 ft. 6 in.
Length	16 ft. 6 in.
Height	6 ft. 0 in.
Wing Area	75 sq. ft.
Engine Make, Model, HP	VW 1600, 70-90 hp
Prop Diameter/Pitch	various
Reduction Ratio	1-to-1
Fuel Capacity/Consumption	12-15 gal.
Gross Weight	900 lbs.
Empty Weight	600 lbs.
Useful Load	300 lbs.
Wing Loading	12 psf
Power Loading	10 lb/hp
Design Load Factors	+6, -6
Construction Time	1500 man-hrs

Flight Performance (100 hp)

Velocity Never Exceed	N.A.
Top Level Speed	170 mph
Cruise Speed	145 mph
Stall Speed (in free air)	55 mph
Sea Level Climb Rate	1,200 fpm
Takeoff Run	800 ft.
Dist. Req'd to clear 50 ft.	N.A.
Landing Roll	1000 ft.
Service Ceiling (100 fpm climb)	N.A.
Range at Cruise	400-500 mi.

Focke-Wulf FW-190
War Aircraft Replicas, Inc.
348 So. Eighth St., Santa Paula, CA 93023, (805) 525-8212, Sales Manager

Rand KR-2

The KR-2 is the two seat version of the KR-1. Ken Rand and I took it up and ran it through the stall through highspeed range. It quits flying about 55 MPH or so and seems to go over 155 indicated using the Revmaster Turbo engine of about 70 HP. The nose waggle when you move the stick indicates not enough vertical fin area, but in general it has a nice responsive feel. Two weeks later, when Ken was coming back from the Sun and Fun Fly-in in Florida, he apparently ran out of fuel because of storms and headwinds. Just 20 minutes from his home field at Meadowlark, a southern California Airport, the airplane fell into a dense snowstorm over Hesperia in the high desert. He radioed Edwards Air Force base for directions to land but seemed

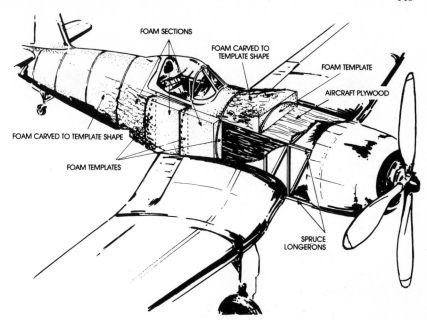

FOAM SECTIONS

FOAM CARVED TO
TEMPLATE SHAPE

FOAM TEMPLATE

AIRCRAFT PLYWOOD

FOAM CARVED TO TEMPLATE SHAPE

FOAM TEMPLATES

SPRUCE
LONGERONS

Fig. 7-5. W.A.R. Corsair depicts foam blocks before, during and after carving to the aircraft's contours.

to lose level flight in the dark clouds and turbulence. The plane probably went into a spiral dive. The last call was, "Down to 3000 feet! I'm going to hit!" I knew the area well so called his wife and offered to fly my motorglider on the search effort. He was found a few days later having dived straight into the ground near a settled area. The storm had been so thick no one had heard or seen the crash. It is sad the creativity of Ken Rand has ended, but his design and airplane had nothing to do with the accident. Over 90 percent of homebuilt airplane accidents are weather related or "pilot error," and not due to the design or construction. Ken's contribution to plastic construction will live on. Some sophisticated structural purists will bemoan the use of foam and glass over a basic spar and fuselage. They wonder why the designer cannot use the glass and foam as a shell as does the Quickie, Long-EZ and Dragonfly. Yes, it is a departure from the ideal, but it is a simple way to make an outside shape to any desired style.

As an example of what can be done, the MOBA sailplane wing was made using foam over structure. Its advantage is that the builder can construct the airplane without jigs or molds. The maker of the ship, Gary Sunderland of Australia, found the method practical and as light as any comparable sailplane of equal size. He made a metal box spar to take all the bending and twisting forces on the wing. Then, he bolted accurate plywood ribs to the spar and filled in the spaces between ribs with urethane foam blocks. The blocks were sanded to the contour of the ribs. Then cloth, in this case two layers of fiberglass, was epoxied over the wing for the final covering which was then

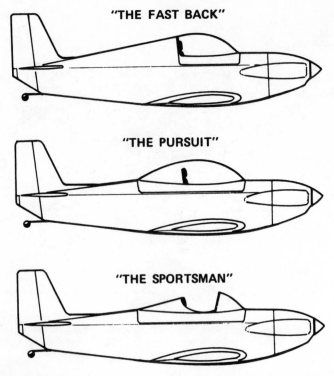

Fig. 7-6. Variations on the KR-1 theme, shows your individuality is readily accommodated by the foam-over-structure method.

filled and finished. With the added strength of the glass and foam, the wing can carry at least 1.3 times over its design stress of 5 G's.

This extra load factor is probably true of all these wood and foam planes such as the KR-1, KR-2 and WAR replicas. They are designed to have the wood structure carry the loads and anything added to the strength by the foam and Glass/Dynel simply adds to the reserve load factor for extra strength.

An important procedure in putting foam blocks over the structure is to be sure the edges of these blocks do not end up feathered. Another point in self-designed airplanes or modifications is to attach the foam to the basic structure with the loads spread over a large area. This can be done using plywood ribs firmly attached to the spars, or bulkheads fastened to the fuselage. Then use the foam to fill in between the spar and the leading trailing back edges.

The technique can be used for additions or modifications to already flying airplanes. Decide on the shape. Make the templates for sections as wide as the blocks of urethane. For complex curves, use smaller sections, a foot to two feet is easy enough to use a knife for rough shaping. Take a two or three foot board an inch thick with rough sandpaper wrapped and fastened

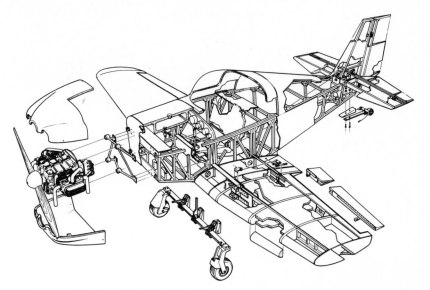

Fig. 7-7. Cutaway of KR-2 two-seater, showing complete structure, as well as foam overlays.

around it. Move it back and forth over the foam until it touches the bulkhead templates.

Since urethane foam doesn't dissolve, I recommend polyester resin be used for the final glassing. It is far cheaper, only $17.75 per gallon, (versus $45.00 for epoxy), less toxic, more flexible and easily strong enough as shaping over a basic structure. Roll on the resin and lay the Dynel or fiberglass smoothly over the foam. Another layer of resin on the outside and it's ready for fill and finish. The kits are probably the least expensive composite aircraft on the market today. Rand/Robinson Engineering, at 5842 K McFadden Ave., Huntington Beach, CA 92649, sells the kit with many parts now premolded, for $2900.

Moldless Fuselages

Another process of making fuselages is found in using a moldless method that can perhaps eliminate much of the great time and expense of plug construction and mold preparation. Although there are no kits using this technique, there is no reason why an ambitious designer/homebuilder cannot use it for the front section of a fuselage where the many compound curves make it difficult to use aluminum and wood. The idea is to use the plug, or inside mold, as the final structure. This will allow skipping a very time consuming part of the process.

First, draw the desired part of the fuselage. (A spar or wing is probably too difficult for most builders). Make a cardboard cross section of the shape every 6 inches. These temporary bulkheads are covered with foam sheets such as Clark Foam about one-half inch thick, or one-quarter inch balsa

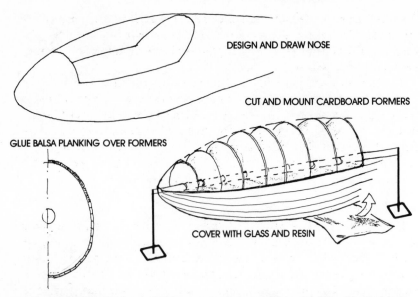

DESIGN AND DRAW NOSE

CUT AND MOUNT CARDBOARD FORMERS

GLUE BALSA PLANKING OVER FORMERS

COVER WITH GLASS AND RESIN

Fig. 7-8. Moldless fuselages are yet another method of composite construction. It involves balsa planking over cardboard formers. Balsa is covered with glass and resin. When the outside is finished, the part is split in two, and the formers discarded. The inside surface is then glassed and resined. Finally, the two halves are glued back together. Cutouts, such as the cockpit opening, are made, and the edges reinforced.

wood planks. For this explanation, let's use balsa wood, but even the foam is likely to be a little easier.

The sheets should be the lightest you can find at the hobby store or homebuilt aircraft supplier. The planks are glued to the cardboard bulkheads and to each other with 5-minute epoxy or any wood glue you like to work with that is easily sanded. After the shape is covered with balsa wood, it is given a coat of resin and the low spots are filled with microballoon-resin mix. Sand until it has a smooth, wave-free surface.

Brush on the resin and spread the fiberglass cloth over the balsa. Use the largest pieces possible without wrinkling. In most compound curve areas near the nose, strips should be cut and laid on, overlapping 3 to 4 inches.

Using a rubber squeegee, the resin is spread out through the glass and the excess removed. Color can be added so paint is not needed. The more resin that can be worked out, the lighter the structure with no loss in strength. Curing time depends on how much hardener you mix and the temperature around the work — it's about 45 minutes at 80° F. After it has hardened, pull out the cardboard bulkheads and throw them away. Perfect accuracy is not needed for areas not in the wing but it should be trimmed and sanded to make it look nice.

Glass cloth is resined to the bottom inside of the shell. Then the shell is turned so that another quarter can be put on until the entire inside is covered. After three layers of fiberglass are on each side, you will have a sandwich of immense strength. The cockpit can be cut out and the edges strengthened.

Plywood can be glassed into the structure at any place where attach points are needed. The cost can be as low as $3.00 per square foot, including the resin, balsa and fiberglass cloth. Each glass lamination will weight 1½ ounces per square foot, per layer of cloth.

The balsa or foam core will weigh about 2½ ounces per square foot. The total will be only little over one-half pound per square foot for this section of the fuselage. In a very narrow fuselage nose, it might be easier to cut it in half, do the inside layers, then glue it back together and cover the seams with extra strips of fiberglass. Plywood reinforcing pieces plus the extra joining strips could add a little extra weight. But in the case of a forced landing accident, a pilot can be well protected by such a strong eggshell structure.

Bagging

Here is another clever method of finishing that saves a lot of time, in wings and tail sections that do not have too much of a sharp curve. First, complete the basic foam structure. Next, the fiberglass is cut and fitted in the proper sequence to give the greatest strength. Instead of putting it on the foam it is laid on a smooth surface for resining. This can be window glass or formica with a thin layer of plastic to keep it from sticking. After the resin is rolled or brushed into the fiberglass, it is allowed to cure. The sheets are smooth and slick on the side facing the surface on which they were made. They are then placed on the foam structure. Brush a layer of resin over the foam structure and place the prelaminated and cured sheets in place.

Wrap the part in a plastic sheeting, like 6 mil thick painter's drop cloth. Tape it shut and stick a household vacuum cleaner into one corner so it sucks the air from the inside of the bag. The assembly will be pulled together for a tight, perfect bond. When it cures the plastic is unwrapped and the part is almost ready to finish, with no long hours of sanding and filling necessary as you would have to do with a regular layup.

Summary

- Foam glued over a basic structure can be made into almost any shape by very inexperienced builders.
- Non critical covering can be dynel or fiberglass in thin layers.
- Easy repair of dents and holes is assured, because the main structure is out of harm's way underneath the foam and glass.
- Moldless parts use cardboard bulkheads and foam or balsa planking for the sandwich. High strength and light weight for one-off fuselages, wheel fairings or nose sections is its greatest asset.
- Precured laminates can be used with vacuum cleaner bagging to reduce much of the work of layups that have been made right over the foam.

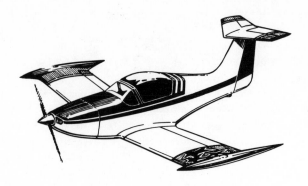

8

Exotic Composite Aircraft

Imagine an airplane that spans 96 feet, weighs only 70 pounds, and flies on the power of a single pedaling human. Or, how about one that takes off and flies hundreds of miles on the immediate electric power generated by the sunshine on its wings and tail. These are examples of some of the incredible flying machines that could never have been made before plastics like Kevlar, carbon fiber, mylar and epoxy resins. Plastics were exclusively used in these most interesting of airplanes to be built in a decade.

Planes like this are not generally considered "homebuilt" but they were done with the simplest of tools and are one-of-a-kind so they really are "homebuilt". There is no reason some of the techniques could not be used for an advanced homebuilt ultralight.

Also, since this is a book on composite construction and I worked on the Gossamer Albatross project, I would be amiss to not share the details of their design and construction. They are an inspiration to homebuilders by showing what can be done with composites.

The Gossamer Albatross
This wonderful airplane flew over thirty miles to cross the waters of the English channel in a flight to France in 1979. The story starts back in 1958

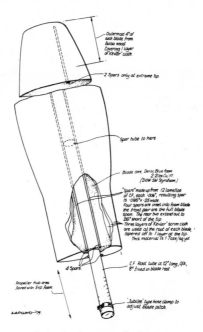

Fig. 8-1. Gossamer Albatross propeller is a basic composite structure.

when the Royal Aero Club of England announced a prize for the first figure of eight flight over a one mile course. This was to include a pass over a ten foot high marker and would define the achievement of human powered flight. Eventually the prize was 50,000 pounds sterling, about $200,000, depending on the value of the pound versus the dollar.

In 1976, my wife and I had just completed a bicycle trip around the world, stopping at lots of airports and getting to fly different kinds of airplanes and gliders. On arrival back home, I got a call from Dr. Paul MacCready to have lunch and discuss a flying project. He had gotten the idea that a huge, very light airplane would carry a person at less than ten miles an hour. That speed is so slow it would need only four-tenths of a horsepower. This is in the range of human power for ten minutes or more. If the airplane could turn and go around the Kremer course, named after the prize's sponsor, Henry Kremer, the money would be won. I joined with Paul MacCready and Peter Lissaman for a share of the prize if we won.

Using 2 inch aluminum tubing, wire bracing, and mylar plastic covering, we built a rough prototype in just ten days. It had plenty of lift at low speed and seemed strong enough, so we made another after moving our operation to Mojave Airport, later home of many composite airplanes.

We made a big propeller, like model airplane wings, attached it behind the wing and connected a plastic bicycle chain driven by pedals at the bottom of the kingpost-mast. With Paul's son Tyler pedaling, it flew almost immediately. One calm evening, flown by racing cyclist Greg Miller, it stayed up over a minute.

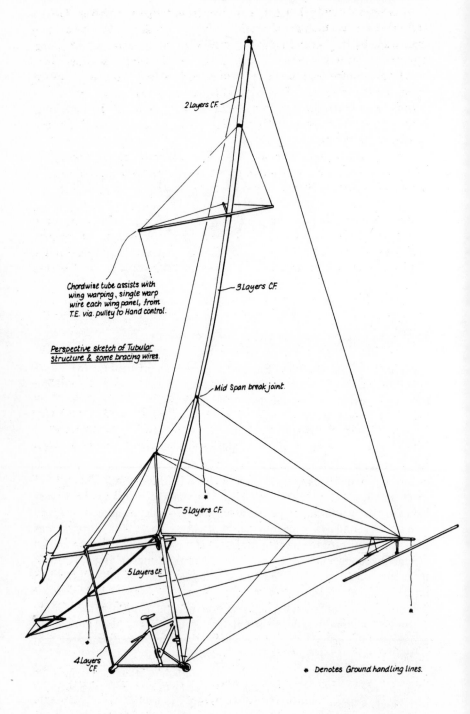

2 Layers C.F.

Chordwise tube assists with
wing warping, single warp
wire each wing panel, from
T.E. via. pulley to Hand control.

3 Layers C.F.

*Perspective sketch of Tubular
structure & some bracing wires.*

Mid Span break joint.

5 Layers C.F.

5 Layers C.F.

4 Layers
C.F.

* Denotes Ground handling lines.

Fig. 8-2. Perspective sketch of Gossamer Albatross's tubular structure and some bracing wires.

After several hundred flights, we moved from Mojave to Shafter Airport and made a new streamlined version. The new airplane made some long flights, and by July, we had solved the turning problem by warping the wings opposite to the way you would expect. The outside wing was twisted by a wire from a control lever which reduced its angle to the air and increased the attack on the inside tip. This allowed the plane to swing around a circle without having the outer wing generate so much more lift than the inner wing. This prevented the wing from rolling the plane too much and forcing it to slide into the ground.

On August 23, 1977, less than a year since the project's start, the rider-pilot, Bryan Allen, pedaled it around the course in seven and a half strenuous minutes and won the 50,000 Pound Sterling Kremer prize that had stood for almost 20 years.

Henry Kremer, through the Royal Aeronautical Society, then announced a new prize. One expected to stand another twenty years. It seemed incredible. A prize of 100,000 Pounds, $235,000. It was the greatest in the history of aviation. The task was for a human powered flight from England to France!

How could a gain in range from one mile to twenty-two miles be accomplished? What "magic" would it take since only man was to be the power?

The magic was crisper design and composite plastic construction. The original Condor needed endurance for the level of human energy which lasts only ten minutes. But, if an airplane could be made to fly on only .25 HP, it could stay up for hours. A human being can produce a quarter horsepower for that period of time. Riding a bicycle at 15 MPH takes a tenth of a horsepower and can be done all day by a person in reasonably good condition. A very fit person can produce the quarter horsepower to ride a bike at 20 to 22 MPH for several hours.

For each pound lighter the plane can be made .75 percent less power is needed. If wing area is cut 30 percent, but span kept the same, both induced and friction drag is less.

To keep the flying speed the same as the Gossamer Condor, the same lift must be created by the smaller wing area. The way to do that is to have a more accurately shaped airfoil so the air is moved down with the least turbulence by the wing's passage. A foam leading edge, more ribs and a stronger wing would allow tighter covering with less billows and wrinkles. A stiffer wing would need less brace wire. The old aluminum tubing Condor had 78 wires to hold the wing resulting in considerable drag, even at the 10 mph flying speed. A stiffer wing would need fewer bracing wires. The carbon fiber Albatross needed only four.

To make all the tubing in the main structure, we kept a roll of pre-preg unidirectional carbon fiber in the refrigerator. The cold kept the epoxy from starting to set. A two-inch aluminum tube was mounted in a holder that would turn slowly, like a lathe. The carbon was wrapped around the tube at an angle. Strips of carbon were laid on the top and bottom for extra strength

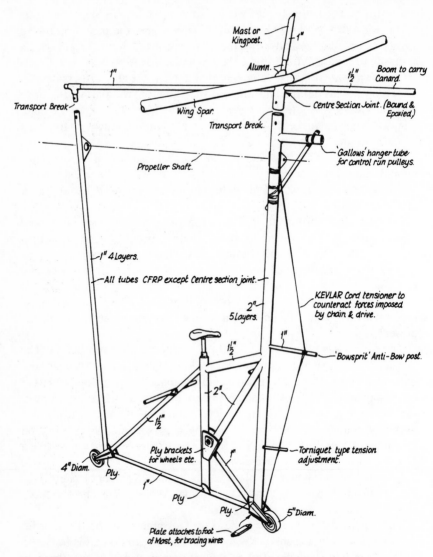

Fig. 8-3. General arrangement of gondola basic structure and attachment of wing unit.

in bending up and down. Then, shrink tape was wrapped around the layup. It was taken off the lathe and put in a cardboard carpet tube. These tubes can be obtained from any carpet store after the material has been sold. A couple of heater blowers were arranged to send hot air into the tubes to cure the pre preg carbon fiber.

After half hour to an hour the carbon would cure. We then took out the aluminum tubes and split off the shrink tape with a razor. The aluminum inside was not necessary because the carbon fiber tubes were so strong. Now to get rid of the aluminum. Trying to pull a twelve foot piece of aluminum out

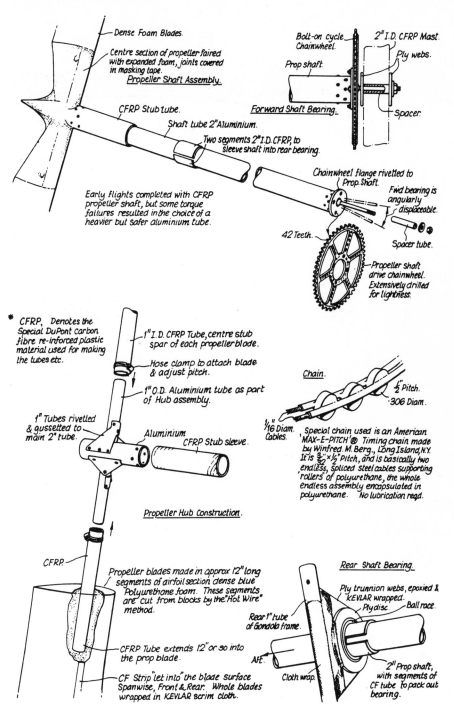

Dense Foam Blades.

Centre section of propeller faired with expanded foam, joints covered in masking tape.
Propeller Shaft Assembly.

CFRP Stub tube.

Shaft tube 2" Aluminium.

Two segments 2"I.D. CFRP, to sleeve shaft into rear bearing.

Early flights completed with CFRP propeller shaft, but some torque failures resulted in the choice of a heavier but safer aluminium tube.

Bolt-on cycle Chainwheel.

2" I.D. CFRP Mast.

Prop shaft.

Ply webs.

Forward Shaft Bearing.

Spacer.

Chainwheel flange rivetted to Prop. Shaft.

Fwd bearing is angularly displaceable.

42 Teeth.

Spacer tube.

Propeller shaft drive chainwheel. Extensively drilled for lightness.

* CFRP, Denotes the Special DuPont carbon fibre re-inforced plastic material used for making the tubes etc.

1" I.D. CFRP Tube, centre stub spar of each propeller blade.

Hose clamp to attach blade & adjust pitch.

1" O.D. Aluminium tube as part of Hub assembly.

1" Tubes rivetted & gussetted to main 2" tube.

Aluminium

CFRP Stub sleeve.

Propeller Hub Construction.

Chain.

½" Pitch.

.306 Diam.

1/16" Diam. Cables.

Special chain used is an American MAX-E-PITCH ® Timing chain made by Winfred. M. Berg., Long Island, N.Y. It is 3/20" x ½" Pitch, and is basically two endless, spliced steel cables supporting rollers of polyurethane, the whole endless assembly encapsulated in polyurethane.   No lubrication reqd.

CFRP.

Propeller blades made in approx 12" long segments of airfoil section dense blue Polyurethane foam. These segments are cut from blocks by the "Hot Wire" method.

CFRP Tube extends 12" or so into the prop blade.

CF Strip "let into" the blade surface Spanwise, Front & Rear. Whole blades wrapped in KEVLAR scrim cloth.

Rear Shaft Bearing.

Ply trunnion webs, epoxied & KEVLAR wrapped.

Ply disc.

Ball race.

Rear 1" tube of Gondola frame.

Aft.

Cloth wrap.

2" Prop shaft, with segments of CF tube to pack out bearing.

Fig. 8-4. Detail or propeller shaft assembly and drive train.

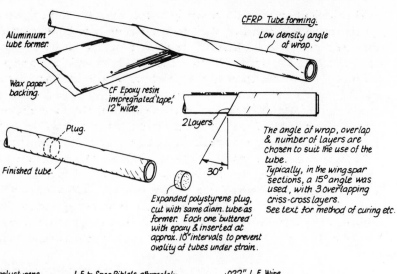

CFRP Tube forming.

Aluminium tube former.

Low density angle of wrap.

Wax paper backing.

CF Epoxy resin impregnated 'tape,' 12" wide.

Plug.

Finished tube.

2 Layers

30°

The angle of wrap, overlap & number of layers are chosen to suit the use of the tube.
Typically, in the wing spar sections, a 15° angle was used, with 3 overlapping criss-cross layers.
See text for method of curing etc.

Expanded polystyrene plug, cut with same diam. tube as former. Each one 'buttered' with epoxy & inserted at approx. 10" intervals to prevent ovality of tubes under strain.

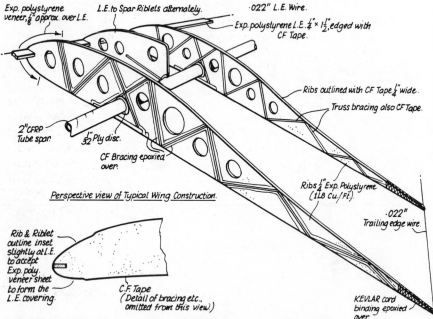

Exp. polystyrene veneer, ⅛" approx. over L.E.

L.E. to Spar Riblets alternately.

·022" L.E. Wire.

Exp. polystyrene L.E. ¼" × 1½" edged with CF Tape.

Ribs outlined with CF Tape ¼" wide.

Truss bracing also CF Tape.

2" CFRP Tube spar.

3/32" Ply disc.

CF Bracing epoxied over.

Ribs ¼" Exp. Polystyrene (1 LB Cu./Ft.).

·022" Trailing edge wire.

Perspective view of Typical Wing Construction.

Rib & Riblet outline inset slightly at L.E. to accept Exp. poly. veneer sheet to form the L.E. covering.

C.F. Tape (Detail of bracing etc., omitted from this view.)

KEVLAR cord binding epoxied over.

Fig. 8-5. Perspective drawing of typical composite used in wing's construction.

of a carbon fiber layup was not possible so the tube was put in a big plastic irrigation pipe with the ends capped. Swimming pool acid was poured in. After about 30 minutes of furious bubbling and boiling the aluminum disappeared and only a pure carbon fiber tube remained. By pushing epoxy coated foam plugs into the tubes at one foot spacing the strength increased another 20% because the foam segments kept the tube from changing shape under load.

The airfoil ribs were made from polystyrene foam. A hot wire first sliced quarter inch sheets from a big block and these in turn were hot wire cut from the sheets using a smooth airfoil template. Strips of carbon fiber were epoxied to the ribs, top and bottom, and across the middle to give great stiffness. A fine tape of fiberglass over the strips spread the loads to the foam rib. Ribs were slid on the fiberglass tubes and epoxy slurried in position. I took sheets of the polystyrene and bent them into shape for the leading edge by heating with a hot blower, and gently pushing the softened sheets into a form mold with gloved hands. These were then glued to the leading edge.

The wing was made in four sections to make it easy to take apart and move to the flying site. Each section weighed only 8 pounds! The entire 96 foot wing scaled only 32 pounds. To me, the most dramatic illustration of carbon fiber application was that the 24 foot wing sections were so light and stiff that without the covering I could hold my hands two feet apart and wave the wing up and down without it bending! Compare that with the aluminum tubed Condor.

I took the Aluminum tube structure Condor to the Smithsonian Institute, and, with Bryan Allen and Vern Oldershaw, hung it in over the "Milestones in Flight" hall. We had to position ourselves evenly and hold each wing to lift it because the alloy was so flexible and floppy it would drape on the floor without its wire braces. The Albatross carbon fiber spar tubes had twice the stiffness and half the weight in comparison with the Condor.

Carbon fiber is strong as the steel used in airliner landing gear but its very stiffness makes for some problems. When it fractures it doesn't break cleanly but splinters into fine needle-like pieces at the break. Slivers of carbon fiber easily get imbedded in your skin. The white blood cells would not work it out as they can a wood sliver. I would notice a prickly pain in my hand for days and find a sliver of carbon under the skin. I had to cut each out with a knife and tweezers. The tubes around the pilot were wrapped in Kevlar, which is very tough, to hold the splinters in any break, so the pilot wouldn't become a pincushion.

The propeller was made like any foam composite. It used carbon fiber tube spar, an airfoil of dense blue foam, covered with Kevlar and finished smoothly. It was heavier than the Balsa wood, Monokote covered prop of the original Condor but extra efficient. Its more complex shape was designed to smooth the lift distribution.

Most of the steel wires of the Condor were replaced with lighter and stronger Kevlar cords.

The pictures and diagrams give you an idea of some of the details more clearly than words.

But a reasonable question about all this is what about the homebuilder who wants to create a practical airplane. The Gossamer Condor and Albatross are not practical airplanes. They had the same mass/size ratio as a dirigible and regulated on almost absolute calm in which to fly, plus a crew of three to five simply to walk it in and out of the hangar. They were unstable at any speed over 15 MPH. Both had the pitch control on the front. This canard

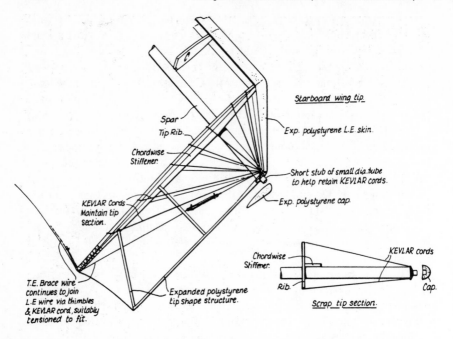

Starboard wing tip

Spar

Tip Rib.

Chordwise Stiffener.

Exp. polystyrene L.E. skin.

Short stub of small dia. tube to help retain KEVLAR cords.

Exp. polystyrene cap.

KEVLAR Cords Maintain tip section.

T.E. Brace wire continues to join L.E wire via thimbles & KEVLAR cord, suitably tensioned to fit.

Expanded polystyrene tip shape structure.

Chordwise Stiffener.

KEVLAR cords

Rib.

Cap.

Scrap tip section.

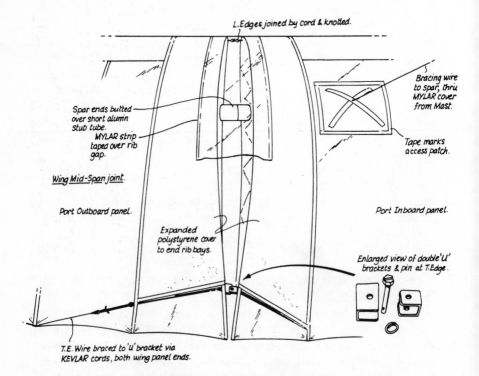

L. Edges joined by cord & knotted.

Spar ends butted over short alumin stub tube.

MYLAR strip taped over rib gap.

Bracing wire to spar, thru MYLAR cover from Mast.

Tape marks access patch.

Wing Mid-Span joint.

Port Outboard panel.

Port Inboard panel.

Expanded polystyrene cover to end rib bays.

Enlarged view of double 'U' brackets & pin at T. Edge.

T.E. Wire braced to 'U' bracket via KEVLAR cords, both wing panel ends.

Fig. 8-6. More details of the Gossamer Albatross's wing structure.

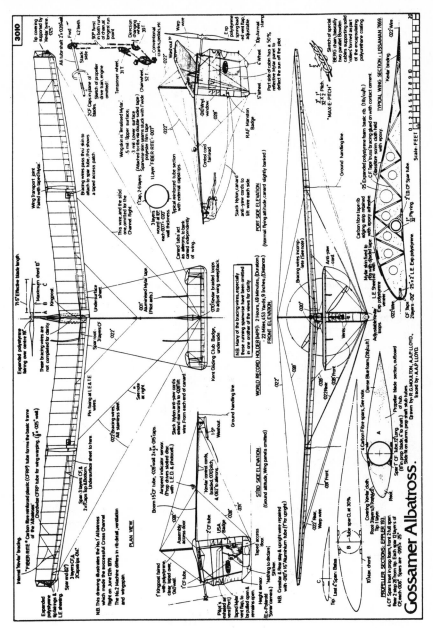

Fig. 8-7. Four-view drawing of the Gossamer Albatross.

carried less lift than the wing per unit area. In a stall the wing dropped before the canard so the plane fell backward. Conventional canard stability, as used on the Long-EZ, with a highly loaded front surface, is far too aerodynamically inefficient for the human powered airplanes which need every bit of performance possible. Flights were three to fifteen feet high and

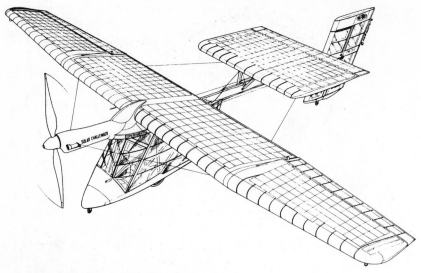

Fig. 8-8. Perspective sketch of the Solar Challenger.

at nine to twelve MPH and the stall occurred in slow motion so it was not critical. At 18 mph the Albatross became unstable and almost impossible to control.

Inspiring as it is, the particular designs of the Condor and Albatross are not the way to go, unless you want the lightest possible slow speed human powered airplane. Then Dupont sponsored Dr. MacCready on a new project that may have a greater influence on airplanes in the ultralight category.

Solar Challenger

I know some people think the only way to make an airplane is with aluminum. As I pointed out earlier, this method is one of the best for production airplanes and present engineering techniques. It is so good, especially for simple shapes, I often wonder if the reason homebuilders use composite construction is actually a rebellion against the pre-planned shapes of alloy machines. With composite plastics, the home designer-builder can piece things together bit by bit using layers of fiberglass, resin and foam, giving a more tactile sense of making the airplane shape.

In the case of the Solar powered airplane however, the challenge could have been won only by using composites. The plane had to be very light because the solar cells alone sending electricity to an electric motor were supposed to power the plane. Before this, only an unmanned, purely sun energized airplane had ever flown. A manned electric machine in England and a hang glider in USA had carried a pilot, but both were actually powered by batteries. That these batteries had been allowed to charge by on-board solar cells does not make them sun powered, anymore than we humans are solar powered, just because we digest vegetables that originally received energy from photosynthesis. Some believe gasoline is from previous sun-

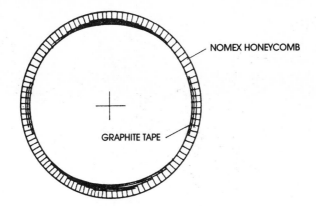

NOMEX HONEYCOMB

GRAPHITE TAPE

Fig. 8-9. Cross section of Solar Challenger composite spar construction.

plant energy so all such motors using that fuel could be considered sun powered. But real solar power should have no stored energy.

The Solar Challenger, in contrast, carried no batteries but ran on direct sun energy from solar cells. It was to fly from Paris to London as a demonstration of solar power. The shape and aerodynamics grew from the need to carry as many solar cells as possible to give it enough power. Flat topped airfoils were used on the wing and tail because the 16,128 thin, square silicon solar cells could not be bent to the shape of a curved airfoil. The lift coefficient was a perfectly normal and average 1.4 for this airfoil again, pointing out the fallacy of the old "the air must go farther over the top to give lift" Bernoulli based explanation of flight.

For efficiency, the huge prop resulted in an extra deep fuselage. Kevlar cords in tension helped stiffen the carbon fiber tubing so that the pilot had 9 G crash protection. A parachute was used to let the entire plane down in case anything broke. Built of composite construction, it was designed to take +6 G loads because it would meet more jolts from turbulence than the Gossamer Albatross.

The spar was a carbon fiber tube like the Albatross but a layer of Nomex honey comb was laid over and two Kevlar cloth laminations put on top of that. The result had all the stiffness and lightness of carbon combined with the toughness of Kevlar. The nomex added thickness for resistance against crushing.

Ribs were hot wire sawn from blocks of foam and recut into the rib pattern again, with hot wire and templates. After sliding them over the tubular spar and fastening with epoxy slurry, the foam leading and trailing edges were glued on and controls installed. Covering was the same as the Condor and Albatross: 4 mil clear plastic mylar stuck on the wings and fuselage and tail with double-sided clear mylar tape. We would stick the tape on the ribs, position the plastic with the "grain" spanwise on the wing, then reach under and peel off the tape cover to expose the stickiness. With helpers holding the plastic out of the way it is not too difficult and requires only a little practice. I

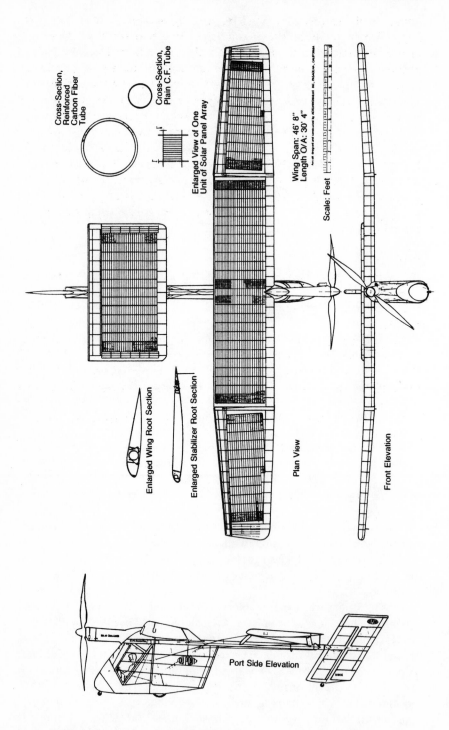

Fig. 8-10. Three-view drawing of the Solar Challenger.

found, in doing one of the Albatross wing sections, that covering is impossible without help. After the outside layer is peeled off the double-sided tape the slightest touch to it by the plastic sheet will adhere it and everything had better be exactly in position. Pulling it back off for a restart makes a mess. A heat gun or flatiron is used to shrink the mylar to a smooth surface. This must be done with some care so as not to overdo on the light structure. It could pull the end ribs and trailing edges in too much, or warp the surfaces.

To see the difference advanced plastic composites can mean in airplanes, consider Solar Challenger. With a 46 foot span wing it can fly 50 mph on 5.7 HP (4100 watts), has an L/D of almost 16, a design load factor of 6, and weighs only 202 pounds. Compare that to most aluminum tube, wire braced, ultralights that weight 254 pounds with at least ten feet shorter wings and an L/D of only 6. An L/D of 12 and 16 HP is representative of the best of the aluminum ultralights.

Summary

- Composites have been used on the most exotic of the advanced low powered airplanes.
- Homebuilders can adapt to carbon fiber and foam construction techniques.
- Carbon fiber spars and construction tubing can be made at home using pre-preg thin tubing and swimming pool acid.
- Foam plugs add 20 percent more strength to carbon tubing.
- Kevlar wrapping for joints and pilot protection from splinters is important for the very strong but brittle carbon tubes.
- Mylar with double sided mylar tape makes very satisfactory covering for speeds up to 50 MPH.

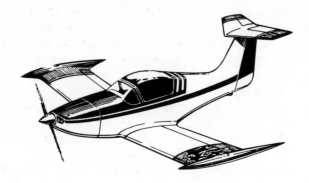

9

Safety In Working With Composite Construction

I once thought I was attacked by a strange malady. It turned out to be epoxy. It happened when I decided to extend the span on my Fauvel Flying Wing glider to decrease it's sinking speed. The longer wing tips would reduce drag when I was flying slowly in thermals.

I got some big chunks of foam, hot wired them to the shape I wanted, and made fittings so they would slip into the present wing. I had often used polyester resin with no problem but, this time I had to use epoxy so the foam would not be softened. The straw colored resin smelled differently than polyester but it wasn't unpleasant so I was soon brushing it on and even using my bare hands to smooth and wipe off the excess.

Epoxy

Pleased with my newly glassed wingtips I drove home, washed for dinner and later went to bed. That night, I was transformed into a monster. My itching burning eyes were swollen shut. My face was puffy and my hands were red. It was from the epoxy but, because of the delay, I didn't know what was happening. There had been no bad reaction when I had been using the epoxy. It's always frightening when you don't know what has gone wrong.

Three days later the swelling receded, leaving baggy skin around my eyes. It had aged me ten years. This happened over twenty years ago. As a matter of fact the lines have even increased since then. A week later, chastened with gloves, goggles and baggy coveralls, I was back at work on my wingtips but again awakened with swollen eyes. The damage had been done. I had become so sensitized that just the smell of the epoxy resin brought on a recurrence.

All the warnings displayed plainly on the can of epoxy about keeping it from the skin, using it in a well ventilated place and keeping it away from the eyes were exactly right. But you know how it is. Who ever takes label warnings seriously? Every product sold is usually covered with warnings thought up by the manufacturer's legal department.

It was some years before I was again able to use epoxy without bad reactions but then only in tiny amounts. I also used strict precautions such as rubber gloves, expendable coveralls, goggles and working outside, to keep the fumes away.

Granted, some people work with epoxy resin continually and often get it on their clothes with no immediate effect. However, I know at least one of my friends who used epoxy for five projects with no problem, but he developed a sensitivity on the sixth building effort. The new safety epoxies being sold are better than those used years ago, but I would be just as careful anyhow.

Epoxy has a greasy texture and is hard to remove, even with soap and water. You must be meticulously careful not to get any on your skin. One builder tied his loose shoelace with epoxy on his gloves. When he removed his shoes in the evening it got on his hands and then his face when he rubbed his cheek. Inspect your clothes and wash-up whenever you finish a work session.

Polyester

Polyester resins are sticky, just like epoxy, but are not nearly as toxic. The catalyst used in the polyester resins can burn the skin however. Once I left a bottle of catalyst in my pocket which leaked into my pants. Wow, did it smart! I had to run into the nearest bathroom, strip and scrub my painful leg. The skin later blistered and peeled just like any burn.

The problem with epoxy is the chemical ethers used to thin the resin and the curing agents with irritating amines in them.

Carbon Fiber, Fiberglass and Kevlar

Carbon fiber and fiberglass are most dangerous when being sanded. The glass is very sharp and irritates the lungs. Cancer of the cervix is said to be of higher incidence in women married to men who work in the fiberglass industry. The tiny glass fibers apparently make a long time irritation to tender tissues. It stands to reason that you shouldn't breath the stuff or get it on your skin. For the homebuilder who doesn't make a lifetime occupation of fiberglass work and takes a long soapy shower, along with leaving the fiberglass dusted clothing outside the house, there is little danger.

Kevlar is an aramid fiber that does not have the brittle consistency of fiberglass, so it is not such an itchy problem, but its dust should not be breathed in anyhow. The other wonder material, carbon fiber, is not glass either but is so strong and stiff it breaks into fine slivers. The needle-like bits of carbon fiber easily poke into your skin but do not work their way out as a normal wood or metal sliver will do, instead it just hurts. Carbon simply does react with the body, and will not get pushed out by being surrounded with white blood cells. A sliver of wood has a little pocket of white blood cells that surround it after a while and by squeezing, you can push it out along with the pus. Carbon fiber splinters must be dug out with a pin, knife or tweezers. Obviously, when sanding and cutting carbon fibers, you should wear a mask to keep the little splinters from getting in your lungs. I haven't heard of anyone suffering from "Carbon-fiber-Black-Lung Disease" yet, but believe any sanding of carbon with a power grinder should be done only while you are protected with a mouth and nose filter. Filters are cheap and can be found in hardware and paint stores.

Fumes

Fumes from resins, thinning agents, catalysts and solvents are, however, not removed with the paper filters. Although they are rather expensive filters that do protect a person from fumes, it is simpler and less expensive to work outside on the patio, under a shady tree or a large airy building. Then fumes can dissipate or waft away on the wind, away from your lungs.

Foams are not toxic as they sit but urethane based foams give off deadly gasses if burned or melted, for example, with a hot wire. These foams are easily sanded and not softened or dissolved by gasoline or polyester resin. Urethane foams are cut and sanded instead of hot wired for shaping. The dust from sanding or saw cutting is very sharp and can irritate the lungs. I always work outside and use a long handled brush to sweep up the gritty sandings and shavings. When using a sanding board in shaping the wing airfoil, there is lots of dust flying off with each stroke of the board. It's common to get down close to the airfoil to check the contours. This is when the sharp little bits can get in the lungs and eyes. Working outside in a wind is my choice for sanding urethane along with shaking out the dusty work clothes followed by a shower. Use caution when sanding or sweeping urethane dust. Smooth, slow sanding strokes keep the dust from swirling in the air. Always wear your nose filter during sanding and clean-up, as well.

Polystyrene foams are soft and do not break into tiny bits, but it will burn giving off irritating fumes.

Fire can be a serious disaster in fiberglass work. The resins can burn easily and are even more flammable. The highly evaporative catalysts, thinners and promoters can actually burst into flame from a small spark. The resins themselves can flame if mixed with too much hardener. The larger the resin mix the more possible it will be to have a fire from "going-off-too-quickly". Always mix an accelerator into the resin before adding the catalyst. If an accelerator is put in after the resin and catalyst have been mixed, there may be an explosive heat-up.

Summary

- Strip and wash your clothing after each work session.
- Use rubber gloves with resin.
- Soak old gloves and tools in soapy water before the resin hardens.
- Run a fan, work outside or do your project in a very large workshop.
- Be on the lookout for fire caused by incorrect mixing of catalyst and accelerators.
- Fiberglass resins have reduced irritation. The accelerators, thinners, catalysts and solvents are a bit more dangerous than resins.
- Be aware of urethane foam-dust. Use a nose filter, shake dust out and wash your clothes daily.
- When using carbon fiber, always check for tiny splinters.

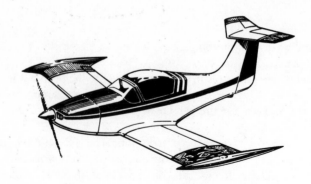

10
Care & Repair Of Composite Structures

Fiberglass is easy to take care of because it is "non-organic". That means, it wasn't part of something alive at one time, such as wood or cotton. Living things go back to "nature". They rot or are eaten by other living things. Composites also have longer fatigue life than aluminum. That means repeated bending does not result in breaking as soon as with metal.

The builders in Germany who pioneered the methods, have tested wings with machines that simulated thousands of hours of flexing at normal flight stress and found little cracking or failure. When stressed to maximum design load, the glass will eventually start showing fractures. This occurs less than with a metal structure, all things being equal. I have seen some stress cracks in the gel coat of old Libelle and Phoenix sailplanes that have been flying since the sixties but these are only surface cracks. The basic fiberglass structure seems unchanged.

For homebuilt fiberglass airplanes, sunshine on a hot day can soften the airplane to 75% of it's cold strength. If the plastic reaches 150 degrees Fahrenheit it will soften enough to bend and take a permanent set when cooled. In fact, wing aerodynamic heaviness can be corrected by painting an

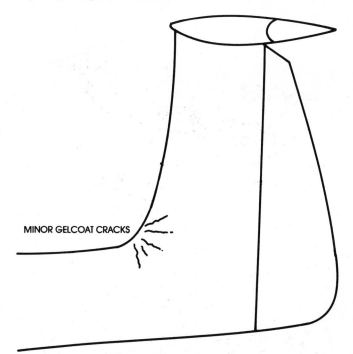

Fig. 10-1. The T-tail of a composite sailplane shows minor gelcoat crack at the root of the vertical stabilizer.

incorrectly twisted wing with black tempura, a poster point easily washed off with water. Let it heat in the sun while bracing with boards or weights to bend it in the desired manner. After several hours in the sun, see if the new twist is correct. Wash the dark water color paint off the wing with water. A test flight will then tell if it has eliminated the wing "heaviness".

Cold doesn't effect fiberglass structures badly. In fact at 20,000 feet it can be 40 below zero. Your airplane is ten percent stronger, here.

Sunshine, over an extended period of time, can break the chemical bonds of the resin and weaken the structure. Fortunately, this is not a serious problem, because almost all mold built parts have a protective gel coat covering. Non-molded construction, usually without gel coat, can be hidden from the sun by two coats of silver paint. The almost mandatory final white finish coat also protects fiberglass from sunshine as well as keeping it cooler.

The worst degradation of fiberglass occurs in engine cowlings, which are thin as well as subject to heat and vibration. These conditions may soften the cowl because the stress direction does not line up with weave. The fiberglass in cowlings is two directional, which does not have the resistance to fatigue found in the uni-directional rovings. Unidirectional rovings are usually laid up for wing spars.

Having seen many cracking fiberglass cowlings, I recommend they be made of sandwich, instead of the solid, which will help stop flexing and cracking.

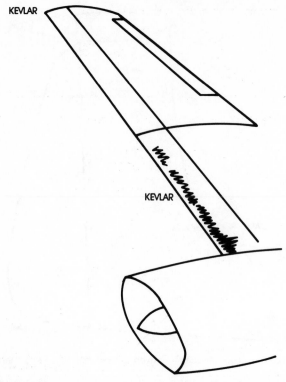

Fig. 10-2. Put Kevlar over leading edges on tractor configurations to protect them from debris thrown back by the propeller.

Regular waxing and polishing keeps fiberglass looking well cared for, and protects it from sand and rain. Homebuilts fly less in bad weather so hail is usually not a problem. In the case of a really important part of the airplane, a layer of Kevlar can be put over the fiberglass. The Gossamer Albatross and Solar Challenger airplanes had Kevlar over the carbon fiber spar tubes. Kevlar is very tough. The D tube of a wing could be protected by Kevlar behind the propeller. An airplane operating from a stony runway or a seaplane where abrasion from high speed water could hurt this critical part of the wing, needs to be so protected.

Repairs

Most damage is not due to crashes, but day to day operation around the airport, such as when a wing tip gets in the way of a runway or taxiway marker. Perhaps a hanger door somehow jumps in the way as you're pulling the airplane out. Or the wing is bumped and dropped when removing it from the trailer. Most damage will be to the surface, a gash or scrape, some will puncture the layers of fiberglass and more rarely go through the glass and into the sandwich. A really bad encounter, such as gear up landing in a rocky field, or into a post, will break through both sides of the sandwich. Let's take one at a time, from least to worst.

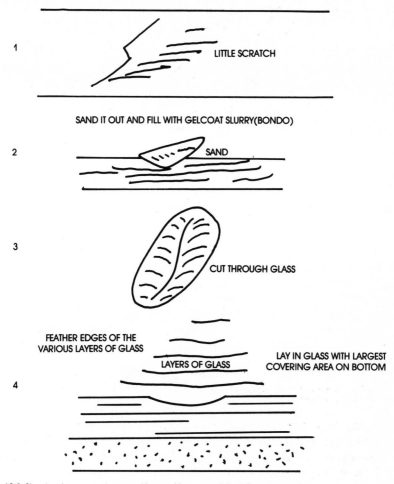

1

LITTLE SCRATCH

SAND IT OUT AND FILL WITH GELCOAT SLURRY(BONDO)

2

SAND

3

CUT THROUGH GLASS

FEATHER EDGES OF THE
VARIOUS LAYERS OF GLASS

LAY IN GLASS WITH LARGEST
COVERING AREA ON BOTTOM

LAYERS OF GLASS

4

Fig. 10-3. Step-by-step procedure used in repairing a scratched fiberglass surface.

Little scratches and dents which do not go through the fiberglass layers are fixed by removing the paint three inches beyond the damage. This must be done by sanding. Paint removers or strong solvents, chlorinated oils and strong acids should never be used, because they may cause softening of the resin. MEK and acetone are not harmful. Now that we have a nice clean surface, mix some resin of whatever kind was used in the structure and paint it over the nicks, scars or ground area you wish to repair. Tape a sheet of smooth plastic, such as .01 thick mylar, three inches beyond the painted edge. Check for any air bubbles or extra resin. Push on the plastic to work out the bubbles and resin. This will allow an almost perfect surface after the cure. A heatlamp, sunshine or heatgun can be used if you are in a hurry. Remove the plastic and block sand the repair. Apply paint and promise yourself to be more careful.

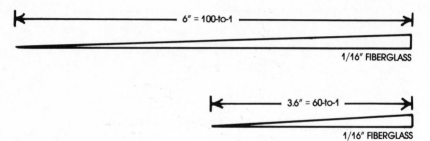

Fig. 10-4. Drawing shows what is meant by 100-to-1 and 60-to-1 tapers, as recommended in contouring a repair area.

If the damaged area is deep enough to cut into the fiberglass layers it must be repaired by pieces of glass fabric. Sand the area three inches beyond the damage, while at the same time contour it out one hundred times the depth of the cut. If the cut was one sixteenth of an inch deep the contour will be 6.25 inches from the center of the damage (16/16ths is 1 inch so a hundred 16ths is 6.25 inches). Put a layer of resin in the depression and lay in the glass fabric until they fill the low place. As usual, tape plastic over and force out the bubbles and extra resin. After it's cured, wet sand with a block to the final "impossible-to-detect-there-was-any-damage", pre-repaired surface.

Often when damage is severe enough, the surface below the outer layers will also be crushed and cut. Remove the outer surface and taper back, as before, then cut and remove the crushed sandwich material be it foam, Klegecell, balsa wood, honeycomb, etc. Glue in the new sandwich material with resin, and sand or grind it to match the previous sandwich material and its position. Finish the repair exactly as explained before by layering in fiberglass pieces, block sanding and matching the undamaged surface.

When a composite sandwich part is smashed all the way through, from one side to the other, the procedure is the same as a double repair, with some obvious differences. One side of the damage must be stabilized so the other can be used to rebuild. This means scarfing each hole to the usual 100 to 1 ratio. Put a support of plywood, for example, covered with a plastic sheet over the hole, to hold the layers of fiberglass. This ensures the repair will be accurate at least on one side. Install the core material and lay in fiberglass to fill the damage on the final side.

One of the more difficult situations, and unfortunately one of the most common, is when you can't get one side because it's inside the wing or tail. This happened to a friend's airplane when he loaned it to a supposedly experienced pilot who proceeded to take off without the canopy latched. The canopy blew into the wing. It punched a three by five inch hole right through the upper surface of the sandwich-composite. There was no way to get on the inside of the wing except through the top. I repaired it by first cutting away the damage using an electric jig saw with a fine blade. I cleaned out the dust and shavings, sand, bugs and a couple odd washers left when the airplane was built.

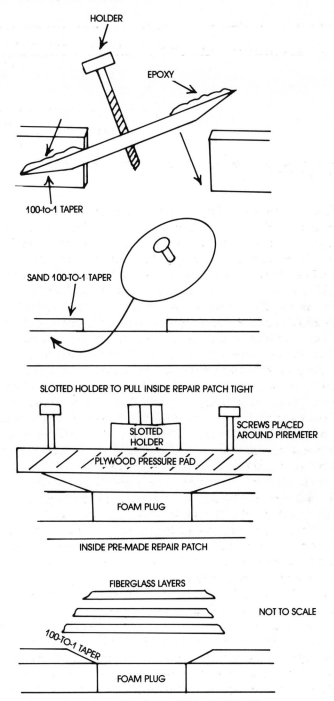

HOLDER

EPOXY

100-to-1 TAPER

SAND 100-TO-1 TAPER

SLOTTED HOLDER TO PULL INSIDE REPAIR PATCH TIGHT

SLOTTED HOLDER

SCREWS PLACED AROUND PIREMETER

PLYWOOD PRESSURE PAD

FOAM PLUG

INSIDE PRE-MADE REPAIR PATCH

FIBERGLASS LAYERS

NOT TO SCALE

100-TO-1 TAPER

FOAM PLUG

Fig. 10-5. How to repair a surface with damage to an inside layer of glass, which is otherwise inaccessible.

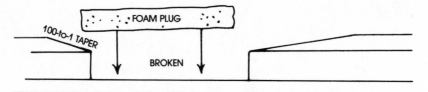

Fig. 10-6. Repairing a surface with the top glass skin and the foam core damaged.

I made a tapered, scarfed and smoothed fiberglass plate three inches bigger than the hole. A "holding" block of 1/2 inch plywood was used on the outside. I drilled holes through this and around the edge of the damage 1½ inches in from the edges and got the screws ready to insert. The inside patch was coated with epoxy glue, slid in edge ways and pulled up tight. A big wood bolt screwed into the center served as a hand hold. Metal screws were tightened from the outer side. This pulled the inside patch up tightly against the hidden side. See Fig. 10-6. After curing I installed the sandwich material with resin on the sides and bottom. Layers of fiberglass filled in the damaged area, which I sanded to precisely fit the contour of the top of the wing. After a little paint, which I hand rubbed using polishing compound a few weeks later, you could not see the repair.

Sometimes, delaminations occur from a bump that does not cut through the surface or even break the outside cover. This minor-type damage can be repaired by mixing a bit of resin and catalyst, inserting it in a hypodermic needle and injecting it into the void. To make sure the delamination is filled, put a little hole at one side and squeeze the resin into the void from the other side. When it starts running out the other hole, you know the area is full. Lay a piece of plastic over the area and weigh it down with a sand bag or a bag of lead shot.

The basic idea in all repairs is to use materials that will be the same as the original so there is no discontinuity in the strength. This would bring about cracking along the edges.

Summary

- Taper edges around damage 100 times the facing material thickness.
- Set core materials in place with resin bonding.
- Make repairs close to the same thickness to eliminate variations in strength.
- Do one side at a time when the sandwich is damaged completely through.
- Cut out the damaged section, taper sand and lay strips of fiberglass in the failed area, and refinish to original contour.
- Fine grit block sanding to match the original surface, followed by painting and hand rubbing, will result in an almost indetectable repair.
- Repair empty spaces and delaminations by injecting catalyzed epoxy into the area and weighting the repair with a hot sand bag or lead shot.
- Use a light colored paint to protect fiberglass from sun and heat.

Appendices

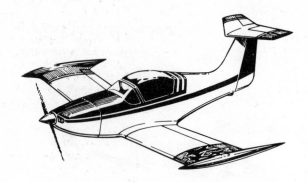

A-1
Reading References
& Composite Suppliers

Here are some of the places to get the foams, resins, tools and various types of woven or unidirectional cloth used in composite aircraft construction. To save time we have included, with permission, parts of the catalog from Aircraft Spruce and Specialties' section on COMPOSITES. You get an idea of prices and various hints on working with some of the products they sell. Be aware that some of the information is of the "sales pitch" variety but interesting and also probably helpful.

SUPPLIERS IN CALIFORNIA
SOUTHERN
Aircraft Spruce and Specialty Co.
POB 424
201 W. Truslow Ave.
Fullerton, 92632 (714) 870 551
Applied Plastics Inc.
612 E. Franklin Ave.
El Segundo, 90245 (213) 322 8050

Visitron (Silmar Division)
12335 S. Van Ness Ave.
Hawthorne, 90250 (213) 757 1801
Clark Foam
25887 Crown Valley Parkway
South Laguna, 92677 (714) 831 1431
RAM Chemicals (Whittaker Corporation)
210 E. Alondra
Gardena, 90248

NORTHERN CALIFORNIA
Chemtron
3525 E. Ventura
Fresno, 93702 (209) 486 7075
Taps Plastic
3011 Alvarado St.
San Leandro, 94577 (415) 357 3755
Vertex Inc.
900 77th Ave.
Oakland, 94621 (415) 569 9681
Pacific Anchor Chemical Corp.
1145 Harbor Way South
Richmond, 94804 (415) 233 7660
Multi Enterprises
7642 S. E. 72nd
Mercer Island, WA 98040

CANADIAN
Sport Aviation Corp
E2651 No 3 Rd
Richmond B.C. Canada V6X2B2 (604) 273 8501
Scientec Epoxy pump
POB 2872 ($19)
Sarnia Ontario, Canada N7TM1

MIDWEST
Rattray Aircraft
2357 Afton Rd
Beloit, Wisconsin 53511 (608) 362 4611
Dow Chemical
(Catalogue)
Midland, Michigan 48640

3M Industrial Specialties
3M Center, Saint Paul, Minnesota 55101
American Klegecell Corp
204 N Dolley St.
Grapevine, Texas 76051 (817) 481 3547
Wicks Aircraft Supply
410 Pine, Highland, Illinois 62249
(618) 654 7447
Ruehle Associates
5594 E. Jefferson Ave.
Denver, CO 80237 (skin protection kit $49.95)
General Mills (Fiberglass)
Minneapolis, Minn
Quality Aircraft Components
16223 93rd St. Bristol, WI 53104.
(414) 857 7419

EASTERN
Columbia Plastics
Box 275
Columbia, MD 21045 (301) 997 1119
DuPont
Centre Board Building
Wilmington, Delaware 19898
Axel Plastics Research
Box 855
58-20 Broadway
Woodside, New York 11377 (212) 672 8300
Dillsburg Aeroplane Works
Dillsburg, Pennsylvania 17019 (717) 432 4589

BOOKS FOR ADVANCED DESIGNERS
AIRCRAFT STRUCTURES by David J. Peery McGraw-Hill 1950

LIGHT AIRCRAFT DESIGN by Pazmany POB 80051 San Diego, CA 92138 ($10)

COMPOSITE AIRCRAFT DESIGN 11082 Bel Aire Ct. Cupertino, CA by Martin Hollmann ($14.95)

PILOTS AERODYNAMICS by Harry Gephart 2140 Rosedale Dr. Las Cruces NM 88005 ($8)

HANDBOOK OF FIBERGLASS AND ADVANCED PLASTICS COMPOS-ITES by George Lubin, Van Nostrand Reinhold Co., N.Y.

BASICS OF BONDED SANDWICH CONSTRUCTION TSB 124 Hexcell Corp, Dublin CA

ANALYSIS OF FLIGHT VEHICLE STRUCTURES by E.F. Bruhn

FORMULAS FOR STRESS AND STRAIN by Ray J. Roark, McGraw Hill 1965

COMPOSITE MATERIALS MODULE FOR THE TI-59/58 CALCULATOR by Stephen W. Tsai who also wrote **INTRODUCTION TO COMPOSITE MATERIALS** Technomic Publishing Co. Westport, CT 1981

MECHANICS OF COMPOSITE MATERIALS by R. M. Christensen, John Wiley and Sons Book Co. 1979.

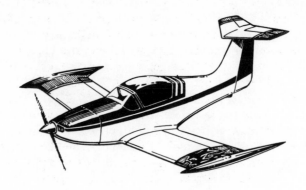

A-2

The Development Of Composite Construction For Homebuilt Aircraft

The Development of Composite Construction

We have followed the development of composite aircraft design with great interest and commitment from 1970 when Ken Rand introduced the KR-1. We were convinced that composite structure represented the greatest breakthrough in materials use since the origin of flight. We immediately featured the building materials in our catalog, although sales were slim. Most builders were skeptical of the reliability of an aircraft put together with foam, synthetic fabric and epoxy. There are many builders who will probably never relate to working with these materials and will continue to build wood and metal designs. There is a percentage of individuals who become sensitized to epoxy and develop either a mild or severe reaction to it in spite of all protective precautions. Until recently these builders have been forced to look to other designs. Now, however, with the development of a new epoxy system of very low toxcitity, composite construction is open to all.

A few builders were working diligently in the early years and the composite war replicas began to appear. Then a young designer, Burt Rutan, introduced his VariViggen which was recognized as an outstanding aircraft and was awarded the Stan Dzik trophy for design contribution at Oshkosh in 1972. Interest was modest, however, and the Skybolts, Stardusters and Pitts continued to roll out of the workshops. Meanwhile, Burt quietly worked on a new design and in July 1976 offered plans for the VariEze. He made a tremendous contribution to the development of composite building by his relentless drive to educate builders in "how-to-do-it". By his step-by-step detailed plans, and the many lectures and building seminars he conducted, he sent forth a contingent of disciples qualified to work with composites and spread the word. It worked well. VE plans sold by the thousands with projects in work all over the world. His introduction of specially woven uni- and bi-directional glass cloths made the process easier and resulted in a much stronger structure than those using the earlier glass and Dynel fabrics. His close control over the materials used in the construction of the VE generated confidence in the builders and gave him peace of mind knowing that proven materials were going into the projects. The Long-EZ program which followed has continued to prove the workability, safety and popularity of the composite design and construction methods.

We wish to recognize the designers who are responsible for developing the outstanding aircraft featured on the following pages. Each has done an exceptional job in meeting the challenge of satisfying the needs of today. All are unbelievably fuel efficient and most economical to build. The lines of each are distinctive and original. Each are a practical, serviceable aircraft – some are even road towable.

In recent years, designers such as the late Tom Jewett and Gene Sheehan of Quickie Aircraft Corp., Gary LeGare of Leg Air Aviation, Joe Alvarez of Polliwagen, and the late George Mead of the Adventure and PAT-1 programs, have utilized and developed the composite construction techniques pioneered by Burt Rutan to produce their own designs. Many of these new creations have been enormously successful in the marketplace, and certainly many more will follow. What an exciting time for the homebuilder!

Composite Aircraft Supply is handling material kits for the Vari-Eze, Long-EZ, Vari-Viggen, Quickie, Q2, Adventure, Polliwagen and Corby Starlet aircraft designs and the American Eaglet self-launching sailplane.

New materials, new methods of handling and new ideas are funneling in from builders and designers to make the process easier, faster and better. There is no limit to the progress that can be made with such a dedicated group working in this new and exciting field of building. Why not join the fun?

It should be noted, however, that a composite structure is not adaptable to amateur design practice. It is an entirely new field which must be developed by the most qualified structural engineers with a composites background. Build one of the proven designs offered by the experts.

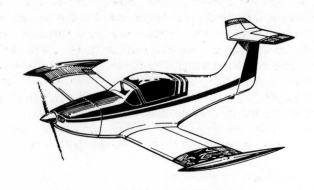

A-3
Materials, Supplies
& Tools

Materials of Construction

The materials featured in this section are those which have been used to construct proven composite designs. We urge all builders to exert great caution in selecting the proper materials for a composite project. A number of needless, fatal accidents have occurred because the aircraft was built of nonstructural materials. We also urge all builders to purchase and diligently study Burt Rutan's manual entitled MOLDLESS COMPOSITE SAND-WICH HOMEBUILT AIRCRAFT CONSTRUCTION. Burt is recognized as the outstanding authority in the field of homebuilt composites — he has written an exceptionally fine manual which sets the guidelines for building all composite aircraft. Start right — STUDY — The fun will follow!

Rutan Fiberglass Cloths

The most basic structural material in building a composite aircraft is glass cloth. The use of glass in aircraft structures, particularly structural sandwich composites, is a recent development. Glass cloth is available commercially in hundreds of different weights, weaves, strengths and working properties. Very few of these, however, are compatible with aircraft requirements for high strength and light weight. Even fewer are suitable for the hand-layup techniques developed by Burt Rutan for the homebuilder. The glass cloth featured here has been specifically selected for the optimum combination of workability, strength and weight. Two types of glass cloth, a bi-directional cloth (RA5277BID) and a uni-directional cloth (RA5177 UND) are used. BID cloth has half of the fibers woven parallel to the selvage edge of the cloth and the other half at right angles to the selvage, giving the cloth the same strength in both directions. UND cloth has 95% of the glass fibers woven parallel to the selvage, giving exceptional strength in that direction and very little at right angles to it. BID is generally used for pieces which are cut at a 45° angle to the selvage, a bias cut, which enables the builder to lay BID into contours with very little effort and provides the needed shear and torsion stiffness for flying surfaces. UND is used in areas where the primary loads are in one direction, such as wing skins and spar caps. Multiple layers of glass cloth are laminated together to form the aircraft structure. Each layer of cloth is called a "ply".

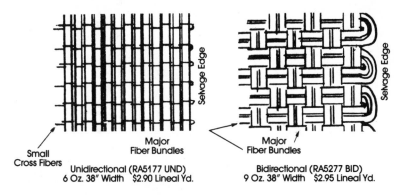

Small Cross Fibers — Major Fiber Bundles — Selvage Edge
Unidirectional (RA5177 UND)
6 Oz. 38" Width $2.90 Lineal Yd.

Major Fiber Bundles — Selvage Edge
Bidirectional (RA5277 BID)
9 Oz. 38" Width $2.95 Lineal Yd.

Glass cloth should be stored, marked and cut in a clean area with clean hands and clean tools. Glass contaminated with dirt, grease or epoxy should not be used. The area used for storing and cutting glass cloth should be separated from the aircraft assembly area because it will be exposed to foam dust, epoxy and other elements which can contaminate the cloth. A pair of good quality, sharp scissors, a felt-tipped marker, a straight board and a tape measure are needed for marking and cutting. The small amount of ink from marking and numbering plies has no detrimental effect on the glass cloth.

Dynel Fabric

Dynel fabric as originally used in a 4 oz./sq. yd. weave in the KR designs is no longer in production. Stock on hand. 66" width. $4.05 Yd.

Standard Fiberglass Cloth

Fiberglass cloth is exactly what the name says - glass. Fine fibers are spun from molten glass marbles, gathered into yarn and woven into a strong, supple glass fabric. It can be folded, rolled or draped, like any other loosely woven fabric - but it can be chemically transformed into solid sheets of tremendous strength. All the fiberglass fabrics listed below are volan treated for maximum strength and resistance to moisture and abrasion. They feature a weave that is tight enough for high strength, yet open enough for thorough wetting by resins.

3.16 Oz./Sq. Yd. Lightweight Industrial Cloth with aerospace applications. Excellent for model building. Only 4 mils thick. Crowfoot weave, which contours nicely. Threads 60 x 58. #120 38" Width

1 Yd.	$2.90
3 Yd. Pack	8.25
5 Yd. Pack	13.00
10 Yds. and Over	2.50 Yd.

3.74 Oz./Sq. Yd. Lightweight Boat or Tooling Cloth. Tight plain weave. Threads 24 x 22.

#1522 50" Width	2.62 Yd.

5.85 Oz./Sq. Yd. Lightweight Boat or Tooling Cloth. Plain weave. Threads 18 x 18.

#3733 60" Width	3.18 Yd.

8.55 Oz./Sq. Yd. Medium Weight - Standard Industrial Cloth. Tight plain weave. Threads 59 x 54.

#7781 50" Width	3.60 Yd.
60"Width	3.95 Yd.

10 Oz./Sq. Yd. Heavy Weight Boat or Tooling Cloth. Plain weave. Threads 16 x 14.

#7500 60" Width	4.73 Yd.

Unidirectional Fiberglass

A unidirectional fabric constructed with Owens-Corning Fiberglass S-2 Glass offering outstanding strength-to-weight ratio, superb glass-resin control to minimize probability of resin-rich and/or resin-dry areas, handleability without distortion and exceptionally high impact resistance.

The integrity of the S-500 is maintained through very fine, adhesive coated fill yarns that are bonded to but not interwoven with the unidirectional fibers of the S-2 Glass. The fill yarns are spaced approximately 1.5 inches apart. The use of short-nap paint rollers is suggested, rolling under pressure, always parallel to the fibers. Use with epoxies, vinyl esters and polyesters. Weight of fabric - 0.56 Lbs. per Sq. Ft. Tensile Strength (hand layup in polyester, air cured) - 128,000 PSI.

12" Wide x 300 Ft. Roll (20 Lbs.) S-500	$192.00
Less than Full Roll	$ .83 Ft.

Glass Mat

100% Fiberglass in a non-woven state. It is used for bulk "build-up" in molding and fabricating components. Also useful for filling holes and badly damaged parts. 1½ Oz. weight. 38" Width. $2.95 Yd.

Fiberglass Tape — Standard Weave

Tape is conventional fiberglass cloth woven into narrow widths with a non-raveling edge. Perfect for glassing seams, corners, edges and for repair jobs.

2" x 50 Yds.	$19.90
3" x 50 Yds.	$25.70

Pre-Cured Fiberglass Laminate

These fully-cured glass cloth laminates with polyester resin binder systems are used in commercial jet aircraft. The .013" thick laminate is made to a Boeing specification and is used in the ceiling and baggage compartments of all 747 aircraft. The .017" thick laminate was made as a high-impact cargo liner material. Both are used as skin material in construction of the Eaglet sailplane. They are compatible with composite construction methods and bond well when epoxied to wood, foam, paper and most low modulus materials. They do not bond to aluminum and other metals. They should be excellent for use as spar caps. Samples furnished on request.

Thickness In.	Sheet Size*	Wt./Sq. Ft. Lbs.	Tensile Strength PSI	Impact Strength Ft. Lbs.	Price per Sheet
.013	48" x 72"	.11	48,000	2	$55.00
.017	48" x 8'6"				$76.00
.017	48" x 17'	.16	38,000	4	$145.00

*Can be rolled for UPS shipment.   Small Cuts - $4.50/Sq. Ft.

Polyester Resin

Standard laminating coating for fiberglass cloth. May be used over urethane foams. Do not use over styrofoam as it will dissolve the foam. An inexpensive coating for conventional glassing applications.

Wt. 9 Lbs./Gal.

1 Qt. Kit with Hardener (Bondo #402)	$6.75
1 Gal. Kit with Hardener (#1520-5)	17.75
5 Gal. Kit with Hardener @ $17.00 Gal.	85.00

Bidirectional Woven Kevlar

"Kevlar" 49 aramid fiber was introduced commercially in 1972 and is the Du Pont registered trademark for its new high strength, high modulus organic fiber. It combines high tensile strength (43,000 PSI) and high modulus (19 million PSI) with light weight and toughness superior to other reinforcing fibers for plastics. It is available in yarns and rovings which meet all FAA requirements for flammability. It shows no degradation in jet fuel, lubricating oils, water, salt water or high humidity. At cryogenic temperatures (-320°F.) performance is excellent with essentially no embrittlement or degradation of fiber properties. Kevlar 49 can offer both a significant weight saving and improved stiffness versus glass in addition to superior vibration damping and good impact resistance. A kayak made with Kevlar 49, for example, weighs about 18 pounds while the weight of a comparable boat made with glass would be over 30 pounds. The advantages over glass in small aircraft are similar - weight savings and improved impact resistance. Kevlar 49 is used in a number of parts on the Lockheed L-1011 because of weight savings of up to 30% compared to similar parts made of glass. One unusual benefit of Kevlar is its "quietness". A cowling made of Kevlar will be quieter and less sensitive to engine vibrations than its glass or graphite counterpart.

Although all of the processes used in combining resins with glass fiber are adaptable to Kevlar 49 with little or no modification, it has been found that the vinyl ester type system is most compatible. The use of polyesters is not recommended because of poor bonding with Kevlar. The modified epoxy resin system featured in this catalog is compatible with Kevlar 49 and has good wetting characteristics.

There are many fabric weaves available using Kevlar 49 fiber but the one most commonly used in the fabrication of aircraft and boat components has a weight of 5.1 oz. per sq. yd., with a scoured finish. We are now offering Kevlar cowls for the Long-EZ as an alternative to the standard fiberglass cowls.

Part No.	Weight Oz./Sq. Yd.	Width	Thickness	W x F	Tensile Strength Lbs/Inch Warp	Fill	Yarn Denier Warp	Fill	Price Per Lineal Yd.
K-49	5.1	38"	.010"	17 x 17	630	630	1140	1140	$13.75

(10% Discount on Orders of 100 Yards)

SPECIAL PRICING ON QUANTITY ORDERS

OFFSET CUTTING SHEARS - Although Kevlar has many advantages over conventional fiberglass weaves, it is very difficult to cut. Special scissors have been developed to facilitate cutting. These scissors have a wear-resistant coating which is metallurgically bonded to the steel substrate. The coating will not chip or peel off and can be sharpened.

WR-10E-4 Shears $49.50

Unidirectional Kevlar

KS-400 is a unique unidirectional reinforcing material which combines the benefits of Kevlar 49 with Owens-Corning Fiberglass S-2 Glass. KS-400 is designed for use in laminates which must have high modulus or stiffness and tensile strength combined with low weight or density. The material is specifically constructed to enhance properties of wet-out behavior, bondability and impact strength in a hand laid-up composite. As compared with woven fabrics of pure Kevlar, KS-400 should produce laminates with better fiber-resin ratios and superior stiffness. The integrity of KS-400 is maintained through very fine, adhesive coated Dacron fill yarns that are bonded to, but not interwoven with, the unidirectional fibers. Only vinyl esters or epoxies should be used as impregnating resins. The presence of the S-2 Glass enables the fabricator to determine visually when the material is properly wet out. Resin bond is far superior to the glass than to the Kevlar. This means increased resistance to delamination. Also, the presence of the S-2 Glass even in such a relatively small amount increases the impact strength of the laminate significantly. In application, it is important that the fabricator does not confuse the appearance of the cross-direction adhesive binder with air bubbles. The impregnating resin will soften this adhesive and it will flow slightly. The adhesive shows up as milky areas on both sides of the fabric within the finished laminate. A gel coat or paint covers these areas effectively.

12″ Wide x 50 Ft. Roll (4 Lbs.) KS-400 $66.00 Roll
Less than Full 50 Ft. Roll $1.72 Ft.
12″ Wide x 300 Ft. Roll (24 Lbs.) KS-400 $366.00 Roll

Bidirectional Woven Graphite

Woven Graphite is a fabric introduced in recent years which has become an excellent alternative to fiberglass and Kevlar - only mils thick with great strength. Although Woven Graphite is very costly, the material saving is appreciable since only one course of Graphite is required for 3 or 4 of fiberglass. It cuts considerably easier than Kevlar. Woven Graphite has an immediate, waiting market in the aircraft building field because of its attractive physical properties of light weight and strength. Woven Graphite is available in plain weaves or impregnated with either polyester or epoxy resins - referred to as "Prepregs". This material need only be heated at 200 to 250° F for about a half hour either by heat lamps or in an oven to achieve a full cure. Working with prepregs saves labor, allows for good control over the part, adds stability and uniformity. Most weaves are 38″ to 42″ wide and cost about $30 to $35 per yard. The prepregs add about 50¢ a yard for polyester resin and $1 a yard for epoxy resin.   Quotations will be furnished on specific requirements. Shown below are specifications on a popular graphite weave, which is carried in stock. This weave was used to produce an excellent run of lightweight Long-EZ cowls. Kevlar has been used on later production runs due to cost differentials, and results have been satisfactory.

Weight Oz./Sq. Yd.	Width	Thickness	W & F	Style Number	Price per Lineal Yd.
5.0	42"	.008"	12.5 x 12.5	F3C211	$29.80

Unidirectional Graphite

Construction is such that the fibers are oriented in a straight or linear manner with no twist and are able to be maintained in that condition while being impregnated by hand. The fabric is formed from rovings or "tows" of fibers similar to that used in making woven fabric. These fibers are locked into position by very fine fill (or cross machine direction) fibers which are encapsulated with an adhesive which is compatible with common impregnating resins. These fill fibers and the encapsulating adhesive will be visible in any clear resin. The resulting "pattern" is normal and should not be interpreted as poor wet-out of the reinforcing fibers. For hand lay-ups, resin may be applied by spray, brush or by pouring action. A short napped paint roller is recommended for spreading the resin. Excess resin should always be rolled out in a direction parallel to the graphite fibers. The final or external layer should be applied with the fill yarns facing down (unexposed). Satisfactory for use with epoxies, polyesters, vinyl esters and other resins. The fabric is rolled with a polyethylene interliner to maintain cleanliness.

Care and cleanliness should be practiced when working with Graphite materials. Unattached graphite fibers are easily airborne. A filter mask should be worn when cutting and fabricating. Itching and irritation caused by broken filaments becoming imbedded in the skin can result from filament breakage during handling.

Tensile Strength - 450,000 PSI, Weight - 0.033 Lb/Sq.Ft.

5" Wide x 250 Ft. Roll	$210.00 Roll
Less than Full Roll	$1.25 Ft.
12" Wide x 50 Ft. Roll	$135.00 Roll
12" Wide x 300 Ft. Roll	$597.00 Roll
Less than Full Roll	$2.72 Ft.

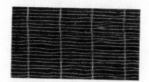

Carbon or Graphite Fibers

High strength (470,000 PSI) from carbon fibers are used as reinforcement in high performance structural composites for aircraft applications, recreational and industrial products. Carbon fiber filaments are finer than a human hair. These filaments are bundled together to make a fiber of 3,000, 6,000 or 12,000 filaments which is called a "tow". The tow is sized with an epoxy compatible material to improve the handling characteristics. It is then wound on a cardboard core holding from 4 to 6 pounds of fiber.

Actual Size	Approx. Yield	Price
3K Tow	2470 Yd./Lb.	$170.00/4 Lb. Spool
6K Tow	1229 Yd./Lb.	$128.00/4 Lb. Spool
		$50.00 Lb.
		$3.95 Oz.
12K Tow	621 Yd./Lb.	$168.00/6 Lb. Spool

It appears that the 6K tow will prove most practical for homebuilding applications. This size will be available in the small units shown. The 3K and 12K sizes are offered in full spools only. The 3K tow is used primarily by weavers. The 12K is difficult to wet out but can be done by diligent brushing.

Epoxy Systems

Just as fiberglass products are extremely varied, epoxy systems also differ greatly in their working properties—some are thick, slow pouring liquids and others are like water. Some allow hours of working time and others harden almost as fast as they are mixed. The RAE epoxy system was formulated to meet the rigid specifications set forth by Burt Rutan at the outset of the VariEze program in 1975. Many builders still prefer the working properties of the RAE system, although most new builders are using the low toxic Safe-T-Poxy introduced in 1980. Both these systems provide the combination of workability and strength required in composite aircraft structures.

Safe-T-Poxy

As hundreds of VariEze projects progressed, one persistent problem plagued many builders - sensitivity to the chemicals in the epoxy system although the RAF system was by far the least toxic of all systems available. A number of builders developed severe cases of dermatitis and were forced to abandon their projects. Applied Plastics, manufacturers of the RAF system, were keenly aware of the problem and genuinely concerned for the safety of the builders. A full scale research project was launched beginning with data accumulated by their Research Director years ago. In only eight months, they were able to develop a system which is so low in toxicity that incidental contact is not hazardous. A tremendous breakthrough!

In addition to the obvious advantages of being safe to use, this new Safe-T-Poxy system, which uses only one speed hardener, has other very desirable characteristics. It has unusually low water absorption and will cure to a dry surface at high humidity at room temperature with a very low exotherm. Since the material actually repels water, it cannot have a surface stickiness as caused by humidity in the early system. Other redeeming features builders will find in using it are:

1. No fillers to settle out.
2. Superior wetting of the fiber with little drain out of resin.
3. Lower density resin that yields a lighter laminate.
4. A 35% reduction in exotherm with no change in cure rate.
5. Cost competitive with the old established systems.

With further respect to the safety features:

1. Previous resins contained glycidyl ethers or various solvents to reduce viscosity for better handling. Most of these are now NIOSH restricted. The new resin contains none of these.

2. Most epoxy curing agents contain amines that will severely irritate the skin. When these are measured by a Draise Skin Irritation Test, in almost all cases they will yield a rating of 5 or worse. The new hardener rates "0" in this test.

Safe-T-Poxy is without qualification the best epoxy system available today.

Mixing Ratio: By Weight 100 parts resin to 44 parts hardener
                        By Volume 100 parts resin to 45 parts hardener

This system will tolerate a ± 5% error in mix ratio with little drop off in physicals.

Pot Life: 45 Minutes at 77°F. (100 grams).

Flash Point: #2410 Resin, 320°F.; #2183 Hardener, 172°F. (Tag closed cup).

Tack-Free Time: 4 Hours at 77°F.

Cure: 10 Hours at room temperature, or temperature set plus 2 hours at 150°F.

Storage Conditions: Keep at a constant room temperature (77°F). Securely close the containers after use.

Storage Life: One Year at 77°F.

Safe-T-Poxy 1¼ Gallon Kit 2410K, consisting of ⅞ Gal. #2410 Epoxy Resin and

2/5 Gal. #2183 Hardener (11 Lbs.)	$47.50
⅞ Gallon #2410 Resin only	38.75
2/5 Gallon #2183 Hardener only	14.90
1½ Qt. Kit (Furnished in Practice Kit)	14.95
1½ Pt. Kit	8.75
¾ Pt. Kit	6.50
½ Pt. Kit, in handy polyethylene squeeze bottles (4 Oz. each) for controlled dispensing	6.35
Five-Minute Kit #9935K (1 Pint #9935 Part A Resin and 1 Pint #9935 Part B Resin Hardener)	21.00
Drum Kit: 1 - 55 Gal. Drum (500 Lb.) #2410D Formulated Resin @ $2.74 Lb.	$1370.00
1 - 30 Gal. Drum (225 Lb.) #2183D30 Hardener @ $2.58 Lb.	$580.00
5 Gal. Pail (40 Lb.) #2410-5G Resin @ $3.04 Lb.	$121.60
5 Gal. Pail (35 Lb.) #2183-5G Hardener @ $2.86 Lb.	$100.10

Drum Kits and 5 Gal. Pails shipped F.O.B. El Segundo, California

EPOXY COMPONENTS SOLD BY WEIGHT RATHER THAN VOLUME

Poxipol II

The epoxy system used for the Polliwagen is basically the same formulation as Safe-T-Poxy with slightly higher viscosity. Ten 1¼ gallon kits will normally be sufficient for the construction of the Polliwagen.

Poxipol II 1¼ Gallon Kit #2410P (⅞ Gal. Resin and 2/5 Gal. Hardener) (11 lbs.)	$47.50
#2410G Resin only (⅞ Gal.)	$38.75
#2183G Hardener only (2/5 Gal.)	$14.95

Drum Kit prices for Poxipol II same as for Safe-T-Poxy

RAE Epoxy System

Some builders who are not sensitive to epoxy toxicity still prefer working with the RAE system as originally developed for use on the VariEze. This system offers two speeds of hardeners: RAES (slow curing) and RAEF (fast curing). Both the RAES and RAEF hardeners use the same RAE resin.

Mixing Ratio: By Volume, 100 parts resin to 25 parts hardener

By Weight, 100 parts resin to 20 parts hardener

Cure Rate: RAEF: Pot Life 20-45 minutes, Cure Time 3-6 hours @ 77° F.

RAES: Pot Life 1-2 hours, Cure Time 10-16 hours @ 77° F.

RAE Kit #2426K: 1 Gal. Resin and 1 Qt. Hardener* (10 lbs., 13 Oz.)

*Specify slow or fast hardener

1 Gal. 2426 Resin only	$44.20
1 Qt. 2176 Fast Hardener Only	$36.65
1 Qt. 2177 Slow Hardener Only	$10.50

Five-Minute Kit Available in Safe-T-Poxy Only

1½ Qt. Kit Available in Safe-T-Poxy Only

A simple check of RAE epoxy pot life - Be sure resin and hardener are at 80° F. Mix about 6 oz. of epoxy in an 8 oz. cup. Stir well and leave the cup undisturbed at 80° F. The fast epoxy should exotherm and become a solid block in about 30 - 40 minutes. The slow epoxy should be solid in about 80-100 minutes.

Epoxy resin and hardener are mixed in small batches, usually 6 ounces or less, even in the largest layups. If mixed in large batches, the heat generated as the hardening progresses speeds the reaction, causing even more heating and resulting in a very fast reaction called an "exotherm". An exotherm will cause the cup of epoxy to get hot and thicken rapidly. If this occurs, discard it and mix a new batch. For a large layup, mix many small batches rather than a few large ones. Unwaxed cups are used for mixing and ratio-ing epoxy and hardener. Do not use waxed cups — the wax will contaminate the epoxy. Mixing is done with a wooden mixing stick.

Foams

Five different types of rigid, closed cell foams are currently being used in proven designs.

Styrofoam FB - Low density (2 lb./ft.³), large cell, fire retardant. Varies in color from white to blue. The large-cell type provides better protection from delamination than the more commonly used small-cell blue styrofoam. Cuts smoothly with a hot wire for airfoil shapes. Do not confuse styrofoam with expanded polystyrene which is the type seen in the average picnic cooler. The compressive strength of polystyrene is too low and it dissolves in most solvents and fuel.

Styrofoam, Orange - Low Density (2 lb./ft.³), used for years in flotation for boat docks and other marine uses. Commonly called a Bouyancy Billet, this orange foam applications and cost are similar to the blue/white type. The prime advantage is the availability in the large billet sizes. This foam is now used in the Q2 design, and should be used with Safe-T-Poxy only. RAE type tends to bleed into the foam which can result in a dry layup.

• Use only epoxy with styrofoam. Polyester will dissolve the foam.

Urethane - Low density (2 lb./ft.³), small cell, colored green or tan. Used extensively in the fuselage and fuel tanks as it is completely fuel proof. Easy to carve and contour with a large knife. Do not hot-wire urethane foam as a hazardous gas is discharged.

Urethane Polyester - Medium and high density, white (4 to 18 lb./ft.³), this is a small cell rigid urethane-polyester foam which can be readily cut and carved and has limited heat forming characteristics. Its fuel compatability makes it suitable for sandwich tank construction. The uniform surface, excellent compressive strength and low cost of this white foam makes it an ideal replacement for some types of PVC foam.

PVC - Medium and high density, Dark Blue (3 lb./ft.³), used in fuselage bulkheads and other areas where higher compressive strength is required. R45 dark blue PVC is the only PVC still used in the composite kits. Other types have recently been replaced by white Urethane-Polyester foams which combine comparable qualities at much lower prices.

• Either epoxy or polyester systems may be used with urethane and PVC.

NOTE: Do not store foams in sunlight

The foam sheet sizes listed are stock sizes as called out in various plans currently offered. Other sizes may be obtained on special order. We also have cutoffs of styrofoam, urethane and PVC in sheet sizes smaller than those shown in the table. In urethane, cutoffs considerably thicker than the thicknesses shown are available from time to time. Write for quotation on your requirements.

Foam Type	Thickness	Sheet Size	Price per Sheet
Styrofoam (Blue) (2 Lb./Ft.³)	½"	24" x 48"	$4.85
	1"	24" x 48"	7.10
	2"	24" x 48"	13.80
	4"	24" x 48"	26.45
	5"	9" x 36"	16.50
	7"	14" x 41"	21.75
	7"	14" x 64"	33.90
	7"	14" x 67"	35.60
	7"	14" x 108"	53.50
Styrofoam (Orange) (2 Lb./Ft.³)	10"	20" x 96"	79.50
	10"	24" x 96"	94.25
Urethane (2 Lb./Ft.³)	½"	24" x 48"	4.70
	½"	48" x 48"	9.40
	1"	24" x 48"	5.75
	1"	24" x 96"	11.50
	1"	48" x 96"	23.00
	1"	48" x 120"	30.90
	2"	24" x 48"	11.45
	2"	24" x 96"	22.90
	2"	48" x 96"	45.80
	2"	48" x 120"	61.80
Urethane (4 Lb./Ft.³)	0.35"	24" x 96"	25.52
PVC (Dark Blue) (3 Lb./Ft.³) Type R45	0.35"	32" x 48"	Aircraft 32.94
	⅜"	32" x 48"	Marine 18.10
	¾"	32" x 48"	Marine 28.24
	1.6"	32" x 48"	Marine 61.59
Clark Urethane/Polyester (White) 4.5 Lb./Ft.³ 180°F	10 mm	24" x 120"	14.25
	¼"	24" x 96"	7.92
	½"	24" x 96"	13.53
	½"*	24" x 96"	14.27
	¾"	24" x 48"	11.20
	¾"	24" x 96"	20.36

Clark Urethane/Polyester	¼"	24" x 48"	4.95
(White) 6 Lb./Ft.³ 180°F	⅜"	24" x 48"	6.95
	1"	6" x 10"	2.95
Clark Urethane/Polyester	1"	16" x 24"	8.84
(White) 8 Lb./Ft.³ 180°F			
Clark Urethane/Polyester	0.200"	12" x 48"	6.98
(White) 18 Lb./Ft.³ 180°F	¼"	12" x 48"	8.78

*Scored one side.
Refer to your plans and newsletters for approved substitutions of White foam for applications formerly using obsolete PVC foam.

WARNING: Working with all foams may be hazardous to health due to inhalation of toxic fumes and dust. All cutting should be done in a well ventilated area with plenty of fresh air. The use of exhaust fans is recommended. Do not hot wire urethane or PVC foams. Styrofoam may be hot wired with good ventilation.

Liquid "X-40" Foam (Two-Component Polyurethane Foam)

This sytem consists of two components - "X-40" Resin and "X-40" Catalyst. When the resin and catalyst are mixed in equal volumes they expand into a rigid closed-cell foam of 2 pound density. Thorough mixing of the two components is essential. "X-40" Foam expands approximately 40 times its liquid volume. Small-batch mixes are recommended. Cured foams can be easily trimmed, cut and shaped with common woodworking tools. Use toluene or MEK for cleanup. "X-40" Foam contains a highly reactive agent and is classified as a toxic material. It is combustible, a strong skin sensitizer and eye irritant. Avoid contact with the skin. Use rubber gloves when handling. Common uses: Flotation, thermal and acoustical insulation, reinforcement and miscellaneous void filling. Most small pleasure boats can be made "sink-proof" with approximately two gallons of "X-40". Data sheet available. "X-40" Foam contains a volatile fluorocarbon and should be stored at 70°F. or lower. "X-40" is used on the Osprey II bottom hull, canopy, nose cone, etc., requiring about four gallons of material (two gallons of each component). Shelf life - at least six months. Users have reported "more than two years shelf life".

Kit Size	Kit Part No.	Approx. Foamed Vol. (Cu.Ft.)	Weight Lbs.	Price per Kit
1 Quart Kit (1 Pt. each component)	M-25	1¼	3	$10.35
2 Quart Kit (1 Qt. each component)	M-26	2½	6	$17.75
2 Gallon Kit (1 Gal. each component)	M-28	10	22	$57.00
10 Gallon Kit (5 Gal. each component)	M-29	50	110	$245.00

Poly-Cel One

New one-component polyurethane foam - requires no mixing. Dispenses like shaving cream from an aerosol can, then sets up to a rigid closed cell foam. Adheres permanently to almost any surface - does not shrink, dry out or become brittle with age.   12 Oz. Aerosol Can $6.95

Fillers—Tapes—Primers

Glass Bubbles - These bubbles are actually hollow glass spheres. Because the high-quality glass is very crush resistant, the foam is much stronger, stiffer and water-resistant than any foam made by chemical foaming. These foams displace 4-6 times their weight in most resins and improve the handling characteristics of the base resin. They have a low bulk density and are nontoxic. Mix resin and hardener as directed, then fold in the glass bubbles. Upon cure, a strong, low-density product results which is easy to sand and file. May be shaped to form compound angles and curves. The term "micro" was applied to the mixture of microspheres and epoxy early in the development of composite structures. Although microspheres have been replaced by glass bubbles, the word "micro" is still commonly used to reference the mixture. "Micro" is used to fill voids and low areas, to glue foam blocks together and as a bond between foams and glass cloth. Micro is used in three consistencies - (1) a "slurry" which is a one-to-one by volume mix of epoxy and glass bubles, (2) "wet micro" which is about two to four parts glass bubbles by volume to one part epoxy, and (3) "dry micro" which is a mix of epoxy with enough glass bubbles to obtain a paste which will not sag or run (about five parts to one by volume). In all instances glass bubbles are added to completely mixed epoxy resin and hardener. Wet micro is used to join foam blocks and is much thicker than slurry (it has the consistency of honey) but can be brushed. Dry micro is used to fill low spots and voids and is mixed so that it is a dry paste and will not sag. Apply with a putty knife. **Never** use micro between glass layers.

One-Pound Bag (Approx. 1 Gal.)	$5.70
Five-Pound Bag (Approx. 5 Gal.)	$27.00

Flocked Cotton Fiber - A structural resin filler. This mixture of cotton fiber and epoxy is referred to as "flox". The mixture is used in structural joints and in areas where a very hard, durable buildup is required. Flox is mixed in much the same way as dry micro but only about two parts flock to one part epoxy is required. Mix in just enough flock to make the mixture stand up. If "wet flox" is called out, mix it so it will sag or run. Flox is often used to reinforce a sharp corner. Paint a light coat of pure epoxy inside the corner, trowel flox in to make a triangular support. The flox corner is done just before one glass surface is applied for a wet bond to one surface.

One-Pound Bag $1.85

Bondo - Automotive body filler, used extensively in composite construction to hold jig blocks in place, and for other temporary fastening jobs. Hardens quickly and can be chipped off without damaging the fiberglass. The color of the mixture is used to judge how fast it will set. As more hardener is added, the brighter in color the mixture becomes and the faster it hardens. The original #211 series automotive plastic filler has been improved using a microsphere formula producing a lightweight body filler which sands easier, spreads smooth. Can be shaped days later. Ideal for the aircraft homebuilder. Used extensively in composite construction.

#261	Pint	(1½ Lb.)	$3.20
#262	Quart	(3 Lb.)	$5.15
#265	Gallon	(12 Lb.)	$15.30

Bondo Mixing Board - A handy, rigid polypropylene sheet, 6"W x 8½"L. Ideal surface for mixing Bondo. Will not stick. When job is finished, let residue dry, flex board and excess Bondo will pop off, leaving board clean.

#359 $1.15

Ultralite - A formulation of polyester resin, talcs and Microspheres used as a lightweight filler on metal and fiberglass. Works easily, sands faster. Only 7.5 lbs. per gallon as compared to 12 lbs. per gallon for conventional fillers.

#392	One Qt.	$5.10
Case of 12 Qts. @ $4.60 Qt.		$55.20
#394	One Gal.	$14.75
Case of 4 Gals. @ $13.55 Gal.		$54.20

Feather Fill - A sprayable polyester filler/primer used for filling of minor surface irregularities such as scratches, blemishes and exposed fiberglass threads before final sanding and painting. It adheres to bare metal, plastic filler and fiberglass with minimal surface preparation. Cures ready to sand and paint in 45 - 60 minutes. Any type of finish — lacquer, enamel, acrylics —can be applied over Feather Fill with excellent adhesion. Quart kit includes catalyst and instructions. Approximately six quarts are required for finishing a VE.

#401	One Qt.	$8.98
Case of 6 Qts. @ $8.35 Qt.		$50.10
#391	One Gal.	$27.80
Case of 4 Gals. @ $25.90 Gal.		$103.60

Micro-Putty - A flexible, lightweight (5½ lbs. per gallon) plastic filler containing 60% by volume glass bubbles and non-bleeding chromate pigments in a polyester resin cured with cream hardener. It will adhere to most clean surfaces - fiberglass, wood and metals. Sets in 10-15 minutes and finishes to a smooth surface with no airborne dust.

MP-1100 Qt. $8.05
Gal. $24.52

Peel Ply - A layer of 2.7 oz. Dacron fabric strips or tape laminated into a layup as if it were an extra ply of glass. The peel coat wets out with epoxy like glass cloth and cures along with the rest of the layup. However, the Dacron does not adhere structurally to the glass and when peeled away it leaves a surface ready for glass-to-glass bonding without sanding. Average tape requirements for small aircraft:

Tape Discounts:
  12 Rolls   Less 10%
  25 Rolls   Less 15%
  May be assorted.

3 Rolls of 1" x 50 Yds. Tape	$3.95 Roll
2 Rolls of 2" x 50 Yds. Tape	$4.90 Roll
1 Roll of 3" x 50 Yds. Tape	$7.95 Roll
1 Roll of 4" x 50 Yds. Tape	$9.50 Roll
Peel Ply Yardage: 50" Width	$1.75 Yd.
66" Width	$2.95 Yd.

Fine Line Tape - A specially extruded matte-finish green polypropylene film tape that is resistant to moisture, solvents and epoxy. Stretches easily for smooth curves, yet tears readily by hand. Although considerably more expensive than masking tape, it saves many hours of work and assures a fine professional finish. Excellent for custom painting applications. 3M #218.

⅛" x 60 Yds. $4.03   ½" x 60 Yds. $3.91
¼" x 60 Yds. $3.00   ¾" x 60 Yds. $4.89
Less 10% on 6 Rolls. Less 15% on 12 Rolls. May be assorted.

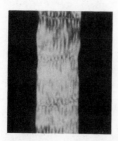

Fiberglass Tape - This is a fibrous glass reinforcement designed to furnish exceptionally high directional strength. Manufactured from parallel strands of glass roving which are held together by a fine woven cross thread. The placement of the cross thread is such that the parallel rovings do not wander or have a tendency to cross over each other. This 100% unidirectional tape can be used instead of unidirectional fabric for spar caps, wings and elevators. Contours well and cuts building time considerably. Wt. 22 oz./sq.yd., .025" thick. May be used with either polyester or epoxy systems. Used on Polliwagen, Long-EZ, Adventure and applicable to all composites.

UND Tape	(Long-EZ)	3" x 180 Yd. Roll (22½ Lbs.)	$63.00
Pollitape	(Polliwagen)	3" x 300 Yd. Roll (40 Lbs.)	$90.00
		Less than Full Roll	.45 Yd.

Primer Surfacers - Du Pont 70-S is a dark gray lacquer primer surfacer which provides an effective ultra-violet radiation barrier with its 15% carbon black content, as well as an excellent finish-sanding surface in preparation for the finish paint.

Qt.	$11.50
Gal.	$29.25

Du Pont 3011-S is the same type of primer-surfacer as 70-S but is for use when the aircraft is to be finished in enamel.

Qt.	$12.15
Gal.	$32.60

Note: 70-S and 3011-S are flammable products requiring special documentation for air shipment overseas.

Zolatone Cockpit Paint - Used to paint cockpit interiors, excellent on fiberglass. Gives a coarse, durable, professional finish. One gallon required for Long-EZ cockpit. Available in #40-59 Charcoal, #40-34 Mottled Brown and #40-52 Mottled Blue. Primer not required when used on fiberglass.

	Qt.	$6.25
	Gal.	$21.50
Primer 99 for Zolatone	Gal.	$19.45

#77 Spray Adhesive - This 3M aerosol spray adhesive works well to laminate styrofoam sheets together. Laminations cut well with a hot wire. Net wt. 17 oz.

23.5 Fl. Oz. Aerosol Spray Can	$8.60

Composite Materials Practice Kit

All designers highly recommend that builders who are considering a composite project purchase this practice kit. It contains the excellent 26 page 11" x 17" manual by Burt Rutan entitled MOLDLESS COMPOSITE SANDWICH HOMEBUILT AIRCRAFT CONSTRUCTION ($14.50) plus the assorted foams, epoxy, fiberglass, filler materials and supplies with which to work. Everything needed to practice the technique of composite building before venturing into a complete aircraft project. $49.95

Helpful Hints and Precautions

It is important to have the entire work area including tables, foam, tools and working materials thoroughly warm before commencing. This may take 3-4 hours. An electric hair dryer may be used to warm local areas, being careful not to overheat the part or epoxy. When, due to cool temperatures, a part is slow to wet out, a few quick passes with a hair dryer will greatly speed the layup time. Do not use a hair dryer to heat a cup of epoxy. This can give local hot spots and ruin pot life.

The epoxy system components should be stored at room temperature. Never keep resin or hardeners in a cold place, even for long-term storage. If the resin appears to crystallize and settle out it should be returned to its normal state as soon as possible, even if prompt usage is not anticipated. Placing the container of resin in hot (160-190° F.) water for several hours will usually decrystallize it and return it to a clear state. Mild agitation will accelerate the process. Leaving the resin hot for 3-5 hours after it clears will reduce its susceptibility to recrystallize. Securely close containers after use.

Never attempt any layup below 70° F. since the higher viscosity of the resin will make it more difficult to wet out the cloth. Ideal working temperature is 85° F. Keep the epoxy at 75° to 85° F. Never work outside in sunlight or in a shop heated with radiant heaters.

Never make a glass layup over a core that is not straight and smooth. The glass panel cannot take the loads if it has bumps or depressions in excess of the allowable values. A wrinkle, depression or bump in a layup which is greater than 1/16" high or low and which is more than 20% of the chord length or 20% of the spar chord is not acceptable and requires repair. A depression can usually be repaired by filling with flox to level and laying over the entire depression the amount of glass that is underneath, lapping outside the depression a distance equal to one inch per ply. Care should be taken not to lay up a depression or bump in the thick main spar caps. The transition of the spar caps into the wing fittings must be smooth and without joggles. These precautions apply only to the flying surfaces. The fuselage and fuel tanks can have relatively large depressions or bumps without affecting structural safety. Care should be taken in the finishing process not to sand through more than one ply on the structure.

Joining foam blocks - (1) Paint a coat of epoxy (no micro) on the joining surfaces. (2) Trowel a wedge of dry micro on the center of one surface. (3) Squeeze the joining surfaces together, wiggling them back and forth to obtain a thin micro joint less than 1/16" thick. It is desirable to have the micro about ⅜" low in the joint (not squeezed out). The low joint is filled with micro before glass is laid over the joint allowing a wet bond between the micro and the glass. If some does squeeze out, wipe the joint low with a mixing stick. Do not try to fill large voids with micro, as there is a possibility of exotherm damage. For a void larger than about 0.1", fill with a sliver of foam with micro on each side.

A paper cutter is excellent for measuring and cutting the many little squares of glass cloth.

Epoxy should be removed from metal tools or parts with acetone, MEK or soap and water before it cures.

Micro slurry should not be applied to glass surfaces being bonded. This weakens the joint.

Do not use Bondo on styrofoam, it has a polyester base which will dissolve the foam. Bondo will not attack urethane or PVC.

Precaution - Be sure layups are not dry, with air present (small flecks of white). Inspect thoroughly before leaving a wet layup. A cured layup that is too dry must be rejected.

Make sure that ample micro slurry is applied over the foam, particularly the urethane. Inadequate slurry allows air to remain under the first ply, decreasing laminate peel strength and surface durability.

Hot wire cutting - A good method to use for judging wire temperatures is the appearance of the cut foam surface. A cratered or rutted surface indicates the wire is too hot. A very light "hair" of plastic strands on the surface is just right. Always adjust the temperature so that the wire will cut one inch in 4 to 6 seconds with light pressure.

Exotherm foam damage - Care must be taken to avoid heavy buildups of epoxy/micro down inside a joint that is insulated by foam, such as the assembly of the wing cores. The gap to be filled by micro when assembling any foam cores should not be thicker than 1/16". In filling a gap greater than 0.1", excessive weight is added and, more importantly, the large mass of epoxy/micro insulated by the foam can exotherm. Heat resulting from the exotherm can be as high as 450° F., which will melt away the foam locally and destroy the joint.

White is the recommended color for composite aircraft since it absorbs very little of the sun's heat (10%) while a black surface will heat up tremendously (95% absorption). Trim colors in noncritical areas are acceptable. Any good quality automotive enamel, lacquer, acrylic or polyurethane is acceptable. A primer-surfacer with an ultra-violet radiation barrier is recommended as an undercoating.

Caution: Do not ever wipe paint thinners on any part of the structure. Minute pin holes in the epoxy/glass skin can allow the thinners to penetrate down to the styrofoam, which dissolves in thinners.

Quality Control

One of the unique features of the glass-foam-glass composite construction technique is the ability to visually inspect the structure from the outside. The transparency of the glass/epoxy material makes it possible to see all the way through the skins and even through the spar caps. Defects in the layup take four basic forms: (1) resin lean areas, (2) delaminations, (3) wrinkles or bumps in the fibers and (4) damage due to sanding structure away in finishing. Resin lean areas are white in appearance due to incomplete wetting of the glass cloth with epoxy during layup. The presence of minor white (lean) areas up to about 2 inches in diameter is not cause for rejection of the piece. Delaminations in a new layup may be due to small air bubbles trapped between plies during the layup. Small delaminations or bubbles up to 2″ diameter may be filled by drilling a small hole into the bubble and filling the void with epoxy. Major wrinkles or bumps along more than 2″ of chord are cause for rejection in the wings, canard and winglet on the VE, particularly on the top. In most cases the rejected part can be repaired by following the basic rule: Remove the damaged area and fair back the area at a slope of at least one inch per ply with a sanding block in all directions. Count the number of plies removed while sanding and replace with same, plus one more ply of BID over the entire patch.

Designer—Approved Tools

The tools offered in this section have been selected by professional designers as being either necessary or highly desirable for working with composite structures.

Calrad Variable Voltage Control - A fine quality control to supply the electrical current for hot-wire cutting of styrofoam and PVC foam. One unit can serve to build many aircraft. Input 115 volts AC. Output variable from 0 to 130 volts AC at 5 amps. Caution - a fuse should be inserted in the secondary to protect the control in the event of a short circuit. $47.50

Safety Wire - Type 302 stainless steel safety wire, for hot wire cutter. Specify .032″ or .041″ diameter wire.

25 Ft. Coil	$1.00
1 Lb. Spool .032″	5.25
.041″	5.00

Epoxy Ratio Pump - This highly recommended pump, aptly called "Sticky-Stuff Dispenser", will save about $50 in epoxy in building a VE type aircraft, plus time, mess, dermatitis, temper and risk of bad batches. Used by individual craftsmen and professionals alike, it is a practical engineering tool especially designed to eliminate the sticky, messy, costly hand proportioning of epoxy resins. It is well built and should last through the construction of dozens of aircraft. The Sticky-Stuff Dispenser assures accurate measurement of low-viscosity (under 3,500 centipoises) unfilled epoxy resin. The standard Model A dispenser pump is set for the Safe-T-Poxy system and delivers a ratio of 100 parts of resin to 44 parts of hardener. Pumps with other ratios (RAE system is 4:1) are available on special order. $150.00

Pump Conversion Kit - A factory conversion kit designed to convert pumps set up for the RAE 4:1 ratio to the 2:1 Safe-T-Poxy system. The converted pumps can then be changed back to 4:1 ratio at any time by the user. Builder's "do-it-yourself" conversion possible. Write for details.
Factory Conversion Kit $40.00

X-Acto Tools
No. 3205 Knife - For heavy work. Plastic handle with metal blade lock. 4¾" long. Complete with No. 19 blade. $2.75
No. 3206 Knife - For heavy work. Solid aluminum hexagonal handle. 4¾" long. Complete with No. 24 blade. $3.95

No. 215 Keyhole Saw Blade - For small interior cuts.   Pkg. of 5 $2.95

No. 11 Blade - Extremely sharp point for fine angle cutting and stripping. Most popular with modelers.   Pkg. of 5 $ .89
                                                                                     100    $14.00

No. 18 Blade - Chisel blade (½" wide). For deep cross cuts.   Pkg. of 5 $1.15

No. 22 Blade - For long cuts. General shaping, whittling, trimming of potting compounds, excess flashing.   Pkg. of 5 $1.95

No. 23 Blade - Double-edged. For close quarter cuts, angled corners, trimming and dressing of potting compounds.   Pkg. of 5 $3.45

No. 24 Blade - For close corner cuts, deburring, trimming, gasket cutting.
                                                                                 Pkg. of 5 $ .99

No. 25 Blade - For general carving, whittling, trimming of potting compounds, excess flashing. Heavy cutting.   Pkg. of 5 $3.45

No. 227 Blade - 3″ saw blade.   Pkg. of 5 $2.95

No. 236 Razor Saw Blade - For fine and accurate cutting, trimming and notching of metal, wood and plastics. Blade is 1¼″ wide x 5½″ long; 24 teeth per inch. Fits No. 5 handle. $1.99

All blades featured will fit handles furnished in No. 5 and No. 6 knives.

No. 5082 Knife Set - Nos. 1, 2 and 5 knives plus 10 assorted extra blades. Handy, fitted chest. $9.95

No. 5083 Knife Set - Nos. 1, 2 and 6 knives plus 14 assorted extra blades in beautiful wooden chest. $13.95

Stripper Rasps - Four styles for shaping, rasping, planing, beveling and removing paint. Also excellent for working Balsa, fiberglass and foam.

No. 7171 Convex Style	$1.29
No. 7172 Flat Style	1.29
No. 7173 Concave Style	1.29
No. 7174 Round Style	1.29

No. 7450 Mini C Clamps - Small clamps of high-grade steel, finished in baked enamel. Cadmium plated screws with slotted ends resist welding splatter. Set of three clamps, with maximum openings of ½″, ⅞″, and 1-7/16″. $4.29

Super No. 1 Knife - Positive lock toggle allows for instant blade change and adjustable blade grip. Perfectly balanced. Resists rolling. Safety cap. Anodized aluminum handle 5″ long with No. 11 blade.

No. 3111 Knife	$4.65
No. 3111 Knife with 100 #11 Blades	$19.65

No. 7356 Needle File Assortment - Twelve assorted styles in heavy plastic storage stand. $17.95

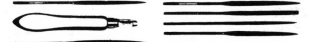

No. 7358 File Set - Three different file styles plus a universal quick-change, comfort-grip handle. $5.75

No. 7361 File Set - A full assortment of six different file styles suited to a wide variety of assignments, plus a universal quick-change, comfort-grip handle.
$10.85

No. 7044 Coping Saw - Steel frame, wooden handle. Adjustable blade grips hold blade taut. Overall length 11″. Complete with one standard and one spiral safety coping saw easy-to-change blades. $4.95

Refill Blades:	No. 734 Coping Saw Blade	Pkg. of 5	$1.95
	No. 735 Spiral Saw Blade	Pkg. of 3	$1.49

Dremel Tools

Dremel Moto-Tool - A versatile, precision power tool with many uses in the construction of composite aircraft. Ideal for wood, plastics and metals. Sturdy, shatter-proof Nylon housing.

Model 250 Moto-Tool: Constant Speed 30,000 RPM. Lubricated bronze sleeve bearings. Amps: 0.8.

List Price	$49.95
Our Price	$44.50

Model 370 Moto-Tool: Variable Speed 5,000-28,000 RPM allows user to select the right speed for every job. Life-time lubricated bronze sleeve bearings. External caps allow for easy replacement of motor brushes. Amps: 0.75 low speed, 0.9 high speed.

List Price	$67.95
Our Price	$61.00

Model 380 Moto-Tool: Variable Speed 5,000-28,000 RPM with 100% ball bearing construction for long life, smooth operation. External caps allow for easy replacement of motor brushes. Amps: 0.75 low speed, 0.9 high speed.

List Price	$77.95
Our Price	$70.00

Moto-Tool Kits:
No. 2501 Kit contains Model 250 Moto-Tool and 25 accessories:

List Price	$58.95
Our Price	$53.00

Qty.	Description
1	Model 250 Constant Speed Moto Tool
1	Kit Box
6	Cut-off Wheels
3	Sanding Discs
1	High Speed Cutter
1	⅛" Drill
1	Wrench
2	Mandrels

Qty.	Description
1	Felt Polishing Wheel
3	Wheel Points
1	Dressing Stone
1	Polishing Wheel
1	Paste Brush
1	Cup Brush
1	Collet (⅛")
1	Drum Sander
1	Sanding Band

No. 3701 Kit contains Model 370 Moto-Tool and 35 accessories:

List Price $77.95
Our Price $70.00

Qty.	Description
1	Model 370 Variable Speed Moto Tool
1	Kit Box
6	Cut-off Wheels
7	Sanding Discs
1	High Speed Cutter
1	⅛" Drill
2	Engraving Cutters
1	Wrench
2	Mandrels

Qty.	Description
2	Felt Polishing Wheels
4	Wheel Points
1	Dressing Stone
1	Polishing Wheel
1	Paste Brush
1	Cup Brush
2	Collets (⅛" & 3/32")
1	Drum Sander
2	Sanding Bands

No. 3801 Kit contains Model 380 Moto-Tool and 40 accessories:

List Price $89.95
Our Price $81.00

Qty.	Description
1	Model 380 Variable Speed Moto-Tool
1	Deluxe Kit Box
6	Cut-off Wheels
7	Sanding Discs
2	High Speed Cutters
1	⅛" Drill
2	Engraving Cutters
1	Wrench
2	Mandrels
2	Felt Polishing Wheels

Qty.	Description
6	Wheel Points
1	Dressing Stone
1	Polishing Wheel
1	Paste Brush
1	Cup Brush
2	Collets (⅛" & 3/32")
1	Drum Sander
2	Sanding Bands
1	Finger Grip
1	Steel Saw

Replacement Motor Brushes (Specify Moto-Tool Model No.) $2.45 Pr.

Moto-Tool Repair Kit for Moto-Tool Nos. 370 and 380 $5.98

No. 407 ½" Drum Sander - Ideal for rough shaping of wood and smoothing of fiberglass. Sander bands are replaceable. Furnished with one band. ⅛" shank. $2.35

No. 408 Drum Sander Bands - ½" dia., coarse grit. Two packages of 6 are required for the VE.   Pkg. of 6 $1.80

Steel Cutters - Can be used for cutting, grooving, shaping and hollowing of most metals, plastics and woods. ⅛" shanks. At least two Nos. 115, 134 and 199 are required for a small homebuilt. Other cutters are very useful for the home craftsman. $3.50 Ea.

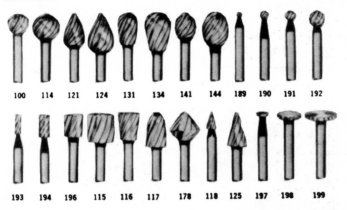

Steel Saws - For slotting and cutting. Fit Mandrel No. 402. Two or three No. 400 required for a composite aircraft.

No. 400 Steel Saw (.023" thick)	$2.35
No. 406 Steel Saw (.005" thick)	$2.35
No. 402 Mandrel (⅛" shank)	$1.80

No. 428 Wire Brush - VE builder reports it works beautifully for cleaning the residual foam and micro off of the canard, wing and winglet trailing edge overlaps in preparation for the top skin layups. Do not run in excess of 15,000 RPM. $1.80

No. 571 Basic Saw/Sander - Rugged steel construction. Includes disc sander and power take-off for additional accessories. 15" throat depth will handle boards up to 1¾" thick. Features front or side mount blade for ripping long

material. Also cuts light gauge metal, plastic, felt, etc. Includes rubber backing pad and adapter, 3 sanding discs and 3 saw blades. Other attachments can be added. Motor 1.4 Amp, 115 V, 60 Hz AC. Wt. 16 lbs.

List Price $95.95
Our Price $86.36

No. 573 Kit - Can be added to Model 571 Saw/Sander. Contains flexible shaft, adapter, drum sander and 4 sander bands, 5 saw blades, 2 emery wheel points, 2 bristle brushes, 1 wire brush, 1 high speed cutter, 1 drill bit, 3 collets and chuck wrench, 1 polishing compound stick, 3 sanding discs, 1 silicon point and 1 buffing wheel. Wt. 2½ lbs.

List Price $34.95
Our Price $31.46

No. 4211 Arbor Adapter - For attaching rubber backing pad and sanding discs and 3″ buffer cloth to power takeoff. $2.05

                - 4″ Dia. rubber backing pad for use with sanding discs. Use No. 4211 Adapter. $1.80

Sanding Discs - Varying coarseness.   Pkg. of 6 $1.90

No. 4227 - Coarse (1/2 Grit)
No. 4228 - Medium (2/0 Grit)
No. 4229 - Fine   (4/0 Grit)

No. 4235 Buffing Wheel - 3″ Dia. buffing cloth. Use with No. 4211 $1.80

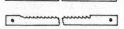

Saw Blades - Fine tooth saw blade.   No. 8029 Pkg. of 5 $1.80
              Coarse tooth saw blade.   No. 8030 Pkg. of 5 $1.90

No. 990196 Flexible Shaft - A 30″ vinyl covered flexible shaft with handpiece and coupling adapter. $19.50

No. 580 Table Saw & Accessories - 4″ Tilt-arbor motorized table saw cuts up to 1″ at 90° and ¾″ at 45°. Includes 4″ dia. combination blade. Blade speed 10,000 RPM. Motor 2.2 Amp, 115 V, 60 Hz AC. Wt. 15 lbs.

List Price $122.95
Our Price $110.66

No. 8003 4″ Combination Blade - 30 Teeth, ½″ arbor. General purpose blade designed for ripping, mitering and cross cutting. $6.75

No. 8004 4″ Fine Blade - 100 Teeth, ½″ arbor. Blade designed for fine smooth cutting in plywood, soft fiber board, sensitive materials. $6.75

No. 8013 Vacuum Attachment - Minimizes mess, fits most size vacuum hoses. $1.90

No. 8014 Sawdust Bag/Attachment - Includes dust bag and No. 8013 vacuum attachment. $6.95

No. 730 Disc-Belt Sander & Accessories - Shapes, sands, polishes most woods, metals and plastics. Disc for rough sanding and shaping. Belt for finish sanding, sharpening and polishing. 3″ throat depth and belt tracking adjustment allows for internal sanding. 45° Tilting table. Comes with two 1″ x 30″ sanding belts and one 5″ sanding disc. Belt speed: 2,700 SFPM. Disc speed: 4,400 RPM. Motor 2.0 Amp, 115 V. 60 Hz AC.

List Price $112.95
Our Price $101.66

Sanding Belts

No. 8040 - 50 Grit (Coarse)	No. 8041 - 80 Grit (Medium)
No. 8042 - 120 Grit (Fine)	No. 8043 - 180 Grit (Extra Fine)
No. 8044 - 240 Grit (Very Fine)	No. 8045 - 320 Grit (Fine Polishing)

Pkg of 2 $4.55

Sanding Discs

No. 8050 - 50 Grit, No. 8051 - 80 Grit, No. 8052 - 120 Grit
Pkg. of 5 $4.55

No. 1522 Soldering Iron - 100 Watt iron with No. 477 ⅜" chisel tip and stand designed for heavy duty use. 120 volts. 1035° F. maximum tip temperature.

List Price	$43.95
Our Price	$39.56

Stanley Tools

Stanley Tape Measure - This 12-ft. steel tape measure, with ½" blade, is graduated in tenths and hundredths of inches and also in fractions of inches (32nds). Very handy for all aircraft construction. A "must" for composite construction.

No. 33-272	$8.99
Replacement Blade No. 32-271	$6.19

Carpenter's Level - A quality level, 24 inches long, with magnesium I-beam construction, three replaceable vials, hand holes and hang hole. Has all the features found in more expensive levels.   No. 42-024 $14.15

Soft-Face Hammer - Renewable tips are made of tough ethyl cellulose that won't mar finely finished surfaces. Handle is stained hickory. Plastic tips are replaceable.   No. 57-594 $12.45

Rubber Mallet - Tough rubber head assembled to a lacquered handle.   No. 57-522 $8.05

Bar Clamp - With quick non-slip adjustment to approximate size, then screws tight to apply firm pressure.   No. 83-157 $5.15

Spring Clamps - Heavy-gauge steel clamps with vinyl grips and tips to prevent marring work. Jaws specially formed to hold flat or round objects. Two sizes available:

Jaw Opening ⅞", Length 4-1/16"	No. 83-261	$2.75
Jaw Opening 1¾", Length 6⅛"	No. 83-262	$4.60

Utility Knife - Aluminum, die-cast in two sections - provides blade storage. Has handy hang hole. Furnished with No. 11-921 blade and blade guard.

No. 10-199 $5.09

Knife Blade - Heavy-duty pointed razor-type utility knife blade for No. 10-199 knife and most other makes of utility knives.

Pkg. of 5 Blades   No. 11-921 $1.65

Hook Blade - For use with No. 10-199 knife and most other makes of utility knives to cut linoleum, roofing material, cartons, etc., without damage. The razor-sharp hooked ends cut to full thickness in one stroke.

Pkg. of 5 Blades   No. 11-961 $4.05

Putty Knife - Blade is 1¼″ wide. Full tang blade permanently fastened to wooden handle.   No. 28-540 $2.89

Surform Plane - A surform plane is one of the fastest and easiest of all cutting and forming tools for use on wood, metals, plastic and fiberglass. Non-clogging razor-sharp cutting edge on hardened tool steel blade - shavings pass through the blade. Cuts with only slight pressure applied.

No. 21-296 $9.69
Replacement Blade   No. 21-293 $3.09

Round File - Enlarges holes fast. Foams and shapes. Black finish hardwood handle. Round, regular cut hardened steel blade is ⅝″ diameter.

No. 21-297 $7.99
Replacement Blade   No. 21-291 $4.39

Wood Chisels - Heavy duty construction - blade and shank forged in one piece, meets shank of steel cap. Blades are forged from high-quality alloy steel. Two blade widths available:

Blade ¼″ Wide x 4″ Long   No. 16-402 $16.75
Blade 1″ Wide x 4″ Long   No. 16-407 $22.29

Circle Cutter - For cutting circles in sheet metal, mild steel, laminated materials, wood. Adjustable bit of high speed steel held in arm with set screw. For use in drill press or drill stand only.   No. 04-418 $16.79

Plumb Bob - Cast in one piece. Cap permits attachment of cord. Hardened replacement tip.   No. 47-171 $6.35

Dovetail Saw - Cuts a true, smooth and narrow kerf. Comfortable hardwood handle provides positive grip. Professional quality.   No. 15-140 $11.49

Miscellaneous Tools and Supplies

Industrial Fabric Shears - Wiss No. 20W heavy-duty shears, ideal for cutting fiberglass cloth and all fabrics. Hot drop-forged steel. $27.50

Disston Abrader - Shapes and sands in one operation. Lasts longer, works faster, costs less than sandpaper. Builder-recommended for use on composite aircraft.   No. 401C $8.95

Rubber Squeegee - Developed especially for working with epoxies, this 6″ wide hard rubber squeegee is superior to the plastic types. Can be easily cleaned and reused many times. $2.85

Paint Brushes - Natural, undyed bristle brushes with smooth, unpainted wooden handles. Unaffected by paints, dopes, resins, thinners or solvents.
1″-Wide Brush $ .40
2″-Wide Brush $ .60

Epoxy Layup Rollers - 3″ wide roller with stipple adhesive cover. Has excellent stippling action for working out air bubbles in layups and has no tendency to lift the cloth. Use on all major layups.
Roller and Cover $2.25
Cover only $1.25

Single-Edge Razor Blades - Used for trimming rough edges of laminates.
.10 Ea.
Box of 100 $5.50

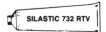

Rubber Sealant - No. 732 RTV general-purpose, clear, one-part silicone rubber. Cures to a firm silicone rubber in 24 hours at room temperature.

4.7 Oz. tube $5.50

Dispenser Bottle - Polyethylene bottle with Yorker (applicator) cap.

4 Oz. Bottle	$ .55 Ea.
	$5.25 Doz.
16 Oz. (1 Pint) Bottle	$ .95 Ea.
	$9.00 Doz.

Industrial Syringe - Made of hi-impact polyethlyene with seamless body and special safety-grip plunger. Capacity 10 cc. Tapered dispensing nozzle can be clipped with scissors at proper diameter to govern output. Excellent epoxy dispenser.

$ .85 Ea.
6 for $3.50

Docken Spray Gun - An excellent tool for use in finding composite structures and all "do-it-yourself" projects. It will handle sprayable fillers, paints, lacquers, solvents and anything a regular gun can spray. Requires no cleanup as it utilizes disposable paper cups as paint reservoirs. Operates on a siphon tube principle. No paint flows through the gun. Use with compressors capable of producing 40 to 120 PSI. Comes with 10 disposable cups and instructions.

	$39.95
Large-Bore Tube for Spraying Dope	$4.95
Replacement Reservoir Cups, Package of 50	$5.50

Epoxy Mixing Cups - Unwaxed, flat bottom paper cups in two convenient sizes for small mixes.

3 Oz. Size, 100 Cups	$3.50
8 Oz. Size, 100 Cups	$6.50

Mixing Sticks - These mixing sticks are medical tongue depressors which work well for mixing small batches of epoxy. Size: ¾" x 6".

Box of 500 $10.70

Straightedge - A 6 ft. long kiln-dried spruce board, ⅛" to 1" thick and 3" to 4" wide, used for checking the straightness of flying surfaces during composite construction. $16.50

6" Steel Ruler - Flexible stainless steel rule graduated in 10ths and 100ths on one side and in quick-reading 32nds and 64ths on the other side.
                                                                    #616 $2.64

Carter's Felt Tip Markers - Used for marking locations on fiberglass throughout construction.

Broad-Point Marker #B-788	$ .69
Bullet-Point Marker #887	$ .89

Sandpaper - The weights and grits listed have been found to be the most effective for sanding fiberglass/epoxy surfaces. Sheet Size: 9" x 11".

		Price per Sheet	
Sandpaper Type		Less than 50 Sheets	50 Sheets (May be Assorted)
Aluminum Oxide 35 Grit	Open Coat "D" Weight	.66	.55
3M Wetordry 100 Grit 220 Grit 320 Grit	Silicon Carbide "C" Weight "A" Weight "A" Weight	.58 .40 .40	.48 .33 .33

3M Electro-Cut Utility Cloth - Mechanic's aluminum oxide cloth. 100 grit.

2" x 50 Yd. Roll	$41.75
Less than Full Roll	$1.05 Yd.

Sanding Block - A hard rubber tool which comfortably fits the hand for scratch - to finish-sanding. Used by professionals for years in all sanding operations. Simply cut a piece of sandpaper 2¾" x 9" and insert each end into the sanding block. Paper is held securely by nail retainers. Makes the sanding operation much easier.   No. 100 $3.25

12" Long Drill Bits - For use with standard electric drill for hard-to-reach jobs.

#10	$5.90
¼"	$6.20

Countersink - This assembly consists of a ½" dia. AT418E-4 100° cutter, a ¼" dia. AT416-65 pilot, and an AT409-1 adapter with ¼" dia. shank for use with a hand drill. The adapter has a collet-like shaft to securely hold the replaceable pilot.   Complete Assembly $26.75

Spotface - A ⅝" dia. counterbore with ¼" dia. pilot and 10" threaded extension for drilling holes in "impossible" places. $29.50

Pop Rivet Puller - The Cherry No. 404 pop rivet puller is an economy tool for small jobs. Adequate for the home craftsman. Furnished with two nosepieces - one for 3/32" and ⅛" dia. rivets and one for 5/32" and 3/16" dia. rivets.
$16.95

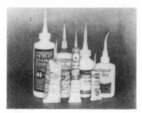

Mini-Sander - A unique sanding tool which uses a 1½" wide strip of sandpaper formed to make a belt. Locked taut by a patented mechanism that snaps into place with a finger pull. Its knife edge sides and padded body sand close to right angle fittings and fit into small concave recesses. Sander body is ⅞" high x 4" long and made of high impact plastic. Buy ready-made belts or make your own (6 belts from standard sheet).   Mini-Sander $2.10
Wetordry Mini-Strips, Pkg of 9 strips (3 - #500, 3 - #320, 3 - #220) $1.50

Mini Glue Tip - Fits most Yorker top dispenser bottles. Just slip a Mini Glue Tip on spout and seal with a pin. Always ready for use - no fuss to fill, no mess to clean. Made of polypropylene - glues don't stick. For shallow tip bends, heat in water, shape with fingers until cool.   Pkg of 4 Tips $1.05

Assorted Supplies For Vari-Eze & Long-EZ

Arrow Stock - Fiberglass arrow shafts used for horizontal canopy bracing. 5/16" O.D. x .028"Wall x 32" Long. $1.60 Ea.

Servo Motor - Activates the VariEze roll trim device.   No. KPS-1511 $17.50

Fiberfrax Paper Insulation - A new material made from washed ceramic fibers with binders added to make a lightweight, flexible insulation which is asbestos-free and economically priced. Withstands temperatures to 2300° F. Excellent for aircraft firewalls. 1/16" Thick x 24" Wide. #970F $1.50 Lineal Ft.

Assorted Springs -

VE	Century Spring (186-C) 2" (3)	Tension	$ .90 Ea.
	Rudder Return Spring 4¼" (2)	Tension	.90 Ea.
	Elevator Trim - Upper 9" (1)	Tension	1.95 Ea.
	Elevator Trim - Lower 13" (1)	Tension	2.50 Ea.
VE and	Landing Brake 10" (2)	Tension	2.10 Ea.
Long-EZ	Compression Spring ½" (2)		1.20 Ea.
	Tension Spring (cut to several pcs.) 30" (1)		4.00 Ea.

Seat Belt/Harness Set - Especially designed for the VE. Also used in the Long-EZ, Quickie and Q2. Belts are made to fit snugly. Aluminum fittings save weight. Two sets per VE, Long-EZ and Q2. One set for Quickie.
$40.25 Set

Upholstery Set - Designed by Burt Rutan for maximum comfort and utility. Durable Nylon tweed fabric in bright blue and black. Consists of one-piece pilot seat, passenger seat, two headrests and two suitcases. Distinctive VE emblem on seat backs and suitcases. Used in VE and Long-EZ. $190.00 Set

Spinner Kit - A four-piece aluminum spinner in a distinctive design. The acorn shape enhances and streamlines the appearance of the aircraft, reducing drag and increasing engine cooling. Furnished complete with hardware and installation instructions. Flight tested and recommended by

Burt Rutan. Specify engine model, prop model, prop hub thickness, bolt diameter, and prop bushing diameter if used. For Lycoming 0-235 engines, specify SAE #1 (4⅜″ dia. bolt circle) or SAE #2 (4¼″ dia. bolt circle) flange. Wt. 2¾ lbs.

Model AC-1 Complete Kit	$87.50
Fwd (Large) Bulkhead Only	$14.50
Aft (Small) Bulkhead Only	$17.00
Spinner Dome Only	$55.00
Fairing Only	$12.00

Air Intake Filter - For VariEze and Long-EZ. Purolator P/N AFP-177, AC P/N 44-8C or NAPA P/N 2904. $8.95

Carburetor Heat Box - For VariEze and Long-EZ. Made to print. $61.50

Fuel Valve - Weatherhead P/N 6749 for VariEze. $20.35

Fuel Filter - The Alondra "View-All" in-line fuel filter can be easily taken apart to clean the filter element. Includes one replacement filter element.

#804 Filter (For ¼″ I.D. Fuel Line)	$5.48
#806 Filter (For ⅜″ I.D. Fuel Line)	$5.48
#896 Replacement Element Kit	
Fits #804 and #806 Filters. Contains	
3 Replacement Elements and 6 O-Rings	$3.95

Oil Breather/Separator - An aluminum reservoir 4″ in diameter with beaded tubing ends for ⅝″ I.D. hose and mounting flange for easy firewall attachment. Minimizes oil loss and allows free breathing of engine. $32.80

P-Strip - Self-adhesive white tubular rubber strip, made in Sweden of 100% EPIM (ethylene-propylene) rubber. Resistant to aging, weather, ozone, ultraviolet sun rays and many chemicals and solvents. Retains resilience at low temperatures (to -45° F.). Used on canopy installations. Excellent for all types of weatherstripping. Furnished as a double-width strip, which splits in the middle to give two P-strips.

#44-56876	.22 Ft.	
50 Ft. Reel (100 Ft. of P-Strip)		$20.50

Long-EZ Panel Marking Set - Complete set of identification and warning placards compiled by Mike Melvill to mark the Long-EZ cockpit, but applicable to other aircraft as well. Contains four each of 35 different callouts plus the Passenger Warning, Limitations, Checklist, Landing and Weight Limits placards. White markings on black background, printed on self-adhesive vinyl. Simply cut out, peel off backing paper and apply. $4.25

YAW TRIM	ROLL TRIM	MAGNETOS
PULL LEFT	LT RT	LT RT

LANDING BRAKE - PULL TO EXTEND
MAX. SPEED 105 MPH/90 KT

Cockpit Placards for VariEze - Set of 22 aluminum placards, with special sponge-type adhesive backing that adheres well to fiberglass. Not applicable to Long-EZ.

Complete Set $6.25

Replacement Placards: Small-letter placards (0.1" high)   .40 Ea.
                        All others (except checklist)   .60 Ea.
                        Checklist only $2.25

Prefabricated Fiberglass Parts For Long-EZ and VariEze

CI	Cowl Inlet	$30.40		CCT-L Cont. Cowl Top	$141.70
NB	Nosegear Box	17.85		CCB-L Cont. Cowl Bottom	141.70
SB	Sump Blister (2)	17.95 Ea.		LCT-L Lyc. Cowl Top	141.70
SC	Strut Cover	17.85		LCB-L Lyc. Cowl Bottom	141.70
CLR	Left Cowl Rib*	15.50		LCT-L-Lite** Lyc. Cowl Top	$448.50 Set of
CRR	Right Cowl Rib*	15.50		LCB-L-Lite** Lyc. Cowl Bottom	Two

* Not used on Long-EZ
**Lite indicates new lightweight Kevlar cowls (for Long-EZ only).
   IMPORTANT - Delete "L" in cowl part no. if ordering for a VariEze.

Wheel Fairings for Long-EZ and VariEze   For 3.40-5 Tires $131.75
                                           For 5.00-5 Tires $155.25

Wheel Fairing Hardware Kits   For 3.40-5 Tires $16.80
                                           For 5.00-5 Tires $23.38

Fiberglass Mold Release - Plastilease 512B, a film-forming, water soluble parting agent, assures clean release of fiberglass parts from molds. For application by brush or spray.   Qt. $6.95

Safety Equipment

The need for adequate safety protection cannot be stressed too highly. Eyes, lungs, and skin are exposed to harmful chemicals and abrasive objects which can either be discomforting or permanently disabling. Always wear glasses when working with the Dremel grinder to protect the eyes from flying particles. Sanding or grinding fiberglass and foams creates dust that can be harmful to the lungs. Use a dust respirator mask or a disposable type. Many individuals will develop an allergy when working with epoxy with bare hands. This "sensitization" is an unpleasant experience so skin protection measures must be taken.

Ply No. 9 Protective Hand Gel - Provides a thin, invisible, flexible film which is an excellent barrier to epoxy resins, rubber adhesives, vinyl plasticizers, polyester resins and glass fibers. Epoxy and gel wash off easily in soap and water. One-Lb. Jar $4.15

Epo-Cleanse Hand Cleaner No. 6001 - Epoxy on unprotected skin should be washed away with Epo-Cleanse. Rub well, rinse with water. Epo-Cleanse restores natural skin oils. One-Pint Bottle $9.35

Polyethylene Gloves - Lightweight, single usage, disposable type.
Dispenser Box of 100 $5.50

Latex Gloves - Disposable but reuseable gloves which resist tearing. Large size. Fit right or left hand. Box of 100 $16.50

Cotton Gloves - Lightweight liners to wear under latex gloves. Adds to comfort and improves sensitivity to work. .95 Pr.
$9.50 Doz.

NOTE: NVER USE PLY 9 AND GLOVES TOGETHER.
USE **EITHER** GLOVES **OR** PLY 9 - NOT BOTH.

Safe-T-Plus

A complete kit of protective materials recommended for use when working with epoxies. The kit contains the best tried and proven items to insure maximum safety in handling these chemicals. Although SAFE-T-POXY is considered completely non-toxic, the system consists of a blend of chemicals and under any circumstances accepted standards of protection should be observed.

Kit Contents:	
1 Pair Deluxe Safety Glasses (completely shielded)	$4.10
50 Disposable Vinyl Gloves	$6.25
6 Disposable Masks	$4.10
1 Jar Specially Formulated Epoxy Cleaner (16 Oz.)	$8.75
Complete Kit	$23.00

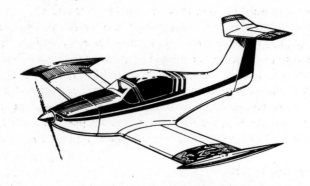

A-4

Kevlar Aramid Fiber For Light Aircraft Construction

Introduction

KEVLAR® aramid fiber, one of the newest and most far-reaching developments of textile research, is helping engineers meet the aircraft design problems of today and the future. Developed by the DuPont Company, KEVLAR has the highest strength-to-weight ratio of any commercially available fiber.

World-famous aeronautical scientist, Dr. Paul MacCready, turned to KEVLAR and other state-of-the-art DuPont products to design and build two remarkable ultralight aircraft.

In June 1979, MacCready's 55-pound human-powered Gossamer Albatross made history when man and machine flew across the English Channel. Two years later, his 195-pound Solar Challenger, first successful manned solar-powered aircraft, soared to 12,000 feet and flew 188 miles in an historic Paris to London flight.

Safety and superior performance are important factors in aircraft design. KEVLAR gives airplane builders a significant design edge by allowing designers to save weight and increase strength in their aircraft.

KEVLAR, generically an aromatic polyamide (aramid) with a very rigid molecular chain, is made by extruding polymer through a die with very small holes. The resulting fibers are collected or joined into yarns. Commercial weavers then manufacture a variety of structural fabrics and woven roving.

KEVLAR has undergone years of extensive development since its introduction. Today, in addition to hundreds of uses which range from powerboats to bullet-resistant vests, from tires to ropes and cables, it is a preferred material in many aircraft and aerospace applications.

Commercial Applications

KEVLAR saved 800 pounds of weight on Lockheed's L-1011 "Tri-Star." The deHavilland DHC-7 STOL aircraft interior and flooring are made from composites reinforced with KEVLAR. This new-technology material helped Sikorsky save 30 percent in airframe weight, enough to increase the passenger capacity of its S-76 helicopter by one person.

KEVLAR is also being used on Cessna's "Citation," Canadair's "Challenger," Piper's "Cheyenne," the Concorde SST, the Airbus A-310, Boeing's new generation 757 and 767 and other fixed and rotary wing aircraft. Uses range from interior components to control surfaces, fairings, propellers, and even complete wings and fuselages in some light aircraft.

Plastic Propeller Blades and Tanks

Composite propeller blades are quieter and lighter than their aluminum counterparts. Blades made from KEVLAR are more damage resistant and easier to maintain. They also have improved vibration damping characteristics and longer fatigue life.

A Spanish CASA 212 twin-turbo-prop commuter aircraft was outfitted with the first set of Hartzell propellers having blades made from an epoxy resin matrix reinforced with KEVLAR. The Federal Aviation Administration has reported that these propellers exhibit outstanding fatigue life at three times actual flight stress. Propeller blades of KEVLAR also have been certified for Beech's "King Air."

Liquid methane has been successfully used to power light aircraft after minor modification to the powerplant fuel system. Aircraft builders who want to use this fuel may wish to consider lightweight pressure bottles filament wound with KEVLAR 49. These tanks save up to 50 percent of the weight of conventional steel pressure bottles.

KEVLAR is making a contribution to our nation's space and defense programs. Rocket motor casings wound with KEVLAR 49 rather than glass fiber have substantially reduced the weight of Trident missiles. Considerable weight savings have been achieved by using KEVLAR in the Space Shuttle program.

Designers and builders of light and ultralight aircraft are generating innovative concepts. KEVLAR can help them turn their dreams into reality.

DuPont's KEVLAR aramid has an outstanding combination of light weight, high strength, outstanding toughness and abuse resistance, and stiffness that can be put to good use in the production of light aircraft.

KEVLAR fibers have a density 43 percent lower than fiberglass and 12 to 30 percent lower than the various graphite and carbon fibers. KEVLAR 49 is 2.5 times as strong as the commonly used E-glass and greater than ten times as strong as aluminum on a specific tensile strength basis. In fact, it has the highest specific tensile strength of any commercially made fiber. (See Fig. 1.)

The tensile modulus, or stiffness, of KEVLAR 49 is greater than twice that of fiberglass on a specific weight basis—an important factor in maintaining aerodynamic shape under load.

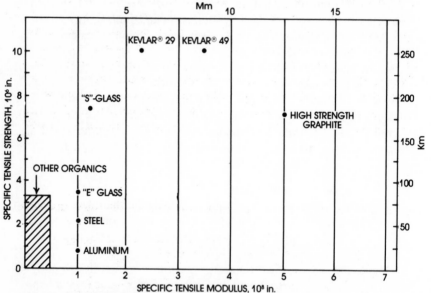

Tested per resin impregnated strand test—ASTMD2343
*Tensile Strength or Modulus Divided by Density

Fig. A-1. Specific* tensile strength and specific* tensile modulus of reinforcing fibers.

KEVLAR 49 displays excellent stability for prolonged periods over temperatures ranging from +300°F to -300°F. (See Fig. 2 for elevated temperature data.) It has good chemical resistance and meets FAA flammability requirements. It does not melt or support combustion.

KEVLAR 29 offers the same broad array of physical and mechanical properties, but has about two-thirds the modulus of KEVLAR 49, providing a less rigid structure, but even better damage resistance.

Composites of KEVLAR are more durable than those of fiberglass and carbon because the aramid fiber provides superior resistance to damage, vibration, (See Fig. 3) and crack propagation as well as excellent fatigue resistance (See Fig. 4). In compression, it exhibits elastic tendencies at low strain and plastic characteristics at high strains, much like aluminum.

In specific applications, designers will find that the low compressive strength of KEVLAR can be either an advantage or disadvantage, depending upon the application. While the compressive strength of composites of KEVLAR is sufficient for some applications, hybrids of KEVLAR and carbon or glass perform well in uses where added compressive strength is needed. Even quantities as low as 5 to 10 percent of KEVLAR as a hybrid reinforcement can dramatically alter the performance of the finished composite.

For instance, Dr. MacCready's Solar Challenger has an extremely lightweight spar with a hybrid construction of carbon tapes with fabric of KEVLAR (See Fig. 5). KEVLAR was used to improve the damage tolerance of the spar, and it raised the compressive buckling resistance as well.

In the case of sandwich structures, the combination of low compressive modulus and high strain-to-failure allows a thin facing laminate of KEVLAR to effectively resist a puncture by indenting into the core, thus changing the initial local facing stress from compression into tension. As penetration continues, the facing then exhibits much added resistance to puncture or failure when compared to either glass or carbon fiber reinforced sandwich facings. KEVLAR 29 should perform even better than KEVLAR 49.

Exposed at Temperature Shown, Tested at Room Temperature Prepared and Tested per ASTM D2343

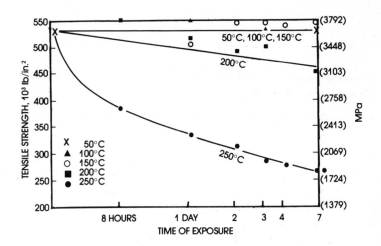

Fig. A-2. Effect of elevated temperature on tensile strength of KEVLAR 49 aramid/epoxy

	Loss Factor*
Stainless Steel	.0006
Ductile Cast Iron	.0030
Graphite/Epoxy	.0017
Fiberglass/Epoxy	.0029
Kevlar®49/Epoxy	.0180
Cured Polyester Resin	.0400

$$^*\text{Loss Factor} = \frac{1}{\pi} \ln\left(\frac{A_n}{A_{n+1}}\right)$$

Where A_n is the amplitude of the nth cycle

Fig. A-3. Decay of Free Vibrations

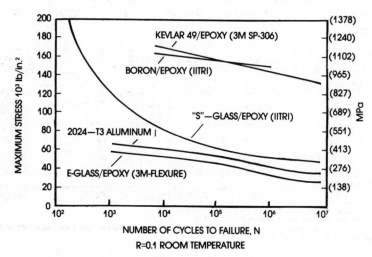

Fig. A-4. Tension-tension fatigue behavior of unidirectional composites and aluminum

Fig. A-5. Cross section of Solar Challenger wing spar. Carbon tube is covered with the two layers of fabric of KEVLAR.

Fabric Selection

Aircraft builders who choose to incorporate the most modern materials can select from several weights and styles of fabric woven from KEVLAR 49 yarns.

Suitable cloth weighing from 1.8 to 6.8 ounces per square yard (61 to 231 grams per square meter), with thickness ranging from 4.5 to 13 mils (0.11 to 0.33 millimeters), can be used to cover light aircraft fuselage, wing, and control surfaces, as well as build other parts and structures. In addition, woven roving of both KEVLAR 49 and 29 is available in thicknesses up to 0.045 inches.

A choice of fabric weaves provides various sought-after design characteristics. Weaves can be selected to give optimum properties such as stiffness, strength, surface conformity, or appearance. The builder selects appropriate fabric of KEVLAR after determining the necessary mechanical characteristics such as strength and modulus (see Table 1). When using a hand layup technique, it is important to select a fabric which readily accepts resin. To help these builders, weaves such as Style 500 are available with an open construction.

In composites, a simple-ply-for-ply substitution for fiberglass layers results in substantial weight savings while enhancing mechanical properties. Some fabrics most useful in aircraft construction are described on the next page.

Fabric Style (DuPont Designation)	Weight oz/yd²(g/m²)	Thickness mils(mm)	Construction ends/in(ends/cm)	Weave	Yarn Denier(Tex)
Cloth					
120	1.8(61)	4.5(0.11)	40x40(16x16)	Plain	195(22)
181	5.0(170)	11 (0.28)	50x50(20x20)	8-Harness Satin	380(42)
220	2.2(75)	5 (0.12)	22x22(9x9)	Plain	380(42)
243*	6.7(230)	13 (0.33)	38x18(15x7)	Crow Foot	1140/380 (127/42)
281**	5.0(170)	10 (0.25)	17x17(7x7)	Plain	1140(127)
285	5.0(170)	10 (0.25)	17x17(7x7)	Crow Foot	1140(127)
500	5.0(170)	10 (0.25)	13x13(5x5)	Plain	1420(158)
335	6.3(210)	13 (0.33)	17x17(7x7)	Crow Foot	1420(158)
Woven Roving					
1350	13.5(460)	25 (0.61)	26x22(10x9)	Basket	2130(237)

*preferred when unidirectional stiffness is required.
**best for prepreg use. Style 500 is preferred for hand layup.

Mechanical properties of laminates constructed from some of these fabrics are given on page 0. Several additional styles are available from fabric manufacturers serving this industry.

Table A-1. Fabrics available for light aircraft.

Fabric Description

Some of the most common DuPont fabric styles for lightweight aircraft construction are shown below.

Fig. A-6. Style 220 is used where an ultra-lightweight fabric is needed.

Fig. A-7. Style 285, a crow foot weave, is used where extra conformability is required in a medium weight cloth.

Fig. A-8. Style 500 is the basic medium weight cloth for canoe, kayak, and small boat construction. It is open enough to conform easily to most hull shapes and to readily accept resin.

Fig. A-9. Style 1350 is the basic woven roving for the boat industry. It is used to replace 24 oz/yd² (800 g/m²) fiberglass woven roving.

Resin Selection

KEVLAR has been successfully used with the commercially available epoxy, vinylester, and polyester resin systems readily obtained from suppliers throughout the country. Each resin system best develops certain characteristics of the fabric which may be valuable in a particular aircraft application.

Epoxy resins produce better adhesion, and flexural and tensile properties than polyester resin. Epoxies have excellent strength-to-weight and modulus-to-weight ratios.

Vinylesters give good adhesion, impact resistance, and mechanical properties which fall between those of epoxy and polyester. Vinylesters are easier to work with than epoxy resins in hand layup applications. Vinylester resins reduce brittle failure and improve toughness because of their high elongation. In addition, some vinylester systems, such as Dow Derakane® XD-8084, are modified with rubber to further enhance toughness.

Additional weight is saved as a result of their lower density versus epoxy systems. Flame retardant vinylesters are also available.

Polyester resins can also be used, especially isophthalic systems, and flexibilized general purpose resins; but they result in lower mechanical properties, particularly interlaminar shear strength, when compared with epoxies or vinylesters.

Comparing vinylester and epoxy resins used with KEVLAR 49 aramid in fabric style 285 crow foot weave, 5 ounces per square yard (170 g/m²)—the use of epoxy resulted in superior mechanical properties. Tensile strength with epoxy was 59,000 pounds per square inch (410 mPa) compared to vinylester's 49,000 pounds per square inch (340 mPa).

Hand Layup Techniques

Aircraft designers start with a basic concept envisioning the shape and structure of their aircraft, the desired performance, and its aerodynamic characteristics. For example, the designer can choose wood, aluminum, composite, or a sandwich structure using foam or honeycomb core of NOMEX® aramid paper for the various parts of a basic airframe. Any combination of these materials may be chosen to help in reaching performance objectives.

Advanced performance objectives in light aircraft can result in sophisticated use of reinforced plastics for structures. Even so, most homebuilders will likely use hand layup techniques in order to simplify construction procedures.

Layup is the same as with fiberglass, using tools such as rollers, squeegees, and brushes. Impregnation, or "wet-out," is best at a resin system viscosity of 300 to 700 centipoise during application. As with fiberglass, higher resin viscosity slows wet-out and could cause voids, "dry spots," or porosity.

KEVLAR 49 aramid, unlike fiberglass, does not become translucent when impregnated, but turns from a bright yellow to a deep gold color. The fabric should be laid into a film of resin so that the resin wicks up through the ply of fabric from the bottom. Dry spots or bubbles become visible on the surface and can be eliminated by rolling, squeegeeing, or adding more resin.

A small test laminate using the planned fabric layup schedule and selected resin will provide practice in visually determining "wet-out," and will allow testing to assure that adequate adhesion has been achieved.

With most resin systems, best results are obtained by laying up entire panels in one session, without allowing layers to completely cure before adding subsequent plies. Some parts of the aircraft will require more plies than others. If a secondary bond (a new wet ply laid over a completely cured previous ply) must be made, excess resin should be squeegeed from the layer before curing. "Roughing" this resin layer prior to bonding is recommended. A nylon peel ply can also be laminated over the last layer of KEVLAR so that removal prior to secondary bonding yields a clean, fiber-rich layer.

Vacuum bagging is a more sophisticated technique used to achieve increased adhesion, higher laminate density, and to better utilize the outstanding properties of KEVLAR. This technique distributes the resin more evenly and helps eliminate air bubbles. Depending on the system used, the resin can cure at room temperature or, if desired and facilities are available, it can be cured in an oven or even in an autoclave to develop maximum mechanical properties in a much shorter time.

Rensselaer Polytechnic Institute is building its second lightweight sailplane using composite materials.

Most of the airframe is constructed of two skins of KEVLAR 49 Style 285 over a thin foam sheet. When additional strength is needed, four layers of KEVLAR—two on each side of the foam core, are used. Ribs and webs are also reinforced with KEVLAR. Capstrips use a hybrid of KEVLAR and graphite.

Homebuilders can employ many of the techniques used by RPI in making their own laminate (Figures A-11-A-16).

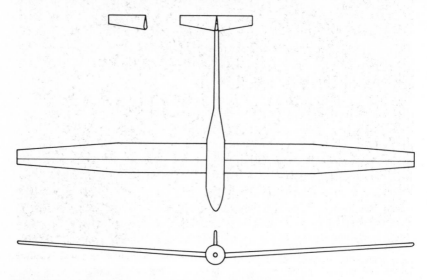

Fig. A-10. Composite sailplane design by Rensselaer Polytechnic Institute.

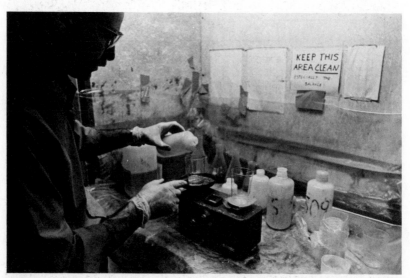

Fig. A-11. Weighing out the exact amount of resin needed for each part ensures optimum resin content and minimizes the chance of adding weight with too much resin. RPI generally uses a 60 percent fiber, 40 percent resin formula.

Fig. A-12. After measuring the space needed to construct the part, a "dam" is laid down on the work table to serve as a vacuum frame.

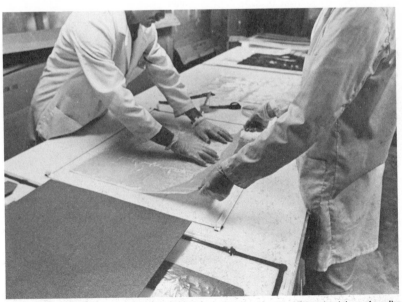

Fig. A-13. Fabric of KEVLAR® aramid fiber is laid on to a film of resin so that the resin wicks up from the bottom. The fabric should be smoothed carefully because it cannot be picked up again once it touches the resin. After the fabric is down, brush or squeegee the resin to ensure complete wet out. Then the foam core, already cut to size, is placed on top of the fabric. If additional skins of KEVLAR are needed, resin and fabric can be added either before or after the foam core.

Fig. A-14. When the laminate is complete, a thin polypropylene sheet is adhered to the vacuum frame and the vacuum nozzle installed. The part may be under the vacuum for 8 to 20 hours, depending upon the resin used.

Fig. A-15. The inboard wing section of the RP-2 can easily be lifted in one hand. The entire RP-2 will weigh only 160 pounds. Standard aluminum and fiberglass construction could raise that figure to more than 400 pounds.

Fig. A-16. KEVLAR aramid fiber is used in the skins, ribs, and webs on the RP-2 being built by the Rensselaer Polytechnic Institute's composites group. Capstrips are KEVLAR sandwiched between graphite.

Cutting and Trimming

Fabric of KEVLAR often will resist cutting by regular tools. However, lighter fabrics of KEVLAR can be cut with sharp, heavy duty upholstery scissors, such as Wiss #4-IS-12″ type. Where practical, parts should be built to net size, trimming during layup, in order to avoid the more difficult trimming of the completed, cured composites. Thin laminates can be trimmed with a utility knife after the resin has cured to a hard, rubbery state. The knife is pulled through the laminate with an up and down slicing motion. Frequent blade changes may be required with standard blades.

Kits of specially designed tools for cutting and machining heavier fabrics and laminates of KEVLAR include shears, sabre saw blades, drills, routers, and razors. These kits and other useful tools are readily available.

Machining composites reinforced with KEVLAR can be compared to wood finishing rather than metal finishing. Aircraft builders will benefit from reading the "Guide to Cutting and Machining KEVLAR aramid" published by the DuPont Company. Other informative publications and technical assistance are available from DuPont.

CONSTRUCTION

Building a small airplane requires construction expertise similar to that needed for a well-designed boat. A lot of the information contained in this section is drawn from experience with marine laminates.

	KEVLAR/ "XD-7818" Epoxy[1]	KEVLAR/ "Epon 826" Epoxy[2]	"Atlac" 382-05 Polyester[3]			
			KEVLAR	Glass	KEVLAR	Glass
Fabric Style	181	181	181	181	120	120
Fabric Volume %	36	39	38	37	37	30
Barcol Hardness	40-45	40-45	-	-	-	-
Interlaminar Shear Strength, PSI	5,120	5,120	3000	5700	3300	6200
Tensile Strength, PSI	65,200	61,200	60,900	40,800	63,600	33,000
Tensile Modulus, 10^6PSI	3.38	3.22	3.26	2.71	3.35	2.23
Flex. Strength, PSI	40,600	37,200	30,300	48,600	32,400	44,900
Flex. Modulus, 10^6PSI	3.54	3.13	2.80	2.24	2.73	2.05
Compressive Strength, PSI	19,100	17,900	15,100	39,100	15,400	37,200
Compressive Modulus, 10^6PSI	3.12	3.13	3.00	2.57	3.24	2.70

(1) Dow resin cured with Jefferson "Jeffamine" D-230 and Jefferson Accelerator A-398.
(2) Shell resin cured with Jefferson "Jeffamine" D-230 and Jefferson Accelerator A-398.
(3) ICI resin cured with MEK peroxide.

Table A-17. Mechanical properties of KEVLAR 49 and fiberglass fabric reinforced composites (epoxy and polyester resins hand-layup room temperature cure).

Solid Laminates

KEVLAR 49 is regularly used in reinforced plastics to reduce weight and increase strength. Careful consideration should be given to aerodynamic stresses and loads to best determine where KEVLAR 49 can be used most efficiently.

Comparative properties of fabrics of KEVLAR 49 and fiberglass follow. This comparison is in pounds per square inch. The numbers favor KEVLAR even more significantly in contrasting strength per unit of weight, using the densities of 1.44 grams per cubic centimeter (g/cc) for KEVLAR and 2.4 g/cc for fiberglass.

Semi-monocoque designs, where skins of KEVLAR 49 are reinforced with longitudinal members, is one method which can be used to enhance modulus while raising compressive strength to meet load requirements. Obviously, one should never exceed speeds which would result in exceeding load limits which have been designed into the structure.

Required mechanical properties can be obtained while reducing the weight of composites through the use of KEVLAR 49 in lieu of fiberglass. Enhanced durability, increased damage tolerance, greater impact resistance, better toughness, higher vibration damping, corrosion, resistance, and a stiffer composite are some of the benefits derived from incorporating KEVLAR 49 in aircraft structural components.

Composites tested showed that substitution of two piles of Style 285 KEVLAR 49 for two plies of Style 181 fiberglass cloth resulted in a 26 percent weight reduction along with a 48 percent increase in tensile stiffness and a 45 percent increase in tensile strength. This thin laminate will act as a membrane, converting aerodynamic loads into tensile forces using the best features of KEVLAR.

Safety is a prime consideration. The Solar Challenger's very thin wing spar tube and fuselage boom were reinforced with KEVLAR overlaid on top of graphite to contain graphite fragments in case of a failure. Laminates of KEVLAR rarely fail catastrophically or fragmentize in the way that is considered normal for composites of graphite, carbon, or glass.

In construction of the Solar Challenger, KEVLAR 49 was used to reinforce the wing ribs which were made of Styrofoam®. A single ply of KEVLAR 49 was used on both sides of each rib to form a sandwich. KEVLAR aramid fiber reinforced the entire fuselage and was also used in the Challenger's landing gear and control cables. Internal bracing where maximum strength and stiffness is required at minimum weight calls for cables of KEVLAR. The cables must be jacketed for protection from abrasion and direct sunlight.

UV Protection

KEVLAR must be protected from the ultraviolet radiation in normal sunlight. A coat of pigmented paint, a layer of aluminized lacquer, or other suitable barrier, can provide this necessary function. Structures of KEVLAR not so protected will gradually deteriorate from the surface inward in much the same way as glass composites do because of degradation of the resin.

Core Laminates

A sandwich panel can be used for components requiring more bending stiffness. Core materials such as balsa wood, honeycomb of NOMEX® aramid, polyvinyl chloride, polystyrene, urethane, and syntactic foams will provide low weight with sharply increased stiffness and bending strength.

Fabrics of KEVLAR 49 are used as face sheets over these cores in place of fiberglass. These sandwich panels are useful for stiffer and stronger ribs, bulkheads, wing shells, fuselage shells, and many other components where increased mechanical properties are required. Hot wire cutting or sanding the foam core to the desired shape and covering it with KEVLAR is a popular and successful technique used by many homebuilders to produce complex shapes.

Results of flexural texts with an 0.33 inch (8.4 millimeter) thick polyvinyl chloride (PVC) foam core sandwich, show that laminates of KEVLAR are superior to those of fiberglass.

When 5 ounces per square yard (170 g/m²) Style 281 fabric of KEVLAR was used in the sandwich laminate construction, the sample with KEVLAR was 79 percent stronger, 10 percent stiffer, and 18 percent lighter than a comparable laminate using a thinner fabric of similar weight fiberglass (See Table III). As a general rule, if stiffness and impact resistance of a particular fiberglass laminate are sufficient, the same or slightly thinner fabric of KEVLAR can be substituted for fiberglass plies and a significant weight savings can be achieved.

The graphs and data in Table IV and V, shown for marine laminates, can be applied to the construction of homebuilt aircraft as well.

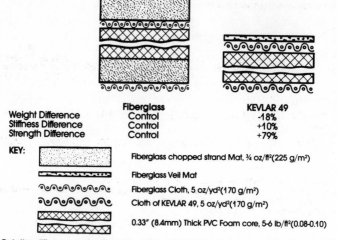

	Fiberglass	KEVLAR 49
Weight Difference	Control	-18%
Stiffness Difference	Control	+10%
Strength Difference	Control	+79%

KEY:

Fiberglass chopped strand Mat, ¾ oz/ft² (225 g/m²)

Fiberglass Veil Mat

Fiberglass Cloth, 5 oz/yd² (170 g/m²)

Cloth of KEVLAR 49, 5 oz/yd² (170 g/m²)

0.33″ (8.4mm) Thick PVC Foam core, 5-6 lb/ft² (0.08-0.10)

Table A-3. Relative differences of weight, strength, and stiffness of sandwich laminates using KEVLAR 49 vs. fiberglass.

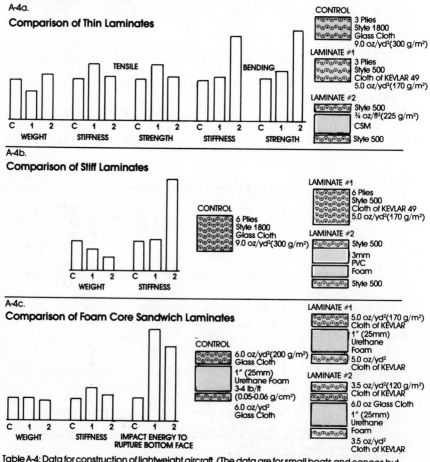

Table A-4: Data for construction of lightweight aircraft. (The data are for small boats and canoes but can be applied to the hand layup of small aircraft as well.

Table A-5. Specifications of various laminates

Table A-5a.

LIGHTWEIGHT LAMINATES

Laminate	Thickness in (mm)	Weight lb/yd² (Kg/m²)	Tensile Modulus 10⁶ psi (GPa)(cm)	Tensile Strength 10³ psi (MPa)	Flex Modulus 10³ psi (GPa)	Flex Strength 10³ psi (MPa)
3 Ply Style 1800 Fiberglass in Polyester	0.04(1.0)	0.34(1.7)	2.2(15.2)	38(262)	2.0(13.8)	32(220)
3 Ply Style 500 KEVLAR® 49 in Vinylester	0.04(1.0)	0.23(1.1)	3.0(20.7)	52(359)	2.1(14.5)	38(262)
Style 500/ CSM*/Style 500 in Vinylester	0.05(1.3)	0.37(1.8)	1.9(13.1)	32(220)	2.1(14.5)	45(310)

NOTE: Some mechanical properties are measured using thicker laminates.
The laminate of KEVLAR/CSM/KEVLAR is actually 5-10% stiffer and stronger in tension and over twice as stiff and strong in flex than the 3 ply glass laminate because of its greater thickness.
*CSM is ¾ oz/ft²(225 g/m²) Chopped Strand Mat

Table A-5b.

LIGHTWEIGHT STIFF LAMINATES*

Laminate	Style 1800 Fiberglass 6 Ply	Style 500 of KEVLAR® 49 6 Ply	Style 500 of KEVLAR® 49 7 Ply**	Style 500 6mm Airex® Style 500	Style 500 Coremat® Style 500	Style 500 3mm Klegecell® Style 500
Weight, lb/ft² (Kg/m²)	0.71 (3.5)	0.51 (2.5)	0.53 (2.6)	0.54 (2.6)	0.73 (3.6)	0.31 (1.5)
Thickness in (mm)	0.08 (2.0)	0.09 (2.3)	0.08 (2.0)	0.31 (7.9)	0.19 (4.8)	0.16 (4.1)
Bending Moment in-lb/in (Kg-m/m)	351 (159)	264 (120)	382 (175)	702 (318)	427 (194)	511 (232)
Apparent Stiffness 10³ in.²-lb.in. (Kg-m²/m)	1.33 (15.3)	1.36 (19.7)	1.65 (19.0)	19.8 (228)	7.41 (85.4)	4.10 (47.2)

*Properties for Laboratory Laminates in polyester resin   **Well squeegeed laminate with high fiber volume (41%)

Table A-5c.

PROTOTYPE FOAM CORE LAMINATES*

LAMINATE			
TOP SKIN	2 ply 6.0 oz/yd² (203 g/m²) Glass Cloth	2 ply 5.0 oz/yd² (170 g/m²) Cloth of KEVLAR	3.5 oz/yd² (119 g/m²) Cloth of KEVLAR 6.0 oz/yd² (203 g/m²) Glass Cloth
BOTTOM SKIN	6.0 oz/yd² (203 g/m²) Glass Cloth	5.0 oz/yd² (170 g/m²) Cloth of KEVLAR	3.5 oz/yd² (119 g/m²) Cloth of KEVLAR
RELATIVE WEIGHT	1.00	1.00	0.92
RELATIVE STIFFNESS	1.00	1.43	1.10
RELATIVE STRENGTH	1.00	1.55	1.48
IMPACT OF BOTTOM SKIN			
Response to 20 in-lb	D	A	A
30 in-lb	E	A	B
40 in-lb	E	B	B
50 in-lb	F	B	C
60 in-lb	—	C	C
70 in-lb	—	C	E

Key
A Very slight indentation; little if any resin cracking; no fiber damage
B Slight indentation; some resin cracking; no fabric rupture
C Large indentation; some resin cracking; no fabric rupture
D Resin cracking; initial fabric rupture
E Moderate damage; fabric clearly ruptured
F Severe damage with core exposed
*Test panels of 1″ thick 3-4 lb/ft³ (0.05-0.06 g/cm³)
Urethane foam with an isopolyester surfboard resin.

Summary

Aircraft designers are finding that KEVLAR aramid fibers are high performance replacements for many materials commonly used in light and ultralight aircraft construction.

We hope you will find the information contained in this publication helpful to your design efforts. We believe it is the best information currently available and is offered as suggestion in experimentation you may care to undertake.

DuPont makes no guarantee of results and assumes no obligation or liability whatsoever in connection with this information. The product user should be satisfied that recommendations are suitable for his own particular use and meet all appropriate safety standards. References to products not of DuPont manufacture do not indicate either endorsement of named products or unsuitability of other similar products.

More Information Available

For more detailed design information and an index of technical literature on KEVLAR, write: Literature Index, KEVLAR Special Products, Centre Road Building, Wilmington, DE 19898.

The FAA's Advisory Circular (AC) system provides much useful information. AC 20-107, "Composite Aircraft Structures," AC 20-44, "Glass Fiber Fabric for Aircraft Covering;" AC 20-27B, "Certification of Amateur-Built Aircraft," portions of AC 65-15A, "Airframe & Powerplant Mechanics Airframe Handbook," and other FAA publications will assist the designer/builder. Other useful material is available from the Experimental Aircraft Association, P.O. Box 229, Hales Corner, Wisconsin 53130. For those interested in exploring both the processes and the materials in more depth, the book "Handbook of Composites," edited by George Lubin, published by Van Nostrand Reinhold, is recommended.

CORE MATERIALS SOURCE LIST

AIREX®	COREMAT™	HONEYCOMB OF NOMEX®
Torin, Inc.	**Firet Corporation**	**ARAMID**
125 Sheridan Terrace	Veenendaal, Holland	**Hexcel Structural Products**
Ridgewood, NJ 07450	Distributed by	11711 Dublin Blvd.
Thomas J. Johannsen	West Point Pepperell, Ltd.	Dublin, CA 94566
201/445-2088	**Lantuck Mill**	Jim Bonner
CONTOURKORE® BALSA	P.O. Box 298	415/828-4200
Baltek Corporation	Faifax, AL 36854	**Ciba-Geigy Corporation**
10 Fairway Court	205/756-7111	Composite Materials Dept.
Northvale, NJ 07647	**KLEGECELL®**	10910 Talbert Avenue
Keith Walton	**American Klegecell**	Fountain Valley, CA 92708
201/767-1400	**Corporation**	E.A. Connell
	204 Dooley	714/964-2731
	Grapevine, TX 76051	**Force Engineering**
	Christopher G. Hart	5329 Ashton Court
	817/481-3547	Sarasota, FL 33583
		John Cloud 813/923-1857

This source is designed to present a representative group of products and suppliers with which we are familiar. It does not include all the products or companies selling the products. It is not an endorsement of any specific manufacturer.

SHEARS AND ROTARY SCISSORS FOR CUTTING KEVLAR®

Manufacturer and Model #	Yarn or Roving	Light & Medium Wt. Fabric, Felt <7 oz/yd²	Heavy Wt. Fabric & Woven Roving >7 oz/yd²	Cured Laminates <0.050"
Pen Associates, Inc. WR-4S-2 (coated*) 2-inch PA1-4A-2 (uncoated)	X			
Pen Associates, Inc. WR-10E-4 (coated*) 4-inch PAI-10E-4 (uncoated)	X	X		
Technology Associates, Inc. ECB4-153 4-inch	X	X		
Pen Associates, Inc. WR-8L-2 (coated*) 2-inch PAI-8L-2 (uncoated)	X	X		
Technology Associates, Inc. CSI-161 (coated*) LDS 2-151 (uncoated) 2-inch	X	X		
Pen Associates, Inc. WR-12C-6 (coated*) 6-inch PAI-12C-6 (uncoated)		X	X	
Technology Associates, Inc. EHD 6-155 6-inch		X	X	
Wiss #4 I.S. (12-inch) Upholstery, carpet & canvas shears		X	X	
Pen Associates, Inc. WR-10M-2 (coated*) 2-inch PAI-10M-2 (uncoated)			X	X
Technology Associates, Inc. MPO-152 1.5-inch			X	X
United Cloth Cutting Machine Co. Electric Shears Model No. LIL 25159		X		
Maiman "Mini-Sphere" Distributed by: Pen Associates, Inc.		X		
Eastman Machinery Co. Eastman Class 355 Lightning Cutter			X	
Maiman "Roto-Sphere" Distributed by: **Pen Associates, Inc.**			X	
Power shears, electric or air Distributed by: **Pen Associates, Inc.**		X	X	X<.100
Black and Decker Power Rotary Cutter 7975	X	X	X	

*Coated for increased durability

CUTTING TOOL SOURCE LIST

SPECIALTY TOOLING
Pen Associates, Inc.
3639 W. Robino Drive
Wilmington, DE 19808
302/995-6868

Technology Associates, Inc.
P.O. Box 7163
Wilmington, DE 19803
302/475-6219

WISS SCISSORS
Dayton-Price, Ltd.
1 Park Avenue
New York, NY
212/532-8470
- or -
Most local hardware stores

ELECTRIC SCISSORS
United Cloth Cutting
Machine Company
1123 Broadway
New York, NY 20010
212/242-2050

Eastman Machinery Company
779 Washington Street
Buffalo, NY 14240
716/856-2200

H. Maiman Company, Inc.
575 Eighth Avenue
New York, NY 10018
212/279-0400

Pen Associates, Inc.
3639 Robino Drive
Wilmington, DE 19808
302/995-6868

Black and Decker
Towson, MD 21204
301/583-3900
- or -
Most local hardware stores

RESINS FOR HAND LAY UP WITH KEVLAR®

ISOPHTHALIC POLYESTERS
AROPOL 7241-T15
Ashland Chem. Co.

KOPPERS 1061
Koppers Co.

REICHHOLD POLYLITE
33-402
Reichhold Chem. Co.

MR 12256
USS Chemicals Co.

VINYLESTERS
HETRON 903
Ashland Chem. Co.

CORROLITE 31-345
Reichhold Chem. Co.

DERAKANE 411-45
DERAKANE 510A-40*
DERAKANE 8084**
Dow Chemical Co.

EPOCRYL 322
Shell Chem. Co.

CO-REZYN 8300
CO-REZYN 8400*
CO-REZYN 8520**
Interplastic Corp.

ATLAC 580-05A
ICI Americas, Inc.

*Flame Resistant
**High elongation, rubber toughened

EPOXY SYSTEMS

Resins		Curing Agents

Resins

low viscosity diluted	medium viscosity
EPI-REZ 507	EPI-REZ 509
Celanese Co.	
EPOTUF 37-127	EPOTUF 37-129
Reichhold Chem. Co.	
ARALDITE 509	ARALDITE 6005
Ciba-Geigy	
DER 324	DER 330
Dow Chem. Co.	
EPON 8132***	EPON 826***
Shell Chem. Co.	

Curing Agents

ACCELERATOR A-398 (4 PHR†)
JEFFAMINE D-230 (28 PHR)
(used w/medium viscosity systems)
Texaco Chemical Co.

VERSAMID V-140*** (40 PHR)
(used w/low viscosity systems)
General Mills Co.

TETA (13 PHR)
(used w/low viscosity systems)
Miller Stephenson Co.

†phr parts curing agent per hundred parts resin
***Also sold by Miller-Stephenson Co.

Rapidly advancing knowledge of new long term toxic effects of many chemicals has emphasized the need to reduce human exposure to many chemicals to the lowest practical limits. Special hazards with respect to chemicals mentioned in this list should be obtained from the manufacturer prior to use. We strongly recommend that processors seek and adhere to manufacturer's or supplier's current instructions for handling each chemical they use.

This source list is designed to present a representative group of products and suppliers with which we are familiar. It does not include all the products or companies selling these products. It is not an endorsement of any specific manufacturer.

RESIN SOURCE LIST

ASHLAND CHEMICAL COMPANY
Polyester Division
P.O. Box 2219
Columbus, OH 43216
Tom Preisel
614/889-3333

CELANESE PLASTICS AND SPECIALTIES COMPANY
1065 West Hill Street
Louisville, KY 40210
Ernie Walker
502/585-8755

CIBA-GEIGY CORPORATION
Resin Department
Ardsley, NY 10502
Robert M. Fisher
914/478-3131

DOW CHEMICAL COMPANY
Designed Products Dept.
Freeport TX 77541
Vinylester: Tom Anderson
713/238-2502
Epoxies: Greg Stevens;
Ed Francis
713/239-3370

ICI AMERICAS, INC.
Wilmington, DE 19897
Ian R. Wilcox
302/575-3561

INTERPLASTIC CORPORATION
P.O. Box 9554
Tulsa, OK 74107
Eugene F. Jacobs
612/331-6850

KOPPERS COMPANY, INC.
P.O. Box 219
Bridgeville, PA 15017
Terry McQuarrie
412/227-2301

MILLER STEPHENSON CHEMICAL CO., INC.
Corporate Office
George Washington Hwy.
Danbury, CT 06810
203/743-4447

LA Office
12261 Foothill Blvd.
Sylmar, CA 91342
213/896-4714

REICHHOLD CHEMICAL CO.
525 North Broadway
White Plains, NY 10603
Polyesters: Edward W. Jansen
914/682-5700
Epoxies: Ken E. Dempsky
914/682-5700

SHELL CHEMICAL COMPANY
P.O. Box 1380
Houston, TX 77001
Epoxies: C. V. Wittenwyler
713/493-7388
Vinylesters: Paul Jones
713/493-7387

TEXACO CHEMICAL COMPANY
4800 Fournace Place
Bellaire, TX 77401
Margaret Pennywell
713/520-3628

USS CHEMICAL COMPANY
1605 W. Elizabeth Avenue
Linden, NJ 07036
Tony Manyak
210/862-5600

GENERAL MILLS COMPANY
4620 West 77th Street
Minneapolis, MN 55435
- or -
425 Broad Hollow Road
Melville Long Island, NY
11746
Dave Carroll
800/645-9462

Chicago Office
6348 Oakton Street
Morton Grove, IL 60053
312/966-2022

COMMERCIAL WEAVERS
FABRICS OF KEVLAR® 29 AND 49 ARAMID

BURLINGTON INDUSTRIAL FABRICS CO.
261 Madison Ave.
New York, NY 10016
Mr. Jerry Zoufaly-Kevlar® 29
212/953-1100

FIBER MATERIALS, INC.
Biddeford Industrial Park
Biddeford, ME 04005
Mr. Gary Williams
207/282-5911

STERN & STERN TEXTILES
1290 Ave. of Americas
New York, NY 10104
Mr. Peter Thornton
212/397-8310

BURLINGTON GLASS FABRICS CO.
1345 Avenue of Americas
New York, NY 10019
Mr. Steve Mischen-Kevlar® 49
212/621-1107

HEXCEL CORPORATION (KEVLAR® 49 ONLY)
11711 Dublin Blvd.
Dublin, CA 94566
Mr. Al Buzdula
415/828-4200

TEXTILE TECHNOLOGY
2727 Philmont Avenue
Huntingdon Valley, PA
19006
Mr. Leon Bryn
215/947-4614

CHEMICAL FABRICS CORP.
P.O. Box 367
108 Northside Drive
Bennington, VT 05201
Mr. Edwin J. Emmet, Jr.
802/442-3122

ORCON CORPORATION
33430 Western Avenue
Union City, CA 94587
Mr. Craig Riley
415/489-8100
(Unidirectional fabrics)

UNIGLASS INDUSTRIES
1440 Broadway
New York, NY 10018
Mr. Bill Boyles
212/564-6000

For Sample Yardage:

CLARK SCHWEBEL FIBERGLASS CORP.
5 Corporate Park Drive
White Plains, NY 10604
Mr. Dieter Wachter
914/694-9090

PRODESCO, INC.
700 Park Avenue
Perkasie, PA 18944
Mr. Jim Batman
215/257-6566

HI-PRO-FORM-FABRICS, INC.
962 Devon Drive
Newark, DE 19711
302/368-0405

PROFORM, INC.
P.O. Box 1046
Seguin, TX 78155
Mr. Keith Hutson
512/379-8830

FABRIC DEVELOPMENT, INC.
10-14 S. Main St.
Quakertown, PA 18951
Mr. Piyush Shah
215/536-1420

INSTRUCTIONS FOR MACHINING LAMINATES OF KEVLAR® ARAMID FIBER

Instructions For Machining Laminates Of Kevlar® Aramid Fiber

A. Drilling: Machine tool and off-hand. "Brad-Point" style drills require no bushings for tool guidance but need rigid backup to prevent delamination when the drill breaks through the laminate.

- Single-point drills require bushings for tool control when off-hand drilling, and rigid backup to prevent delamination.
- Core drills require no guide bushings, but must also have backup to prevent delamination; use of a rotary impact drill will improve core drill performance when off-hand drilling.
- Conventional twist drills will not produce satisfactory holes under any conditions unless drilled through a sandwich of upper and lower sacrificial plates.
- Carbide tipped hole saws are the most practical way to produce holes larger than ½-inch in diameter.
  Drill Speed — 25-250 surface feet/minute
  Feed Rate — .001" per cutting edge/revolution

B. Countersinking — Down-cutting of the laminate by the countersink will produce the best hole; however, adjustable-stop tooling is required when countersinking with a hand-held drill. Radial cutting edge countersinks, whether with single or multiple cutting edges, will not produce acceptable holes. The tool performs best when piloted at speeds of 200-800 revolutions/minute.

C. Sawing — Band sawing and sabre sawing are preferred versus circular sawing. There will be some "fuzzing" (uncut fibers) of the laminate on the exit side of the cut which can be trimmed by belt sanding, using 80-150 grit sanding belts in a hand sander or bench sander. Cutting the KEVLAR® "fuzz" with modified hand shears (see source list) is an alternate edge-trimming technique.
Saw Speed — 3000-6000 feet/minute
Fine Tooth — 14-22 teeth/inch raker set, moderate feed rate

D. Routing — Specialty router bits have been developed for use with laminates of KEVLAR. No conventional style bits have produced acceptable cuts.
Router Speed — 18,000-25,000 revolutions/minute

General Remarks On Cutting KEVLAR® Laminates

Tools selected to cut KEVLAR should only be used on KEVLAR because the material is particularly sensitive to cutting edge quality. Very sharp, defect-free cutting edges are an *absolute necessity* and, if any quantity of cutting is to be done, carbide-edged tools should be considered for extended tool life. The most effective technique for cutting this material is to cause the material to fail (to be cut) in compression; avoid having the cutting tool work the material in tension.

SOURCE OF TOOLS	Drills up to ½" φ	Counter-sinks	Hole Saw ½" φ & Larger	Router	Shears
Airtech International 2542 East Del Amo Blvd. P.O. Box 6207 Carson, CA 90749 (213) 603-9683	X	X			
ATI Industries 2425 West Vineyard Avenue Escondido, CA 92025-2591 (714) 746-8301		X			
Comp Tool 12139 North Linden Road Clio, MI 48420 (313) 687-5450	X				
International Carbide 1111 N. Main Street Wauconda, IL 60084 (800) 323-7550	X	X			
Morris Tool Ltd. G-4006 Corunna Road Flint, MI 48504-5891 (313) 732-3550			X		
Onsrud Cutter 800 Liberty Drive Libertyville, IL 60048 (312) 362-1560				X	
Pen Associates 2639 W. Robino Drive Wilmington, DE 19808 (302) 995-6868	X	X	X	X	X
Starlite Industries 1111 Lancaster Avenue Rosemont, PA 19010 (215) 527-1300	X			X	
Technology Associates P.O. Box 7163 Wilmington, DE 19803 (302) 475-6219	X			X	X

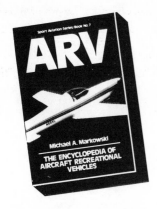

ARV

The Encyclopedia of Aircraft Recreational Vehicles

Michael A. Markowski
320p/160il. $17.95

This is the only book on the newest kitplanes - ARVs. It describes aircraft you can build for the cost of an ultralight - fast, efficient, cross-country aircraft. Learn why ultralight and lightplane pilots are switching to ARVs. This manual shows you how they are built and how they fly.

ARV tells you what you need to know - before you buy:

- Skills, parts, tools, shop facilities, building techniques, and costs of each aircraft.
- Hundreds of three-views, inboard profiles, cutaways, and photos.
- How ARV technology developed, and details of six future ARVs...still in design or prototype stages.
- You'll save over $250 in not having to send for information packages to individual manufacturers.

Some of the aircraft described include: Eaglet, Zia, XTC, Zippy Sport, Goldwing ST, Beta Bird, Hummel Bird, Avid Flyer, LM-1, P-38, Super Wing, Monerai-P, Moni, Questor, Solitaire, Guppy, Starlite, Windwagon, Cricket, eight VW-powered designs, and 43 other unique aircraft.

The Appendix alone is worth the price of the book. It includes: An explanation of how to register your airplane, *including the necessary FAA forms.* FAA's Recreational Pilot's License proposal, so you can get your license easier. A "mini-dictionary" so you can speak the kit builder's jargon. Lists of ARV magazines and organizations. Plus, *Bill-of-Sale forms,* if you decide to sell your kitplane.

Mike Markowski, the author, has been designing, building, flying and writing about sport aircraft for over 15 years. He's an FAA-rated pilot, graduate aeronautical engineer, and member of EAA, SSA, and NASAD. He has written 35 magazine articles and six books on sport aviation.

ARV covers it all, from aerobats to motorgliders...from canards to biplanes...even taildraggers, twins, and two-seaters. If you want a "puddle jumper" or a transportation machine, ARV gives you the facts to help you decide. This is the guide you've waited for.